D0894389

RICHARD III:
THE ROAD TO BOSWORTH FIELD

Fotheringhay Castle, Northamptonshire, birthplace of Richard of Gloucester, and seat of the Yorkist family. The church where Richard's parents the Duke and Duchess of York are buried can be seen in the background.

Portrait of Richard III, a copy made about 1513. It is thought to be the most authentic surviving portrait with no signs of any attempt to make the king appear deformed. Once owned by the Paston family.

RICHARD III:
THE ROAD TO
BOSWORTH FIELD

P.W. HAMMOND
and
ANNE F. SUTTON

CONSTABLE · LONDON

First published in Great Britain 1985
by Constable and Company Limited
10 Orange Street, London WC2H 7EG
Copyright © 1985 by P.W. Hammond and Anne F. Sutton
Reprinted 1986
Set in Monophoto Plantin by
Servis Filmsetting Limited, Manchester
Printed in Great Britain by
BAS Printers Limited, Over Wallop, Hampshire

British Library CIP data
Hammond, P.W.
Richard III: the road to Bosworth Field
1. Richard III, *King of England*
I. Title   II. Sutton, Anne F.
942.04'6'0924   DA260

ISBN 0 09 466160 X

CONTENTS

ILLUSTRATIONS

[5]

ACKNOWLEDGEMENTS

We would like to thank the following for permission to publish material in their possession, or for which they hold the copyright: Her Majesty's Stationery Office (Nos. 12, 122, 179, 180), Alan Sutton Publishing Limited (Nos. 96, 100, 168), Canterbury and York Society (No. 54), Corporation of London Record Office (Nos. 6, 124), Dean and Chapter of Westminster Abbey (No. 98), Dean and Chapter of York (No. 114), Early English Text Society (No. 156), Guildhall Library (Nos. 22, 90, 95, 117, 143, 163), Longman Group Limited (No. 77), Mercers' Company (Nos. 66, 71, 73, 84, 94, 167), Oxford University Press (Nos. 52, 68, 78, 80, 82, 86, 93, 116), Public Record Office (Nos. 60, 99, 118, 135, 174), Richard III Society (Nos. 92, 97, 102, 104–6, 108–11, 113, 121, 134, 137–8, 140–1, 147–9, 151–2, 154–5, 157, 159–62, 169–71, 177), Selden Society (No. 153), Yorkshire Archaeological Society (Nos. 75, 83, 175, 184, 189–90).

We would also like to thank Dr Lorraine Attreed for allowing us to use her transcript of the York House Books, which she is preparing for publication, and Patricia and Robert Hairsine for extracts from their transcripts of PRO C81 and E404, which they are preparing for publication, also Julian Rowe for his drawings, in particular his reconstruction of Fotheringhay Castle, and David Cottrell for his help and advice with photography.

Last, but not least, we want to thank Miss Doris Ogden and Mrs Carolyn Hammond for typing the manuscript, and the latter for her help and advice.

[9]

Since memory is frail, sayings and deeds have to be reinforced by the evidence of writing, so that neither length of time nor the cunning of posterity can obscure the knowledge of past events.

(from a twelfth century notification by William de Braose of a grant of lands to Sele Priory: British Records Association)

FOREWORD

By H.R.H. THE DUKE OF GLOUCESTER G.C.V.O.

Patron, Richard III Society

The reign of King Richard III was but brief and filled with crises – political, personal and military – they were resolved inevitably in that age of violence by the shedding of blood. To both participant and spectator alike the excitement lay in anticipating whose blood would be shed next.

Today we cannot speculate about the score, with the notable exception of the fate of the little princes in the Tower, all that is well recorded. Our role as students of history is to speculate on the motives and the moral decisions taken by the participants in those mysterious and distant times. We are impelled to do so because of the very powerful image created by Shakespeare for his Tudor masters; this sub-human creature – crippled in mind and body – betraying friend and foe alike in his quest for total power, and brought his just deserts by the Tudors whose sense of duty brought them to save their country from the tyrant.

For many years supporters of Richard III, particularly those from the North of England where his original popular support was based, have collected evidence to reverse this image and give a truer image of a decent man overcome by the sudden development of events forced to take a gamble that led him ultimately to Bosworth and defeat, his betrayers blackening his reputation to justify themselves.

Every man must choose for himself, which image they find most credible, but this book with its wealth of contemporary writings – both friendly and hostile – is like an archaeologist's plan on which the historian must reconstruct the edifice, weighing fact with supposition, and each assumption with our own experience of life.

Richard Duke of Gloucester, later the last Plantagenet King of England, was born in 1452, the youngest son of Richard Duke of York, the Yorkist claimant to the throne (see Genealogical table). He was the eighth son (but the fourth living) of the Duke, and thus of very little importance when he was born. When he became King in 1483, as Richard III, his reign lasted only twenty-six months, and he died in his thirty-third year. Consequently it might be thought that he was of no great importance at any time and that there would be very little to say about him. In fact he is one of the best-known of English monarchs, possibly the most denigrated, certainly the subject of almost endless controversy.

The reason for all the discussion and controversy is that Richard of Gloucester has been given one of the worst characters of any English monarch, the character of a man whose every action was designed towards his own advancement, and who has been accused of a number of atrocious crimes, culminating in the murder of his nephews, the sons of his brother Edward IV (the 'Princes in the Tower'). This picture of a man of unrelieved evil is familiar from Shakespeare's well-known play. In fact, most of the accusations against him depend on statements by later, Tudor, writers. Contemporary writers treated Richard's behaviour in a much more matter of fact way. By the later writers he was accused of helping to murder Edward of Lancaster, only son of Henry VI, of murdering Henry VI, being responsible for the execution of his brother George Duke of Clarence in a butt of malmsey wine, and of murdering his wife and the Princes in the Tower, as well as a number of political opponents. That Richard was a much more normal human being, most of whose crimes, if not all, were imaginary, a man capable of benevolent actions as well as of political violence, is demonstrated in the contemporary records printed in this book.

The depiction of Richard as a monster has extended to his physical appearance, in reflecting ancient opinion that an evil mind is inevitably housed in a twisted body – Shakespeare describes him as a hunchback with a withered arm. This, too, is at variance with known facts. There is no detailed description of Richard, but there are brief references to his appearance by a number of writers from which a picture can be built up. John Rous for example, a contemporary (and after 1485, a hostile) witness, who had seen Richard, says that his right shoulder was higher than his left and that he was short in stature. Had the inequality of shoulders extended to a hunchback we can be sure that Rous would not have failed to mention it. Even this inequality is open to doubt since Thomas More, who was writing some thirty years after Richard's death but who had undoubtedly spoken to people who knew him, says that his left shoulder was higher than the right. He also says Richard had a crook back. It seems therefore certain that some slight deformity existed, though probably not enough to make a definite impression, and this deformity seems confirmed by the epithet 'crouchback' given Richard in 1491 by a hostile citizen of York, who had probably seen him. An inequality of shoulder height is, however, a very common characteristic. It has been argued that Richard may have been very tall and perhaps stooped as such people often do, since Nicholas von Poppelau, a Bohemian knight, and a man of known great strength, says that Richard, whom he met in 1484, was 'three fingers' taller than himself. However, it does not necessarily follow that Richard was very tall as von Poppelau may have been short and stockily built. That Richard was in fact on the short side seems to be borne out by a speech made by Archibald Whitelaw, Scottish Ambassador in 1484, in which he referred to the King in his presence and quoted Statius, the Roman poet, to the effect that never had so great a mind been in so small a body. Lastly, John Stow the sixteenth-century London historian is reported to have spoken to old men who had seen Richard (Stow could have done this, being born c. 1525), and they reported that Richard was not deformed, but low in stature. It would therefore appear that Richard III was probably of less than average height, with an inequality of the shoulders. That he had no major deformity, particularly of the arms, is shown by his prowess as a soldier, which in the fifteenth century demanded physical as well as mental prowess. Concerning his features, we know that he was personable enough, with a pale and thin, but not unattractive face, since we have a portrait dating from within thirty years of his death. This portrait (see Frontispiece) was undoubtedly derived from one painted in Richard's lifetime.

We may similarly attempt to evaluate the evidence for Richard's moral character, although this is a particularly difficult task after five hundred years for someone who left few personal letters. Those letters that do survive have been included in this book, such as that to his mother, the famous postscript in the King's own hand about the treachery of the Duke of Buckingham, and the letter about Mistress Shore's marriage to his solicitor, Thomas Lynom. Recourse to an analysis of the few books we know Richard owned is equally unrewarding for the predominance of pious and historical works is what one would expect from a man of his time. We have to fall back upon Richard's actions. In government, the administration of justice and his concern for the ordinary subject Richard is hardly to be faulted – in the words of his predominantly hostile biographer, Charles Ross. He appears to have had a strong appreciation of his vocation or profession as duke and then as king and may have consciously followed the precepts on how to be a 'good prince' laid down in so many books of advice to princes in the middle ages. There is no shortage of documents testifying to Richard's benevolent rule, as the reader will discover.

It is a few 'political' acts that appear to conflict with the image of well-intentioned king and loyal brother. The dismemberment of estates, particularly that of his mother-in-law, has become a fashionable charge to level at him as duke, but this was an activity engaged in by any noble or gentleman in a position, as Richard was, to do so through influential connections and marriage, or merely through the use of money and inside knowledge. Similar acts were carried out by acquisitive lawyers or merchants eager to invest in land and gentility. This is not an activity to be singled out for particular criticism or favour – it was, and is, how power and land change hands. It is certainly not a major guide to character. More seriously one can consider the charge that Richard encouraged and profited by the execution of his brother the Duke of Clarence, a charge recently revived by Dr Michael Hicks the biographer of Clarence. No contemporary ascribed to Richard any ill-intentioned involvement in the matter, not even Dominic Mancini who might particularly have been expected to record such contemporary suspicion, as his sources in 1483 were close to the Woodvilles and the supporters of the Edwardian court party. Mancini records precisely the opposite: that Richard deplored the execution and held the Woodvilles in particular responsible. Mancini did not get this from Richard and his supporters, as Clarence's biographer maintains, for his text shows clearly that he knew none of them. Richard's acquisition of a firmer hold on certain lands and certain offices after Clarence's death similarly cannot be interpreted as meaning he desired his brother's death to acquire such things, which could have been his for the asking.

[15]

Such accusations place much dependence on the charge of hypocrisy, first made by Polydore Vergil. Hypocrisy is always a dangerous charge to bring because it involves the accuser in a vicious circular argument and a committed disbelief in the words of almost everybody. This caveat, so popular again with recent historians, seems to derive in spirit from the current media attitude to politicians. As regards Richard it is instantly attractive because it enables the historian to ignore anything 'good' done by the king. A more common-sense and realistic approach would be to emphasize the ambiguity of personality and event after five hundred years but most writers on Richard III seem to prefer the certainty of condemnation, invariably provoking an equally positive counter-assertion.

In turning to the other specific actions by Richard which are condemned by historians, we may ignore the major crimes listed above, since these are dealt with in the text, and are in the main not now accepted by modern writers. We may mention however the executions of Rivers, Grey, Vaughan and Hastings in June 1483. All were undoubtedly political executions carried out to safeguard Richard's position. The first three were among the Woodville faction: Rivers, the maternal uncle and tutor of Edward V; Grey his nephew, son of Queen Elizabeth by her first husband, and half-brother of Edward V; and Vaughan, an old servant of the Yorkists and identified with the Woodville party. Their arrest, before they could conduct Edward V into London for his coronation, was greeted with delight by such as Lord Hastings, leader of the other main court party. Whether there had been a plot by those arrested to deal with Richard in a similar fashion, which had back-fired, will remain a matter for speculation. When Richard mooted their execution for such a plot, before he made any claim to the throne, the rest of the Council would not agree. Once he was accepted as king he ordered the executions immediately to secure his position. Similar conclusions must be drawn over the execution of Hastings. Hastings wanted Richard as Protector and his old enemies, the Woodvilles, out of power, but he was an old servant and personal friend of Edward IV and he wanted Edward V as king. There are three alternative explanations for his execution: either he responded unfavourably to an actual suggestion from Richard, probably via Buckingham, that Richard was rightfully king; or he concluded early in June, without any such approach, that Richard aimed at the throne; or, thirdly, he decided he would do better as an ally of the Woodvilles, now that Buckingham was clearly going to be Richard's chief adviser instead of himself. As a result of any of these alternatives Hastings must have taken some action to prevent any coup by Richard; he may have plotted to murder him. Whether there was a full-blown conspiracy remains a debating point, but it is surely incredible to maintain, as do some historians, that Hastings was blindly secure and oblivious to how events were progressing. Essentially, however, Hastings died because he would not tolerate the displacement of Edward IV's children.

We have a king of excellent intentions as a monarch and we have a political coup securing him the throne which involved the execution of four persons and encompassed the disappearance of two children. The coup was coupled with a moral claim to the throne that was precise and complex on a point of canon law. Arguments will always remain whether one part of the evidence buttressing this legal argument which made the princes illegitimate was a fabrication – the pre-contract to Eleanor Butler. It remains important, however, that this precise claim was put forward as it may indicate something of the king's character – a strong desire to do the right thing. We have a man of piety, some culture, a lover of music and jewels. The ambiguity remains – it seems a pity to discard it for the villain or for the hero.

In this book we have tried to show this, to depict Richard of Gloucester through the eyes of his contemporaries, and to provide the material for an informed appraisal of his acts and character.

The main sources used are the records of the central government of Richard's England, such as the Rolls of Parliament, and the Patent and Close Rolls. The most useful source for Richard's protectorate and reign is the register of the Signet Office, known as British Library Harleian Manuscript 433, a unique survival of Richard's administration. Other government records used include some from the Exchequer. Local government records from cities such as York and London have also been quoted. Private records of the fifteenth century are few, the Paston and Stonor letters being the best-known. Contemporary chroniclers are useful for filling the gaps between the other records: major use has been made of three of them – the Chronicler of Croyland, Dominic Mancini and John Rous.

The authorship of the 'continuation' or part of the Croyland Chronicle (from Crowland Abbey, Lincolnshire) covering the Yorkist period has been the subject of controversy. The author is known to have been a doctor of canon law and to have gone on diplomatic missions for Edward IV. He was certainly well placed to know what was going on. He may most plausibly be identified as John Russell, Bishop of Lincoln and Chancellor to Richard III. Other suggested authors include Henry Sharp of the Chancery and Richard Lavender, Archdeacon of Leicester. It is generally accepted that the chronicle was finished around April 1486.

Dominic Mancini was an Italian clergyman in the service of the Archbishop of Vienne who happened to be in England in 1483 to collect information for his master. He is unlikely to have known any English and would have been dependent on people who knew Latin, Italian or French for his information. He presumably had no bias himself on English affairs, although his French connections were undoubtedly hostile to England, but his sources seem to have been predominantly from circles hostile to Richard and in favour of the supporters of Edward V. He shows no personal acquaintance with Richard or anyone connected with him. He left England very soon after Richard's coronation and wrote up his account before the end of 1483. His manuscript was not known until it was discovered in Lille Library by C.A.J. Armstrong, who edited it for publication in 1936.

John Rous was a priest and antiquary of Warwick. He wrote a number of works including a history of England and what is known as the Rous Roll, a history of the Earls of Warwick with a paragraph of description and a drawing of each personage. He wrote the first version in English during the reign of Richard III and included a laudatory passage on Richard, and then rewrote this in Latin under Henry VII reviling Richard in strong terms.

EDITORIAL PRACTICE

To make the more difficult transcriptions easier for the non-professional historian to read, the punctuation and capitalisation have been modernised where confusion could arise, and Anglo-Saxon and superscript letters have been changed to modern forms. Omission of part of any text is shown by a line of dots, except for deletions and crossings-out in the original manuscripts which are omitted silently. Editorial additions not in the original manuscript are shown by square brackets.

York and Lancaster

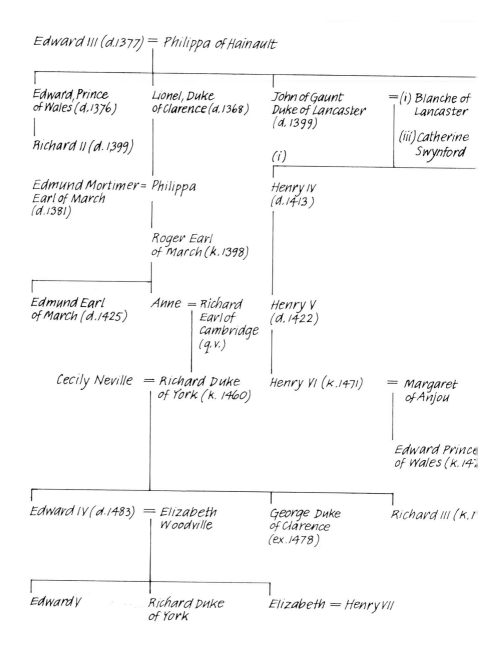

Edward III (d.1377) = Philippa of Hainault

Edward, Prince of Wales (d.1376)

Richard II (d.1399)

Lionel, Duke of Clarence (d.1368)

John of Gaunt Duke of Lancaster (d.1399)

=(i) Blanche of Lancaster

(iii) Catherine Swynford

(i)

Edmund Mortimer = Philippa
Earl of March
(d.1381)

Henry IV
(d.1413)

Roger Earl of March (k.1398)

Edmund Earl of March (d.1425)

Anne = Richard Earl of Cambridge (q.v.)

Henry V (d.1422)

Cecily Neville = Richard Duke of York (k.1460)

Henry VI (k.1471) = Margaret of Anjou

Edward Prince of Wales (k.14?)

Edward IV (d.1483) = Elizabeth Woodville

George Duke of Clarence (ex.1478)

Richard III (k.1

Edward V

Richard Duke of York

Elizabeth = Henry VII

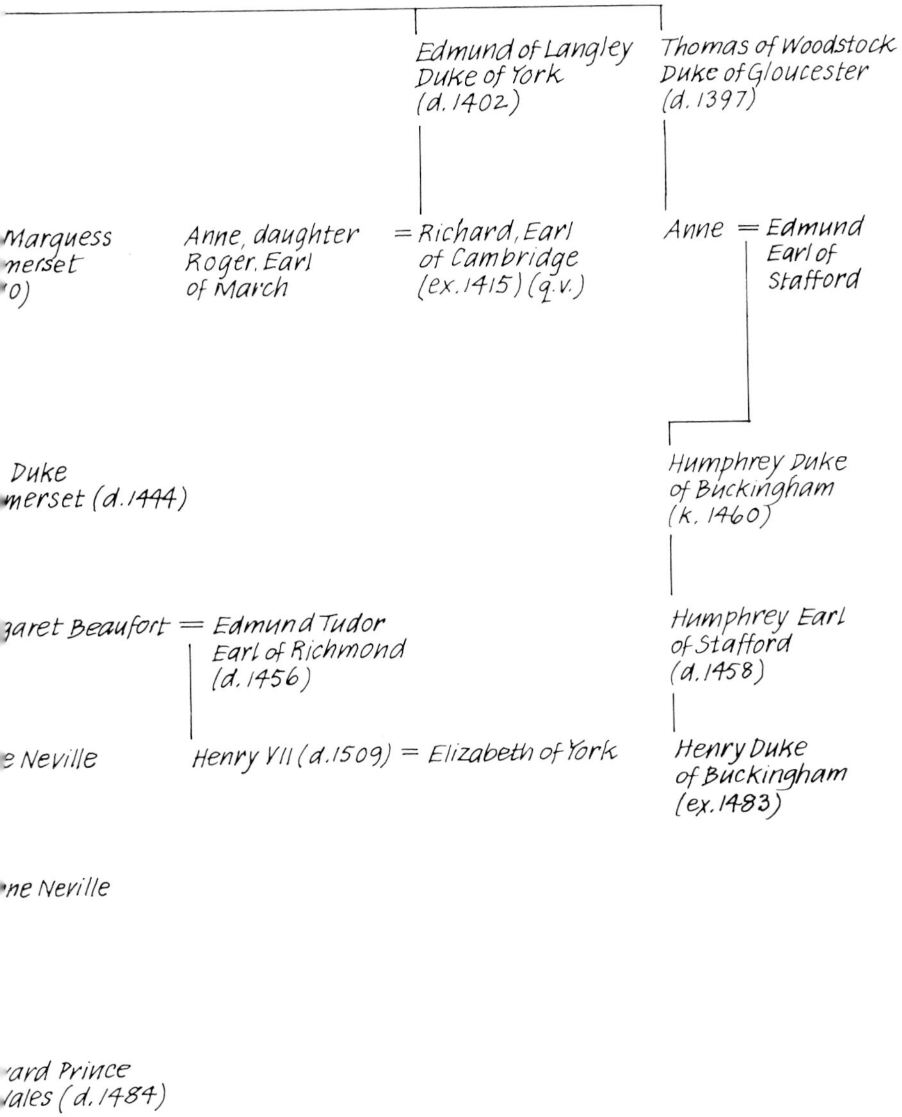

Edmund of Langley
Duke of York
(d. 1402)

Thomas of Woodstock
Duke of Gloucester
(d. 1397)

Marquess
merset
0)

Anne, daughter
Roger. Earl
of March

= Richard, Earl
of Cambridge
(ex. 1415) (q.v.)

Anne = Edmund
Earl of
Stafford

Duke
merset (d. 1444)

Humphrey Duke
of Buckingham
(k. 1460)

garet Beaufort = Edmund Tudor
Earl of Richmond
(d. 1456)

Humphrey Earl
of Stafford
(d. 1458)

e Neville

Henry VII (d. 1509) = Elizabeth of York

Henry Duke
of Buckingham
(ex. 1483)

ne Neville

ard Prince
Vales (d. 1484)

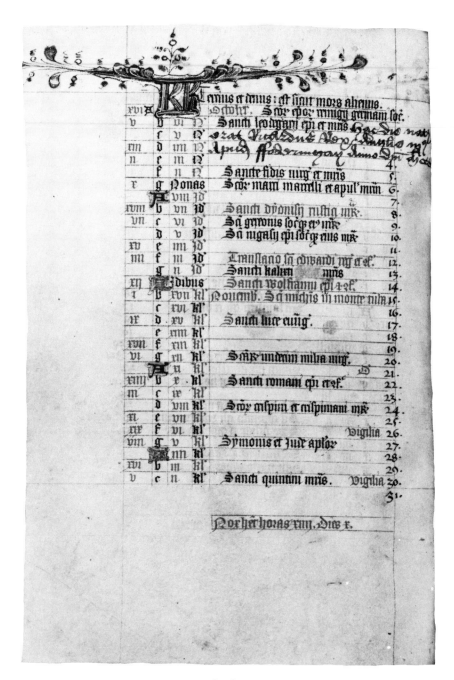

Lemius et deus: est sicut mors aliends.

				October. Scor epor uuigui germani soc.
xvia	A		Kl	
v	b	vi	N	Sancti leodegarii epi et mris
	c	v	N	erat Dietrich Nov — — — —
iiii	d	iiii	N	Aprid A die mozgay Anno — —
ii	e	iii	N	4.
	f	ii	N	Sancte fidis uirg et mris 5.
x	g	Nonas		Scor marii marcelli et apul min 6.
	A	viii	Id	7.
xviii	b	vii	Id	Sancti dyonisii ruftia mr 8.
vii	c	vi	Id	Sci geronis socior et mr 9.
	d	v	Id	Sci nigasii epi socior eius mr 10.
xv	e	iiii	Id	11.
iiii	f	iii	Id	Translacio sci edwardi regis et cf. 12.
	g	ii	Id	Sancti kalixti mris 13.
xii	A	Idibus		Sancti wolfganni epi et cf. 14.
i	b	xvii	kl	Novemb. Sci michis in monte tuba 15.
	c	xvi	kl	16.
ix	d	xv	kl	Sancti luce euang. 17.
	e	xiiii	kl	18.
xvii	f	xiii	kl	19.
vi	g	xii	kl	Scar undecim milia uirg. 20.
	A	xi	kl	21.
xiiii	b	x	kl	Sancti romani epi et cf. 22.
iii	c	ix	kl	23.
	d	viii	kl	Scor crispini et crispiniani mr 24.
xi	e	vii	kl	25.
xix	f	vi	kl	Vigilia 26.
viii	g	v	kl	Symonis et Iude aplor 27.
	A	iiii	kl	28.
xvi	b	iii	kl	29.
v	c	ii	kl	Sancti quintini mris. Vigilia 30.
				31.

Nor het horas xiiii, Dies x.

THE YOUNGEST BROTHER

The future Richard III was born at Fotheringhay Castle on 2 October 1452, the eleventh of twelve children born to Richard, Duke of York, and Cecily Neville, his wife. A contemporary verse records the names of all the children and the fact that Richard had a sickly infancy.

> Sir, aftir the tyme of longe bareynesse
> God first sent Anne, which signyfieth grace,
> In token that al her hertis hevynesse
> He, as for bareynesse, wold fro hem chace.
> Harry, Edward, and Edmonde, each in his place
> Succeedid, and aftir tweyn doughtris came,
> Elizabeth and Margarete, and aftirward William.
>
> John aftir William nexte borne was,
> Which bothe be passid to Godis grace.
> Georgè was next, and after Thomas
> Borne was, which sone aftir did pace
> By the path of dethe to the hevenly place.
> Richard liveth yit; but the last of alle
> Was Ursula, to Hym whom God list calle.[1]

Education followed conventional, pious lines, like those advised by Peter Idley, whose widow, Anne, was to be the mistress of the nursery of Richard's own son.

Opposite: Richard III's Book of Hours: calendar showing 2 October with a note added recording Richard's birth.

[23]

First God and thy kyng thou love and drede;
Above all thyng thou this preserve.
Faile not this for no maner nede,
Thoughe thow therfore shold perissh and sterve.
A man ony tyme fro his trowthe to swerve
Hymsilf and his kynne doith grete shame;
Therfore ever kepe the fro suche maner blame.

Allso thy fadre and modre thow honoure
As thou wolde thy sone shold to the;
And every man after riche and pouere,
As ever thow wilt have love of me;
And in rewarde it is geve unto the
The blessyng of thy fadre and modre:
Goode soone, that thou deserve noon other.

I have herde saide in old romaunce,
He that in youthe woll doo his diligence
To lerne, in age it woll hym avaunce
To kepe hym fro alle indigence.
Therefore in youthe leave thy necligence
And thynke on thy daies oolde:
After warme youthe cometh age coolde.[2]

Richard's education was interrupted by the civil war that came to a head in 1459 between his father and the party of Queen Margaret of Anjou. Richard, his brother George and his sister Margaret may have been at the sack of Ludlow with their mother.

Ande thys same yere there was a grete afray at Lodlowe by twyne the kynge and the Duke of Yorke, the Erle of Salusbury, the Erle of Warwyke, the Erle of Marche. The Duke of Yorke lete make a grete depe dyche and fortefyde it with gonnys, cartys, and stakys, but hys party was ovyr weke, . . . And thenne the duke fledde fro place to place in Walys, and breke downe the bryggys aftyr hym that the kyngys mayny schulde not come aftyr hym. And he wente unto Irlonde . . .

Opposite: Sir Richard and Lady Croft, from Croft Church. Lady Croft had been governess to Richard as a boy, her husband was his Treasurer of the Household as King.

Also that same yere the Duchyes of Yorke com unto Kyng Harry and submyttyd hyr unto hys grace, and she prayde for hyr husbonde that he myght come to hys answere and to be ressayvyd unto hys grace; and the kynge fulle humbely grauntyde hyr grace, and to alle hyrs that wolde come with hyr, and to alle othyr that wolde com yn with yn viij dayes. . . .

The mysrewle of the kyngys galentys at Ludlowe, whenn they hadd drokyn i-nowe of wyne that was in tavernys and in othyr placys, they fulle ungoodely smote owte the heddys of the pypys and hoggys hedys of wyne, that men wente wete-schode in wyne, and thenn they robbyd the towne, and bare a-waye beddynge, clothe, and othyr stuffe, and defoulyd many wymmen.

The Duchyes of Yorke was take to the Duke Bokyngham and to hys lady, for they two ben susters, and there she was tylle the fylde was done at Northehampton, and she was kept fulle strayte and many a grete rebuke.[3]

The Yorkist cause recovered in 1460 with the battle of Northampton, won by Richard's brother, Edward, and the Earl of Warwick. The youngest York children went to live in the great mansion once owned by Sir John Fastolf across the Thames from the Tower.

Christopher Hanson to John Paston, 12 October 1460:

Right worschipfull Sir and Maister, I recomaund me un to you. Please you to wete, the Monday after oure Lady Day there come hider to my maister ys place, . . . the Harbyger of my Lord of Marche, desyryng that my Lady of York and hir tw sonnys, my Lorde George and my Lorde Richard, and my Lady Margarete hir dawztyr, whiche y graunt hem in youre name to ly here untylle Mychelmas. And she had not ley here ij. dayes but sche had tythyng [tiding] of the londyng of my Lord at Chestre. The Tewesday next after, my Lord sent for hir that sche shuld come to hym to Harford [Hereford] and theder sche is gone. And sythe y left here bothe the sunys and the dowztyr, and the Lord of Marche comyth every day to se them.[4]

The Duke of York's defeat and death at Wakefield on 30 December 1460 made it imperative that his two youngest sons be sent to safety, in the lands of the Duke of Burgundy. They were treated with considerable honour in Bruges by the Duke, particularly after it was certain that York's eldest son was victorious and had consolidated his position as King Edward IV with a massive defeat of the Lancastrians at Towton.

[26]

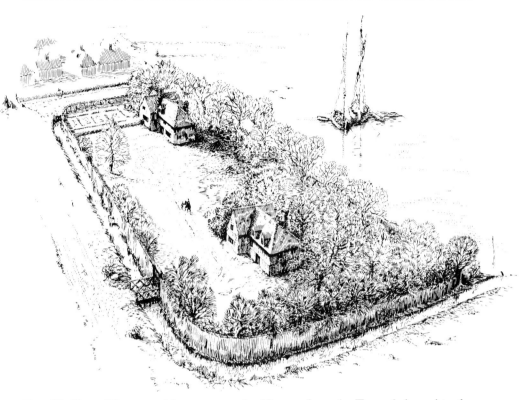

Fastolf's Place. The moated house across the Thames from the Tower belonged to the executors of Sir John Fastolf when Richard with his brother George and sister Margaret stayed there in the summer of 1460, and were visited by their eldest brother, the future Edward IV.

Prospero Camulio, Milanese Ambassador to the French Court, to Francesco Sforza, Duke of Milan, from Bruges on 18 April 1461:

Since I wrote today the two brothers of King Edward have arrived, one eleven and the other twelve years of age. The duke, who is most kind in everything, has been to visit them at their lodging, and showed them great reverence.

Richard and George returned to England via Calais. At both Canterbury and London they were received with ceremony. At London, on 1 June 1461:

[27]

Philip Duke of Burgundy and his son Charles the Bold, Count of Charolais, who married Richard's sister Margaret.

It was agreed that all the Common Council and the most worthy citizens of the guilds should meet tomorrow at Billingsgate the Lords George and Richard, brothers of the Lord King, in their liveries according etc. and that the Mayor and Aldermen be in crimson.[6]

After his attending the coronation on 28 June, honours and offices fell thick and fast on Richard. He was made Duke of Gloucester, elected to the order of the Garter, and made Admiral of England.

Westminster October 12, 1462. Grant for life to the king's brother Richard, duke of Gloucester, of the office of admiral of England, Ireland and Aquitaine, with all accustomed profits and powers, provided that he have no cognisance of affairs within the counties or of wreck of the sea. He is to have cognisance of death and maiming however committed in great ships in the middle of the great rivers, but only in the ports of those near the sea.[7]

Little is known of Richard's actual life until about 1465 when he was placed in the household of Richard Neville, Earl of Warwick, and his Countess, the heiress Anne Beauchamp, to learn the arts of war from the Earl's master of henchmen (well-born boys receiving their education in a lord's household) and the arts of peace, partly at least, from the Countess. John Rous of Warwick, who must have met her, has left a sketch of her:

. . . . . which goode lady had in her dayes grete tribulacon for her lordis sake Syre Rychard Neeuel, son and eyr to Sir Rychard, Eorl of Salisbury, and by her tityll Eorl of Warrwik, a famus knyght and excellent gretly spoke of thorow the moste parte of all christendam. This gode lady was born in the manor of Cawersham by redyng in the counte of Oxenford and was euer a full devout lady in Goddis seruys fre of her speche to euery person familiere accordyng to her and thore degre. Glad to be at and with women that traueld of chyld, full comfortable and plenteus then of all thyng that shuld be helpyng to hem. And in hyr tribulacons sho was euer to the gret plesure of God full pacient, to the grete meryte of her own sowl and ensample of all odre that were vexid with eny aduersyte. Sho was also gladly ever companable and liberal, and in her own persone semly and bewteus, and to all that drew to her ladishup as the dede shewid full gode and gracious, her reson was and euer shall.[8]

[29]

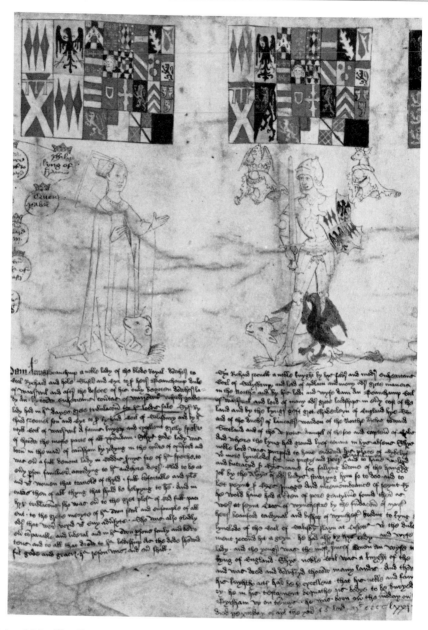

Richard Neville, Earl of Warwick and Anne Beauchamp his wife. Both contributed to Richard of Gloucester's education.

To Richard, Earl of Warwick, for costs and expenses incurred by him for the Lord Duke of Gloucester, the King's brother, and for an exhibition, &c., of the wardship and marriage of the son and heir of the Lord de Lovell,– £1000.[9]

Ceremonial and family duties included attendance at the lavish investiture banquet of his cousin, George Neville, as Archbishop of York. In 1468 he accompanied his sister, Margaret, to the English coast where she took ship to the Low Countries before her marriage to Charles, Duke of Burgundy.

Partriges	—	—	—	—	500
Wodcockes	—	—	—	—	400
Curlewes	—	—	—	—	100
Egrittes	—	—	—	—	1000
Stagges, Buckes, and Roes	—	—	500 and more		
Pasties of Venison colde	—	—	—	4000	
Parted dysshes of Gelly	—	—	—	1000	
Playne dysshes of Gelly	—	—	—	3000	
Colde Tartes baked	—	—	—	3000	
Colde Custardes baked	—	—	—	3000	
Hot pasties of Venison	—	—	—	1500	
Hot Custardes	—	—	—	—	2000
Pykes and Breames	—	—	—	608	
Porposes and Seales	—	—	—	12	

Spices, Sugered delicates, and Wafers plentie.

....

Estates syttyng in the cheefe Chamber

The Duke of Glocester the Kynges brother. On his ryght hande the Duches of Suffolke (his sister Elizabeth). On his left hande the Countesse of Westmorlande, and the Countesse of Northumberland, and two of the Lorde of Warwickes daughters.[10]

....

The Friday, the xviij day of June the viij[th] yere of the Reygne of our said soverayne Lorde, the sayd Princesse went from a place in London callid the Kynges Wardrape, devoutely toward her marriage, as ensuyth.

[31]

The coronet of Margaret of York. This coronet was probably originally made for Margaret to wear at the coronation of her brother Edward in 1461, and was later modified for her use as a marriage coronet at her wedding to Charles of Burgundy in 1468.

Furste unto the churche of Seynt Paule in London a bovesaid, and there made hur offring with grett devocion: and after hur offring soo made, she toke hur hors and rode toward the said cite; the Erle of Warrewyke riding before hur on hur hors, and with hur other Erlez and Barons, grett numbre, the Duchez of Norfolcke and other ladyez and gentilwemen of grett noumbre. And att hur entre into the Chepe, the Maiore of London and his brethern the Aldermen presentid hur a peyre of riche bassonis, and in the said basynnys a c li. of golde. And the same nyght she loggid att the Abbay

Richard's Garter Stall Plate as Duke of Gloucester. Richard was elected a Knight of the Garter in 1465, when he was 13 years old. It is the custom for all knights when elected to have an enamel plate of their arms erected at the back of the stall they occupy in St George's Chapel, Windsor.

The Battle of Barnet, from the Ghent manuscript, a contemporary report of the recovery of the throne by Edward IV.

of Strattforth, where the Kyng and the Quene laye the same nyght. And from thens she toke hur pilgremage unto saynte Thomas of Canterbury. And after hur departyng toward Canterbury, it pleasid the Kyng to send after hur and to see hur shippyng.

The Friday nexte after the Nativite of Seynt John Baptiste, she shippid at Margate; and there she toke leve of the Kyng and departid. There wente a yeyne with the Kyng, the Duc of Clarence, the Duc of Gloucestr, the Erle of Warrewike, the Erle of Sherewysbury, the Erle of Northhumburland; and there a bode with my Lady attendyng hur in hur shipp, my Lorde Scalez hur presenter, my Lorde Dacre hur chamberlayne, Sir John Widdevyle, Sir John Hayward, with many other famose knytes and esquirez. And she was shippid in the new Elyn of London, and in hur navy and compayne, the John of the New Castell, the Mary of Salesbury, and many other roiall shippis: and on the morowe landed att Scluse in Flaundrez.[11]

On 16 January 1469 Richard sat on the commission that tried and found guilty of high treason various persons, including Thomas Hungerford, in the presence of the King at Salisbury. Richard was granted many of the Hungerford lands and he came to an agreement with Thomas's mother, Margaret Lady Hungerford, whose husband also had been executed by the Yorkists after the battle of Hexham. Arrangements included provisions to enable her to carry out the foundation of a charity, almshouse and school.

14 May, 1469. Indenture of agreement, made between Richard Duke of Gloucester and Margaret Lady Hungerford and Botreaux, to the following effect:- (*i*) She to allow him and his heirs to have and enjoy the Castle and Manor of Farleigh [Hungerford], co. Somerset, with the park and all the appurtenances and the Advowson of the church, together also with a certain toft in Hungerford, co. Berks, called Hungerford Court, all which premises once belonged to Walter Lord Hungerford; to hold without interruption by her or by the feoffees of the said Walter. (*ii*) She, or feoffees to her use, to have and enjoy five Manors in Wiltshire . . . without interruption by him. (*iii*) She to hold for her life, without interruption by him, another seven Manors in Wiltshire . . . in which Manors she claimed to have an estate for her life and in dower. (*iv*) The feoffees of Robert, late Lord Hungerford, to hold during her life without interruption by the Duke a further seven manors and three Hundreds, she receiving the issues and

profits. (*v*) She to have and enjoy seven Manors in Cornwall and all the manors, lordships, lands and tenements in England which once belonged to Walter Lord Hungerford or Robert Lord Hungerford, his son, and of which she received the profits—save only the premises in (*i*) above. (*vi*) With regard to another six Manors in Wiltshire and Dorset of which certain persons had been enfeoffed by both Walter Lord Hungerford and Robert Lord Hungerford, for the establishing of a chantry of two priests in Salisbury Cathedral and an almshouse of St. Katherine, for twelve poor men with two women to attend to them, in Heytesbury, and for the finding of a schoolmaster in Heytesbury—the feoffees to hold the said premises, the Duke applying to the King within twelve months for a licence for such foundations.

Margrete Hungerford.[12]

Later in 1469 Richard accompanied the King on his progress through Norfolk. While at Castle Rising he wrote the first letter of his that has survived. The rest of the year was taken up with the plots of the Earl of Warwick and George of Clarence to gain control of the King. It is possible that Richard, together with Lord Hastings, was instrumental in rescuing Edward IV from imprisonment by Warwick in the North. In September Richard entered London with Edward and was soon rewarded for his loyalty with lands and the Constableship of England, the highest military office. His first independent command followed soon after.

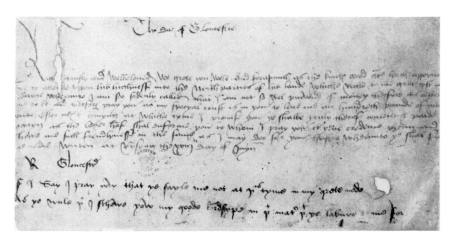

Richard of Gloucester's signature and a motto *Tant le desieree* on a folio of his copy of the romance of *Ipomedon*, in an English prose version. *Ipomedon* was a story of the perfect ideal knight. It is likely this is a teenage signature of Richard's.

Opposite: Letter from Richard to a person unknown, written from Castle Rising in 1469, borrowing money.

[35]

The Duc of Gloucestre.

Right trusty and welbeloved We grete you wele. And forasmuch as the Kings good Grace hathe appoynted me to attende upon His Highnesse into the North parties of his lande, whiche wolbe to me gret cost and charge, whereunto I am soo sodenly called that I am not so wel purveide of money therfore as behoves me to be, and therfore pray you as my specyal trust is in you, to lend me an hundreth pounde of money unto Ester next commyng, at whiche tyme I promise you ye shalbe truly therof content and paide agayn, as the berer herof shal enforme you: to whom I pray you to yeve credence therin, and showe me such frendlynesse in the same as I may doo for you herafter, wherinne ye shal find me redie. Writen at Risyng the xxiiij^{th} day of Juyn.

R. GLOUCESTR.

[A Postscript entirely in the Duke's hand adds]

Sir I say I pray you that ye fayle me not at this tyme in my grete nede, as ye wule that I schewe yow my goode lordshype in that matter that ye labure to me for.[13]

Westminster. 17 October 1469. Grant for life to the king's brother, Richard, duke of Gloucester, of the office of constable of England, with the accustomed fees and profits, in the same manner as Richard, late earl Rivers, had it.[14]

Grant to the King's brother Richard, duke of Gloucester, of full power and authority to reduce and subdue the King's castles of Carmardyn and Cardycan in South Wales, which Morgan ap Thomas ap Griffith, 'gentilman', and Henry ap Thomas ap Griffith, 'gentilman', with other rebels have entered into and from which they raid the adjacent parts, and to put them under safe custody and governance and to promise pardon to such rebels within them as shall be willing to submit and take an oath of fealty.

December 16, 1469, Westminster   By the King[15]

[36]

THE KING'S RIGHT ARM

The disturbances continued in 1470, beginning with a dangerous rebellion by Lord Welles, planned by the Earl of Warwick and the Duke of Clarence. They were proclaimed traitors by Edward IV and in March fled to France, only to return in September with troops, and now as allies of Margaret of Anjou and Henry VI. They in their turn, aided by Warwick's brother the Marquess Montague, drove out Edward IV, who fled to Flanders. Warwick now proclaimed Henry King again, and consolidated his position. Edward IV was accompanied in his flight by his brother Richard, a small part of his court and a few troops. The indigent refugees were received by Edward's brother-in-law the Duke of Burgundy and his agents.

But anone one of the oste went ouste frome the fellawschippe, and tolde Kynge Edwarde alle manere of thynge, and bade hym avoyde, for he was noȝt stronge enoghe to gyff batayle to Markes Montagu; and then anone Kynge Edwarde haysted hym in alle that he myght to the towne of Lynne, and ther he toke schyppynge one Michaelmesse day, in the x. yere of his regne, with Lorde Hastynges, that was the Kynges Chamberleyne, Lorde Say, withe dyverse other knyghtes and squyers, passed and saylede overe the see into Flaunders, to his brother-in-lawe the Duke of Burgeyne, for socoure and helpe, &c.[16]

By chance the Lord de Gruthuse, the Duke of Burgundy's governor in Holland, was at that place where and when King Edward wished to land; who by some persons put on shore, was immediately informed of his miserable condition and the danger he was in by reason of the Easterlings. The governor sent immediately to the Easterlings to charge them to be still, and went on board the King's ship himself, and invited him on shore; whereupon the King landed, with his brother the Duke of Gloucester (who

[37]

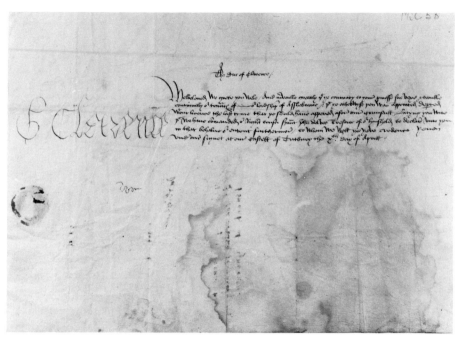

Letter signed by George Duke of Clarence in 1468, from Tutbury Castle.

was called afterwards King Richard III), and about 1500 men in their train. The King had no money about him, and gave the master of the ship a gown lined with beautiful martens, and promised to do more for him whenever he had an opportunity; but sure so poor a company was never seen before; yet the Lord of Gruthuse dealt very honourably by them, for he gave many of them clothes, and bore all their expenses till they came to the Hague, to which place he safely conducted them.[17]

Item paid by order of my Lord of Boucham the bailiff of Veere which he had loaned, when my Lord of Gloucester travelled in Holland 3 pounds 2 shillings 3 pennies[18]

King Edward and his brother were well treated in Burgundy, and were supplied with troops, supplies and ships by Duke Charles. They sailed from Flushing in March 1471, and landed at Ravenspur at the mouth of the Humber on the fourteenth of the month.

Opposite: The house of Louis de Gruuthuse in Bruges, where Richard stayed while in exile in 1470–1.

[39]

The Kynge, with his shippe aloone, wherein was the Lord Hastings, his Chambarlayne, and other to the nombar of v^c well chosen men, landed within Humber, on Holderness syde, at a place callyd Ravenersporne, even in the same place where somtime the Usurpowr Henry of Derby, aftar called Kynge Henry the IV. landed, aftar his exile, contrary and to the dissobeysance of his sovereigne lord, Kynge Richard the II. whome, aftar that, he wrongfully distressed, and put from his reigne and regalie, and usurped it falsely to hymselfe and to his issve, from whome was linially descended Kynge Henry, at this tyme usinge and usurpinge the corone, as sonne to his eldest sonne, somtyme callyd Kynge Henry the V. The Kyng's brothar Richard, Duke of Glowcestar, and, in his company, iij^{c}men, landyd at an othar place iiij myle from thens. The Earle Rivers, and the felowshipe beinge in his companye, to the nombar of ij^c, landyd at a place called Powle, xiiij myle from there the Kynge landyd, and the reminaunt of the felowshipe wher they myght best get land.[19]

From Ravenspur they made for York, where Edward was admitted when he said he had come only to claim his Duchy of York. He then marched south, eluding pursuit by the Marquis Montague and gathering men. At Coventry on the 29th March he proclaimed himself King, and moved on to Warwick where, with the aid of the Duke of Gloucester, he was reconciled with his brother Clarence.

The Kynge, that tyme beinge at Warwyke, and undarstondynge his neere approchinge, upon an afarnone isswyd out of Warwike, with all his felowshipe, by the space of three myles, into a fayre fylde towards Banbery, where he saw the Duke, his brothar, in faire array, come towards hym, with a greate felaship. And, whan they were togedars, within less than an halfe myle, the Kynge set his people in aray, the bannars [displayed] and lefte them standynge still, takynge with hym his brothar of Glocestar, the Lord Rivers, Lord Hastings, and fewe othar, and went towarde his brothar of Clarence. And, in lyke wyse, the Duke, for his partye takynge with hym a fewe noble men, and levinge his hoost in good order, departyd from them towards the Kynge. And so they mett betwixt both hostes, where was right kynde and lovynge langwage betwixt them twoo, with parfite accord knyt togethars for evar here aftar, with as hartyly lovynge chere and countenaunce, as might be betwix two bretherne of so grete nobley and astate. And than, in lyke wyse, spake togethar the two Dukes of Clarence and Glocestar, and, aftar, the othar noble men beinge there with them,

[40]

whereof all the people there that lovyd them, and awght them theyr trew service, were right glade and ioyous, and thanked God highly of that ioyows metynge, unitie, and accorde, hopynge that, therby, shuld growe unto them prosperows fortune, in all that they shud aftar that have a doo. And than the trompetts and minstrels blew uppe, and, with that, the Kynge browght his brothar Clarence, and suche as were there with hym, to his felowshippe, whom the sayd Duke welcomyd into the land in his best manner, and they thanked God, and hym, and honoryd hym as it apparteygned.

Aftar this, the Kygne, yet levinge his hooste standynge still, with the sayd few persons went with his brothar of Clarence to his hoste, whome he hertily welcomyd, and promised hym largely of his grace and good love, and, from thens, they all came hoole togethars to the Kyngs hooste, when ethar party welcomyd and jocundly receyvyd othar, with perfect frindlynes; and, so, with greate gladnes, bothe hostes, with theyr princes, togethars went to Warwyke, with the Kynge, and ther lodged, and in the countrie nere adioyninge.[20]

And in this meane whyle woord was browght that the duke himself was at hand (near Warwick) with an huge army; which when King Edward understoode, he raisyd his camp and went to mete the duke. Howbeyt, because yt showld not seme soome suttle practyse concludyd betwixt them two, he marchid in good order of battaylle, as one that myndyd to fight. The duke dyd the lyke. But whan they came within view thone of thother, Richard duke of Glocestre, as thowghe he had bene apoyntyd arbyter of all controversy, first conferryd secretly with the duke; than he returnyd to King Edward, and dyd the very same with him. Fynally, not warre but peace was in every mans mouth; than, armour and weapon layd apart uppon both sydes, the broothers gladly embracyd one an other.[21]

From Warwick the royal army marched to London, where the gates were opened to them on Maundy Thursday, the 11th of April. Edward went to Westminster where his queen had taken sanctuary, to greet her and his heir, who had been born during the winter. Two days later, on the eve of Easter Day, Edward marched his army north again to meet the Earl of Warwick. The vanguard was commanded by the Duke of Gloucester. The two armies met at Barnet, ten miles north of London, and on Easter Sunday a great battle took place.

[41]

[42]

And Kyng Edward upon the same daye rode wyth grete pompe thorwth the Cyte when he had dynyd, and King Henry was conveyed secretly afftyr hym, and soo held on his waye to Barnet, and that nyght lodgid hym and his people abowth the toun. . . .

Upon the morn soo sone as the day dawid, the Captaynys embataylyd theyre people upon eythir syde, the duke of Glowcetyr ledyng the vaward of Kyng Edward.[22]

But it happenede that he withe his oste were enterede into the toune of Barnet, before the Erle of Warwyke and his host. And so the Erle of Warwyke and his host lay witheoute the towne alle nyght, and eche of them loosede gonnes at othere, alle the nyght. And on Ester day in the mornynge, the xiiij. day of Apryl, ryght erly, eche of them came uppone othere; and ther was suche a grete myste, that nether of them myght see othere perfitely; ther thei faughte, from iiij. of clokke in the mornynge unto x. of clokke the fore-none. And dyverse tymes the Erle of Warwyke party hade the victory, and supposede that thei hade wonne the felde. But it hapenede so, that the Erle of Oxenfordes men hade uppon them ther lordes lyvery, bothe before and behynde, which was a sterre withe stremys, wiche [was] myche lyke Kynge Edwardes lyvery, the sunne with stremys; and the myste was so thycke, that a manne myghte not profytely juge one thynge from anothere; so the Erle of Warwikes menne schott and faughte ayens the Erle of Oxenfordes menne, wetynge and supposynge that thei hade bene Kynge Edwardes menne; and anone the Erle of Oxenforde and his menne cryed "treasoune! treasoune!" and fledde awaye from the felde withe viij. c. menne. The Lorde Markes Montagu was agreyde and apoyntede with Kynge Edwarde, and put uppone hym Kynge Edwardes lyvery; and a manne of the Erles of Warwyke sawe that, and felle uppone hyme, and kyllede hym. And whenne the Erle of Warwyke sawe his brothere dede, and the Erle of Oxenforde fledde, he lepte one horse-backe, and flede to a wode by the felde of Barnett, where was no waye forthe; and one of Kynge Edwardes menne hade espyede hyme, and one came uppone hym and kylled hym, and dispolede hyme nakede. And so Kynge Edwarde gate that felde. And ther was slayne of the Erle of Warwykes party, the Erle hym self, Markes Montagu, Sere William Tyrelle, knyghte, and many other.[23]

Opposite: The London trained bands going out to fight before the Battle of Barnet in 1471. The hostage, Henry VI, is escorted by Edward IV. By J.H. Amschewitz at the Royal Exchange.

[43]

The Yorkist victory was greeted with popular acclaim:

On the Recovery of the Throne by Edward IV

Remembyr with reverens the Maker of mankynde,
  How myghty, how mercyfulle, how glorius he is,
Alle erthly creaturus in thayre reasonys byn blynde,
  Whan they compar with his power thay do alle
      amys.
  Agaynste his power no thynge impossible is;
Wherefore lett us say in wele and in woo
Good Lorde, evermore thy wille be doo.

How mervelous to man, how dowtfulle to drede,
  How far paste mannys resoun and mynde hath it
      bee,
The comyng of kynge Edwarde, and his good spede,
  Owte of Dochelonde into Englonde over the salte see.
  In what parell and trowbill, in what payne was
      hee!
Whan the salte water and tempest wrought hym
      gret woo;
But in adversite and ever, Lorde, thy wille be doo.

His knyghtehode, his power, his ordinance, his ryghte,
  Agaynst this trowblis tempest avaylid hym no
      thynge.
What may manhode do agaynst Goddes myghte?
  The wynde, the water spareth nodyr priynce ne kyng.
  Haply that trowbill was for wickyd lyvyng;
God wolde every creature his Maker shulde know,
Wherefore, good Lorde, ever more thy wille be doo.
              ....

To Westmynster the kyng be water did glide,
  Worshypfully resayvid with processioun in ffeet,
Resayvid with reverence, his dewte not denye;
  The cardenall uppone his hede the crowne did sett,
  The septure in his honde, withowte intrumpcioun or
      lett.

[44]

Then to seynt Edwardes shryne the priynce did goo,
Thus in every thyng the wille of God is doo.

The kyng comfortid the quene, and other ladyes eke;
  His swete babis full tendurly he did kys;
The yonge priynce he behelde, and in his armys did bere.
    Thus his bale turnyd hym to blis;
    Aftur sorow joy, the course of the worlde is.
The sighte of his babis relesid parte of his woo;
Thus the wille of God in every thyng is doo.

How sodenly that tyme he was compellid to parte
  To the felde of Barnet with his enmys to fyghte.
God lett never prynce be so hevy in his herte
  As kynge Edwarde was all that hole nyghte.
    And aftur that shone a ster over his hede full
      bryghte,
The syght of the wiche made his enmys woo;
It was a tokyn of victory, Goddis will was soo.
          ....

"Avaunce, baner," quod the kyng, "passe forthe anone,
  "In the name of the Trinyte and oure Lady
      bryghte,
"Seynt Edward, seynt Anne, and swete seynt Johan,
  "And in the name of seynt George, oure ladis
      "knyghte,
"This day shew thy grett power and thy gret
      "myghte,
"And brynge thy trew subjectes owte of payne and
      "woo;
"And as thy wille is, Lorde, thys jorney be doo."

There was shotyng of gonnys and arows plente;
  There was showtyng and crying that the erth did
      quake;
There was hewyng of harnes, pete was to see;
  For fere of that fray many man did shake.
  There was tremelyng and turnyng thayre woo did
    wake.

[45]

There was hewyng of helmettes and salettes also;
Hit plesid God that seasoun it shulde be soo.

There was jollyng, ther was rennyng for the sove-
    reynte,
  There was rorynge and rumbelynge, pete to here;
Fayne was the waykyer away for to flee.
    That day many a stowte man was ded there;
    Warwicke and Mowntegew were slayne in fere,
Knyghtes and gentilmen and other men moo.
In all thynges, good Lorde, every thy wille be doo.

There was rydynge and rennyng; sum cryed, "Wayle-
    'away!"
  Unknowyng to many man who the better hadde.
Sum soughte thayre maysters, sum hit thaym that day,
    Sum ran here and there like men that were madde;
    Sum were ryght hevy and harde bestadde,
Ryght besy in thayre wittes away to goo.
Alle was for the best, oure Lorde wold it shulde be so.

Kynge Edward and his brothere, dowtyng no fere,
  Lordis and other gentilmen in the kynges ryghte,
Stidfastyly and worshypfully thayre parte did there,
    Manly and freshely that day did thay fyghte.
    To kynge Edwarde fille the victorye, throw Goddes
    myghte.
Many one whan thay wist thay were rughte woo.
Hit bootid hem not to stryve, the wille of God was soo.

To London com the kyng whan the batell was doo,
  Levyng behynde hym many a dede man;
Sum hurte, sum slayne, sum cryinge "Alas!"
    Gretter multitude than I con telle.
    Sum waloyng in blood, sum pale, sum wan.
Sum sekyng thayre frendis in care and in woo.
In every thynge, Lord, thy wille be doo.

            ....

The duke of Glocetter, that nobill prynce,
  Yonge of age and victorius in batayle,
To the honoure of Ectour that he myghte comens,
  Grace hym folowith, fortune, and good spede.
  I suppose hes the same that clerkis of rede,
Fortune hathe hym chosyn, and forthe wyth hym
    wil goo,
Her husbonde to be, the wille of God is soo.

In the kynges forwarde the prynce did ride,
  Withe nobill lordis of grett renowne;
The erle of Penbroke, the lorde chamberlayne be his
    side;
  Many other knyghtes and yomen of the crowne;
  With trumppus and clarions thay rode to Londone.
In the kynges forwarde were viij. m.[1] and moo.
Thus in every thynge the wille of God is doo.
      ....

Then to the gate the kynge did ride,
  His brethir and his lordis in ordre, a good sighte to see.
iiij. m[1] harnessid men the kynge did abide,
  And worshypfully resayvid hym into the cite.
  Cryste preserve the pepull, for his grett pete!
xx. m[1], I suppose, and many one moo,
Welcomyd kyng Edward, the will of God was soo.[24]

On the same day as the Battle of Barnet was being fought, Queen Margaret, with her son Edward and his wife Anne Neville (younger daughter of the Earl of Warwick and recently married to the Prince to cement the alliance), landed in Weymouth. They marched west with fugitives from Barnet, making for Wales in the hope of linking up with Jasper Tudor. Edward hastily gathered his army and on the 24th of April set off from Windsor in pursuit. After a series of forced marches Margaret and her forces were brought to bay at Tewkesbury, near Gloucester, where another great battle took place, the Duke of Gloucester again commanding the van. The Lancastrians were again defeated.

[47]

Diorama of the Battle of Tewkesbury. King Edward's position is the left foreground, the melée in the centre left represents the charge of Richard of Gloucester. The position of Queen Margaret of Anjou is centre top.

And Quene Marget, and Prince Edwarde hire sonne, with other knygtes, squyres, and other menne of the Kyng of France, hade navy to brynge them to Englond: whiche, whenne thei were schipped in Fraunce, the wynde was so contrary unto them xvij. dayes and nyghtes, that [thei] myght not come from Normandy with unto Englonde, whiche withe a wynd myght have seylede it in xij. oures; whiche at the xvij. dayes ende on Ester day at the evyne the[i] landed at Weymouthe, and so by lande from Weymouthe the[i] roode to Excetre; and mette withe hire, at Weymouth, Edmunde Duke of Somersett, the Lorde Jhon his brother, brother to Herry Duke of Somerset slayne at Exham, and Curteney the Erle of Devynschyre, and many other. And on Ester mounday was brought tithingys to them, that Kynge Edwarde hade wonne the felde at Barnett, and that Kynge Herry was put

[48]

into the Toure ayene. And anone ryghte thei made oute commaundementes, in the Quenes name and the Prynce, to alle the weste
countre, and gaderet grete peple, and kepte hire wey towarde the toune of
Brystow. And when the Kynge herd that thei were landede, and hade
gaderede so myche peple, he toke alle his hoste, and went oute of Londone
the wennysday in Ester weke, and manly toke his waye towarde them; and
Prynce Edwarde herd thereof; he hastede hym self and alle his oste towarde
the towne of Glouceter, but he enteryd noght into the towne, but held
forthe his wey to the towne of Teukesbury, and ther he made a felde noght
ferre from the ryver of Saverne; and Kynge Edwarde and his oste came
uppone hym, the saturday the fourth day of Maij, the yere aforeseide of
oure Lorde a m^l. cccclxxj., and the xj yere of Kynge Edwarde.[25]

Upon the morrow followynge, Saterday, the iiij. day of May, [the
Kynge] apparailed hymselfe, and all his hoost set in good array; ordeined
three wards; displayed his bannars; dyd blowe up the trompets;
commytted his caws and qwarell to Almyghty God, to owr most blessyd
lady his mothar, Vyrgyn Mary, the glorious martyr Seint George, and all
the saynts; and avaunced, directly upon his enemyes; approchinge to theyr
filde, whiche was strongly in a marvaylows strong grownd pyght, full
difficult to be assayled. Netheles the Kyngs ordinance was so conveniently
layde afore them, and his vawarde so sore oppressyd them, with shott of
arrows, that they gave them right-a-sharpe shwre. Also they dyd agayne-
ward to them, bothe with shot of arrows and gonnes, whereof netheles they
ne had not so great plenty as had the Kynge. In the front of theyr field were
so evell lanes, and depe dykes, so many hedges, trees, and busshes, that it
was right hard to approche them nere, and come to hands; but Edmond,
called Duke of Somarset, having that day the vawarde, whithar it were for
that he and his fellowshipe were sore annoyed in the place where they were,
as well with gonnes-shott, as with shot of arrows, whiche they ne wowld nor
durst abyde, or els, of great harte and corage, knyghtly and manly avaunsyd
hymselfe, with his fellowshipe, somewhat asyde-hand the Kyngs vawarde,
and, by certayne pathes and wayes therefore afore purveyed, and to the
Kyngs party unknowne, he departyd out of the field, passyd a lane, and
came into a fayre place, or cloos, even afore the Kynge where he was
enbatteled, and, from the hill that was in that one of the closes, he set right
fiercely upon th'end of the Kyngs battayle. The Kynge, full manly, set
forther even upon them, enteryd and wann the dyke, and hedge, upon
them, into the cloose, and, with great vyolence, put them up towards the
hyll, and, so also, the Kyng's vaward, being in the rule of the Duke of
Gloucestar.

[49]

Here it is to be remembred, how that, whan the Kynge was comyn afore theyr fielde, or he set upon them, he consydered that, upon the right hand of theyr field, there was a parke, and therein moche wood, and he, thinkynge to purvey a remedye in caace his sayd enemyes had layed any bushement in that wood, of horsemen, he chose, out of his fellashyppe, ij^c speres, and set them in a plomp, togethars, nere a qwartar of a myle from the fielde, gyvenge them charge to have good eye upon that cornar of the woode, if caas that eny nede were, and to put them in devowre, and, yf they saw none suche, as they thowght most behovfull for tyme and space, to employ themselfe in the best wyse as they cowlde; which provisyon cam as well to poynt at this tyme of the battayle as cowthe well have been devysed, for the sayd spers of the Kyngs party, seinge no lyklynes of eny busshement in the sayd woode-corner, seinge also goode oportunitie t'employ them selfe well, cam and brake on, all at ones, upon the Duke of Somerset, and his vawarde, asyde-hand, unadvysed, whereof they, seinge the Kynge gave them ynoughe to doo afore them, were gretly dismaied and abasshed, and so toke them to flyght into the parke, and into the medowe that was nere, and into lanes, and dykes, where they best hopyd to escape the dangar; of whom, netheles, many were distressed, taken, and slayne; and, even at this point of theyr flyght, the Kynge coragiously set upon that othar felde, were was chefe Edward, called Prince, and, in short while, put hym to discomfiture and flyght; and so fell in the chase of them that many of them were slayne, and, namely, at a mylene, in the medowe fast by the towne, were many drownyd; many rann towards the towne; many to the churche; to the abbey; and els where; as they best myght.[26]

Many were killed on both sides in the battle. The contemporary sources make it clear that Prince Edward was killed on the field and not murdered afterwards by Edward IV and his brothers, as Tudor sources claimed.

And Edmunde Duke of Somersett, and Sere Hugh Curteneye, went oute of the felde, by the whiche the felde was broken; and the moste parte of the people fledde awaye from the Prynce, by the whiche the feld was loste in hire party. And ther was slayne in the felde, Prynce Edward, whiche cryede for socoure to his brother-in-lawe the Duke of Clarence.[27]

In the wynnynge of the fielde such as abode hand-stroks were slayne incontinent; Edward, called Prince, was taken, fleinge to the towne wards, and slayne, in the fielde. Ther was also slayne Thomas, called th'Erle of Devonshire; John of Somarset, called Marqwes Dorset; Lord Wenloke; with many othar in great nombar.[28]

This Kyng tooke to his wyfe Margarete the Kyngus doughtur of Cicile, whit wham he had his sone Edward, Pryns of Wales, that aftur that he come from Fraunce with his modur with a gret ost was sley at the Batel by syde Tewkesbury, the yere of Oure Lord MCCCCLXXII [sic].[29]

George, Duke of Clarence, wrote to Henry Vernon from Tewkesbury, 6 May 1471:

Right trusti and welbeloved we grete you wele, lating you wite that my lord hath had goode spede nowe in his late journey to the subduyng of his enemyes, traitours and rebelles, of the which Edward late called Prince, the late Erl of Devon with other estates, knightes, squiers, and gentilmen, were slayn in playn bataill, Edmund late Duc of Somerset taken and put to execucion, and other diverses estates, knightes, squiers, and gentilmen taken. And for soo much as my said lord and we bee fully pourposed with the grace of our Lord to comme in all goodly haste into the north partyes for theestablishement of pease, tranquillite and restful rule and governance of the same, we desire and for your wele advyse you, and also in my said lordes name charge you, to dispose you to comme and attende upon us with so many men defensibly arrayed as ye can make, and that at ferthest ye bee with us at Coventre the xij day of this present moneth. Yeven under our signet at Tewkesbury the vj day of May. (*Signed:-*) G. Clarence.[30]

Having conquered all his enemies King Edward re-entered London in triumph on Tuesday 21st May with his brothers and the captured Queen Margaret. That same night, in the Tower of London, Henry VI died. It seems probable that his death was ordered by the King (and that he did not die of melancholy as the official account in the *Arrivall* says – unless this refers to a heart attack when he heard of the death of his son), and that the Duke of Gloucester bore the order to the Tower. This he would have done as Constable of England. The execution must have been ordered by the King, Gloucester is unlikely to have murdered Henry on his own initiative without the King's knowledge, as later chronicles accuse him of doing.

[51]

Here it is to be remembred, that, from the tyme of Tewkesbery fielde, where Edward, called Prince, was slayne, thanne, and soone aftar, wer taken, and slayne, and at the Kyngs wylle, all the noblemen that came from beyond the see with the sayde Edward, called Prince, and othar also theyr parte-takers as many as were of eny might or puisaunce. Qwene Margaret, hirselfe, taken, and browght to the Kynge; and, in every party of England, where any commotion was begonne for Kynge Henry's party, anone they were rebuked, so that it appeared to every mann at eye the sayde partie was extincte and repressed for evar, without any mannar hope of agayne quikkening; utterly despaired of any maner of hoope or releve. The certaintie of all whiche came to the knowledge of the sayd Henry, late called Kyng, being in the Tower of London; not havynge, afore that, knowledge of the saide matars, he toke it to so great dispite, ire, and indingnation, that, of pure displeasure, and melencoly, he dyed the xxiij. day of the monithe of May. Whom the Kynge dyd to be browght to the friers prechars at London, and there, his funerall service donne, to be caried, by watar, to an Abbey upon Thamys syd, xvj myles from London, called Chartsey, and there honorably enteryd.[31]

And the same nyghte that Kynge Edwarde came to London, Kynge Herry, beynge inwarde in presone in the Toure of Londone, was putt to dethe, the xxj. day of Maij, on a tywesday nyght, betwyx xj. and xij. of the cloke, beynge thenne at the Toure the Duke of Gloucetre, brothere to Kynge Edwarde, and many other; and one the morwe he was chestyde and brought to Paulys, and his face was opyne that every manne myghte see hyme; and in hys lyinge he bledde one the pament ther; and afterward at the Blake Fryres was broughte, and ther he blede new and fresche; and from thens he was caryed to Chyrchesey abbey in a bote, and buryed there in oure Lady chapelle.[32]

On the vigil of this feast, king Edward entered London in state for the third time, with a retinue far greater than any of his former armies, and with standards unfurled and borne before him and the nobles of his army. Upon this occasion many were struck with surprise and astonishment, seeing that there was now no enemy left for him to encounter. This prudent prince however, fully understanding the fickle disposition of the people of Kent, had come to the resolution that he would not disarm until he had visited those ravagers with condign punishment for their misdeeds at their own doors. For this purpose, he proceeded into Kent with his horse in hostile

[52]

form; having done which, he returned, a most renowned conqueror and a mighty monarch: whose praises resounded far and wide throughout the land, for having achieved such great exploits with such wondrous expedition and in so short a space of time.

I would pass over in silence the fact that at this period king Henry was found dead in the Tower of London; may God spare and grant time for repentance to the person, whoever he was, who thus dared to lay sacrilegious hands upon the Lord's anointed! Hence it is that he who perpetrated this has justly earned the title of tyrant, while he who thus suffered has gained that of a glorious Martyr. The body was exhibited for some days in Saint Paul's church at London, and was carried thence by the river Thames to the conventual church of the monks at Chertsey, in the diocese of Winchester, fifteen miles from the city; a kind of barge having been solemnly prepared for the purpose, provided with lighted torches.[33]

Very soon after his triumphant arrival back in London King Edward took the opportunity of the presence in the City of many of his nobles and knights to obtain their subscription to an oath of loyalty to his new-born son Edward. Richard of Gloucester was the second member of the laity to sign his name, after his brother Clarence.

Memorandum that on 3 July 11 Edward IV at Westminster in the chamber of parliament, Thomas cardinal archbishop of Canterbury and other lords spiritual and temporal and knights whose names are underwritten, made recognisance and gave their oaths to Edward eldest son of King Edward, prince of Wales, duke of Cornwall and earl of Chester, in form following, and in corroboration of their promise, signed their names with their own hand.

I Thomas Cardinall Archbishop of Caunterbury knowlege, take, and repute you, Edward Prince of Wales, Duke of Cornwayll, and Erle of Chestre, furste begoten son of oure sovereigne lord Edward the IIIIth King of England and of Fraunce and Lord of Irland, to be verey and undoubted heyre to oure seid sovereigne lord as to the corones and reames of England and of France and lordship of Ireland; and promitte and swere, that in cas hereafter it happen, you by Goddis disposition to outleve our seid sovereigne lord, I shall then take and accepte you for true, veray, and rightwis Kyng of Englond, &. And feith and trouth to you shall bere. And yn all thyngs truely and feithfully behave me towardes you and youre heyres, as a true and feithfull subject oweth to behave hym to his sovereigne

[53]

lord, and rightwys Kyng of Englond, &. So help me God, and Holidome, and this holy Evaungeliste.[34]

T. Cardinall Cantuar

. . . .

R. Gloucestre

. . . .

Map of Croyland, Lincolnshire, from John Thorpe's Survey, 1617. Richard and Edward visited Croyland in 1469. The Abbey Chronicle is one of the main sources for the reigns of Edward IV and Richard III.

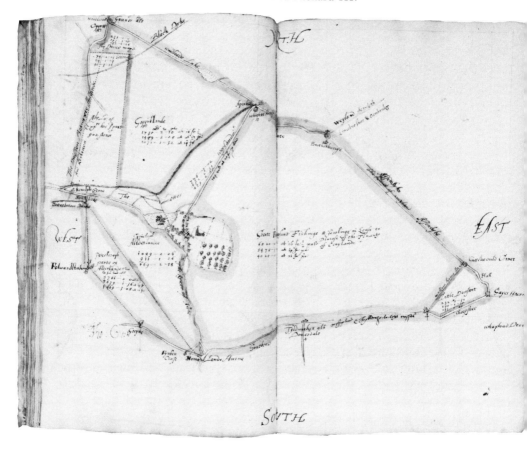

[54]

At some time in the summer of 1471, a great quarrel broke out between the Dukes of Clarence and Gloucester. The latter had been granted the estates of the Earl of Warwick in July, but Clarence seems to have believed that these estates, and those held by the Earl in right of his wife Anne Beauchamp, should come to him as husband of Isobel, the Earl's elder daughter. Richard, who wished to marry Anne Neville, the younger daughter, not unnaturally disagreed. Clarence even went to the length of hiding Anne so that Gloucester could not marry her. The quarrel went on for a considerable time, until brought to an end by the King dividing the estates between the two dukes, after the marriage of Anne and Richard, some time in 1472–3 or early 1474.

Grant to the King's brother Richard, duke of Gloucester, and the heirs male of his body of the castles, manors and lordships of Midelham and Scyrefhoton, co. York, and the castle and lordship of Penreth, co. Cumberland, with their members and all other lordships, manors and lands in those counties which were entailed to Richard Neville, late earl of Warwick, and the heirs male of his body or any ancestor whose heir male he was in like manner, with all knights' fees, advowsons, members, hamlets, meadows, feedings, pastures, fisheries, moors, marshes, turbaries, forests, chaces, parks, woods, warrens, hundreds, fairs, markets, free customs, wards, marriages, escheats and services of tenants.

July 14, 1471, Westminster   By the King[35]

A Jehan Paston Esquier, soit doné (17 February 1472)

. . . .

Yisterday the Kynge, the Qween, my lordes of Claraunce and Glowcester, went to Scheen to pardon; men sey nott alle in cheryte; what wyll falle, men can nott seye.

The Kynge entretyth my Lorde off Claraunce, ffor my Lorde of Glowcester; and as it is seyde, he answerethe that he may weell have my Ladye hys suster in lawe, butt they schall parte no lyvelod, as he seythe; so what wyll falle can I nott seye.

. . . .

John Paston, K.[36]

[55]

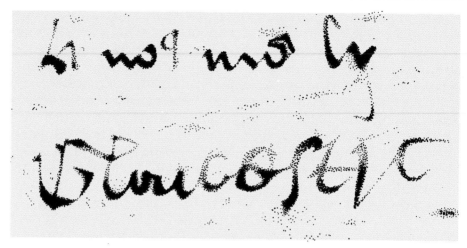

Richard's signature and motto 'A vos me ly' written in his copy of the Wycliffe translation of the Bible.

It is my intention here to insert an account of the dissensions which arose during this Michaelmas Term [1472] between the two brothers of the king already mentioned, and which were with difficulty quieted. After, as already stated, the son of king Henry, to whom the lady Anne, the youngest daughter of the earl of Warwick had been married, was slain at the battle of Tewkesbury, Richard, duke of Gloucester, sought the said Anne in marriage. This proposal, however, did not suit the views of his brother, the duke of Clarence who had previously married the eldest daughter of the same earl. Such being the case, he caused the damsel to be concealed, in order that it might not be known by his brother where she was; as he was afraid of a division of the earl's property, which he wished to come to himself alone in right of his wife, and not to be obliged to share it with any other person. Still however, the craftiness of the duke of Gloucester so far prevailed, that he discovered the young lady in the city of London disguised in the habit of a cookmaid: upon which he had her removed to the sanctuary of Saint Martin's. In consequence of this, such violent dissensions arose between the brothers, and so many arguments were, with the greatest acuteness, put forward on either side, in the king's presence, who sat in judgment in the council-chamber, that all present, and the lawyers even, were quite surprised that these princes should find argument in such abundance by means of which to support their respective causes. In fact, these three brothers, the king and the two dukes, were possessed of

[56]

such surpassing talents, that, if they had been able to live without dissensions, such a threefold cord could never have been broken without the utmost difficulty. At last, their most loving brother, king Edward, agreed to act as mediator between them; and in order that the discord between princes of such high rank might not cause any hindrance to the carrying out of his royal intentions in relation to the affairs of France, the whole misunderstanding was at last set at rest, upon the following terms; the marriage of the duke of Gloucester with Anne before-named was to take place, and he was to have such and so much of the earl's lands as should be agreed upon between them through the mediation of arbitrators; while all the rest were to remain in the possession of the duke of Clarence. The consequence was, that little or nothing was left at the disposal of the real lady and heiress, the countess of Warwick, to whom for the whole of her life the most noble inheritance of the Warwicks and the Despencers properly belonged.[37]

Arms of Anne Neville, impaled with those of Richard III, and showing her descent from the Nevilles and Beauchamps. From the plaque in Westminster Abbey erected by the Richard III Society.

[57]

To John Paston, Esquier, at Norwych, be thys delyvered (6 November 1473)

Wyshypfull and well belovyd brother, I comand me to yow, letyng yow weet that the worlde semyth qwesye heer; ffor the most part that be abowt the Kyng have sende hyddr ffor ther harneys, and it is seyd ffor serteyn that the Duke off Clarance makyth hym bygge in that he kan, schewyng as he wolde but dele with the Duke of Glowcester; but the Kyng ententyth in eschyewyng all inconvenyents to be as bygge as they bothe and to be a styffeler atweyn them . . .

J.P., K.[38]

To John Paston Esquyer by thys delyvered   (22 November 1473)

. . . .

As for other tydynges I trust to God thatt the ij Dukes of Clarans and Glowcester shall be sette att one by the adward off the Kyng. . . .

. . . .

John Paston, K.[39]

Edward Prince biforesaid, son to King Harry the vi. . . . maryid [at Amboise] Anne yongist dougter of the erle of Warwik: the which Anne was weddid to Ric. duke of Gloucestre aftir in the yere of our Lorde M.CCCC.LXXIIII [1474] att Westmonstre, aftir the deth of the same prince Edward.[40]

THE Kyng, by th'advis and assent of the Lordes Spirituelx and Temporelx, and the Commens, in this present Parlement assembled, and by auctorite of the same, for dyvers grete and notable causes and considerations, hath ordeyned, established and enacted, that George Duc of Clarence, and Isabell his wyf, Richard Duc of Gloucestr', and Anne his wyfe, doughters and heires to Richard Nevill late Erle of Warwyk, and doughters and heires apparantes to Anne Countes of Warwyk, late wyfe to the seid Erle, shall from hensforth have, possede, enherit and enjoy, as in the right of their seid wyfes, all Honours, Lordships, Castels, Townes, Maners, Londes, Tenementes, Liberties, Fraunehises, Possessions and Enheritaments, which were or be belongyng to the seid Anne Countes of

[58]

St Stephen's Chapel, attached to Westminster Palace, probably where Richard of Gloucester and Anne Neville were married.

[59]

Warwyk, or any other persone or persones to hir use; to have and to hold to the seid Dukes, and their seid wyfes, and to the heires of their seid wyfes, in like maner and fourme, as yf the seid Countes were nowe naturally dede: . . . And that the said Countes, be barrable, barred and excluded, aswell of all maner joyntours, dower, actions, executions, right, title and interesse, of, in, and for all Honours, Lordships, Castelles, Townes, Maners, Londes, Tenementes, Libertees, Possessions and Enheritaments, that at eny tyme were the seid Erle's late her husbond, or any other persone or persones to his use, as of all other Possessions and Enheritaments whatsoever, that were of the Auncestres of the seid Countes; . . .

And also it is ordeyned by the same auctorite, that yf the same Anne the doughter dye, the seid Richard Duke of Gloucestr' hir overlyvyng, that then the same Duke have, possede and enjoye, for terme of his lyfe all Honours, Castelles, Townes, Lordships, Maners, Londes and Tenementes, Rentes, Revercions, Advousons, Liberties, Fraunchises, and other Enheritaments whatsoever, that by reason of this Acte, or otherwise of right belongeth or belonged to the same Anne.

It is ordeyned by the same auctorite, that yf the seid Richard Duke of Gloucestr' and Anne, bee hereafter devorced, and after the same be lawfully maried: That yet this present Acte be to theym as good and vaillable, as yf no such devorce had ben had, but as yf the same Anne had contynued wyfe to the seid Duke of Gloucestr'.

And over that, it is ordeyned by the seid auctorite, that yf the seid Duc of Gloucestr' and Anne, hereafter be devorced, and after that he doo his effectuell diligence and contynuell devoir, by all convenient and laufull means, to be laufully maried to the seid Anne the doughter, and duryng the lyf of the same Anne the doughter, and duryng the lyf of the same Anne be not wedded ne maried to any other woman: That yet the seid Duke of Gloucestr', shall have and enjoy a moche of the premisses, as shall apperteigne to the seid Anne, duryng the lyf of the seid Duke of Gloucestr'.[41]

Following the grant to him of the northern estates of the Earl of Warwick, Richard seems to have made his home in the north with his wife. Anne's mother, taken north by Sir James Tyrell, a known retainer of Richard, may have lived with them. Here he maintained order on behalf of his brother, establishing good relations between himself and Henry Percy, Earl of Northumberland, the other power in the north.

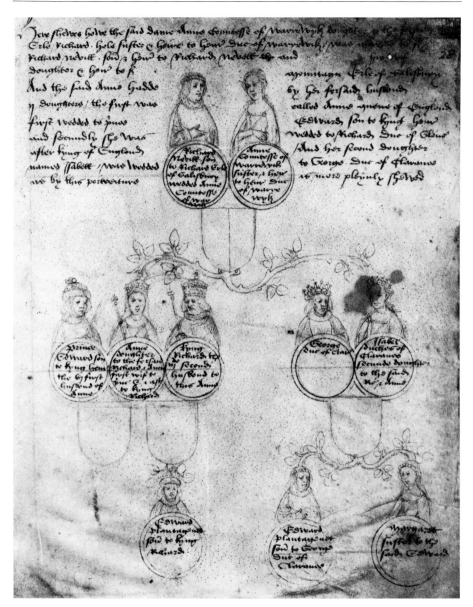

Family tree showing Richard Neville the 'Kingmaker', his wife Anne Beauchamp, heiress of the Beauchamp Earls of Warwick, and their daughters Isabel and her husband George of Clarence and Anne and her two husbands, Edward of Lancaster and Richard III, with their children.

[61]

To Master John Paston, or to my mestresse hys modre, be thys letter delyveryd in hast   [30 April 1472]

· · · · · · · · ·

Item as ffor tydyngs the Erle of Northomberlonde is hoome in to the northe, and my lorde off Glowcester schall afftre as to morow, men seye.[42]

· · · · · · · · ·

To John Paston Esquiere by thys delyveryd

· · · · · · · · · · ·

Item, how that the Cowntesse off Warwyk is now owt off Beweley Seyntwarye, and Sir James Tyrell conveyth hyr northwarde, men seye by the Kynges assent, whereto som men seye that the duke off Clarance is not agreyd.

John Paston, K.[43]

[28 July 1474]. An Indenture between Richard Duke of Gloucester and Henry Earl of Northumberland.—The Earl promiseth and granteth to the Duke to be his faithful servant, the said Duke being his good and faithful lord. And the said Earl to do service to the Duke at all times lawful and convenient when he thereunto by the said Duke shall be lawfully required; the dutie of the allegiance of the said Earl to the King, the Queen, his service and promise to Prince Edward the first begotten son, and all the King's issue begotten and to be begotten first at all times reserved. The Duke promises to be the Earl's faithful Lord, and that he will not ask or claim any office or fee that the Earl hath of the King's grant or of any other person or persons at the making of these presents, or take any servant retained by the Earl of fee, clothing, or promise, according to the appointments taken between the Duke and Earl by the King and Lords of his Council at Nottingham the 12th of May in the 13th year, except John Wedryngton.[44]

In 1475 Edward IV mounted a great expedition to France, in order to assert his claim to the throne. He took with him some 1500 men at arms and 11000 archers, raised by indentures, i.e. each magnate undertook to bring so many men at so much per head.

[62]

Middleham Castle. Richard lived here while in the Earl of Warwick's household from 1462 to 1464. The castle was granted to him in 1471 and he seems to have lived mainly here with his wife until he succeeded to the throne.

The Duc of clarence	10 chevaliers, 100 lances, archers 1000, Black bull
The Duc of gloucester	10 chevaliers, 100 lances, archers 1000, Whitt bore
The Duc of norffolke	2 chevaliers, 40 lances, archers 300, Whytt lyon
The Duc of Suffolke	2 chevaliers, 40 lances, archers 300, Lyon of gold the kew forched

[63]

The Duc off Bokyngham   4 chevaliers, 40 lances,
                               archers 400,   the Stafford Knot
                               Reversus domum[45]

The expedition was not a success in military terms, since no fighting took place. Edward IV quarrelled with his chief ally, Charles Duke of Burgundy, and came to terms with Louis XI, King of France. Louis bribed the English chief officers to help them agree to terms, the Duke of Gloucester almost alone wanted to continue the war.

After this, a conference was held between the two kings, for the purpose of more firmly establishing the peace that had been made between them. Indeed, there was no kind of pledge, promise, or oath made in public, which king Louis would not willingly give in order to guarantee the due performance of the terms agreed on. Accordingly, our lord the king returned to England, having thus concluded an honourable treaty of peace: for in this light it was regarded by the higher officers of the royal army, although there is nothing so holy or of so high a sanction, that it may not have contempt thrown upon it by being ill spoken of.[46]

The King of England was accommodated by the King of France with whatever he wanted, even to the very torches and candles. The Duke of Gloucester, the King of England's brother, and some other persons of quality, were not present at this interview, as being averse to the treaty; but they recollected themselves afterwards, and the Duke of Gloucester waited on the king our master at Amiens, where he was splendidly entertained, and nobly presented both with plate and fine horses.[47]

Soon after the French expedition Edward IV decided to give his father and brother Edmund a more fitting burial; after their deaths at the battle of Wakefield in 1461 their bodies had been hastily interred at Pontefract. He sent his brother Richard to Pontefract to oversee their removal and transfer to the Yorkist foundation at Fotheringhay. At the requiem Mass held in Pontefract Richard acted as chief mourner and offered the alms.

In order to which upon the 22nd of July 1476, the said bones were put into a chariot, covered with black velvet, richly wrapped in cloth of gold and royal

Plaque with joined initials R and A found at Middleham. This may be a belt or horse harness ornament, and could be associated with Richard and Anne Neville or with Richard Neville and Anne Beauchamp.

Page from an English manuscript of the Visions of St Matilda of Hackenborn, a German mystic, recording the ownership of Anne Warrewyk and her husband R Gloucestr'.

[65]

habit, at whose feet stood a white angel, bearing a crown of gold, to signifie that of right he was King. The chariot had seven horses, trapped to the ground, and covered with black, charged with escocheons of the said Prince's arms, every horse carried a man, and upon the foremost rode Sir John Skipwith who bore the Prince's banner displayed. The Bishops and Abbots went two or three miles before, to prepare the churches for the reception of the Prince, in *pontificalibus*. Richard Duke of Gloucester followed next after the corps, accompanied with a number of nobles, the officers of arms being also present. In this equipage they parted from Pontefract, and that night rested at Doncaster, where they were received by the convent of Cordeliers, in grey habit; from thence by journeys to Blithe, to Toxford in the Clay, to Newark, to Grantham, to Stamford, and from thence on Monday the 29th of July, to Fotheringhay, where they arrived betwixt two and three of the clock in the afternoon, where the bodies were received by several bishops and abbots in *pontificalibus*, and supported by twelve servants of the defunct prince.

At the entry of the churchyard was the King, accompanied by several dukes, earls and barons, all in mourning, who proceeded into the heart of Fotheringhay church, near to the high altar, where there was a herse covered with black, furnished with a great number of banners, bannerols and pencills, and under the said herse were the bones of the said prince and his son Edmond.

The Queen and her two daughters were present, also in black, attended by several ladies and gentlewomen. Item, over the image was a cloth of majesty, of black sarcenet, with the figure of our Lord, sitting on a rainbow, beaten in gold, having on every corner a scocheon of the arms of France and England quarterly, with a vallans about the herse also of black sarcenet, fringed half a yard deep, and beaten with three angels of gold holding the arms within a Garter, in every part above the herse.[48]

An indenture was made on 17 July 1477 between Richard, various of his trustees for the Lordship of Foulmere in Cambridgeshire, which once had been the property of Elizabeth Countess of Oxford, and the President and Fellows of Queens' College Cambridge. In return for the gift of this lordship the College was to admit four priests 'wele

Opposite: A medieval king in his robes of estate, holding a sceptre. The initial letter introducing Richard III's statutes from Cartae Antiquae, a manuscript made for the City of London in the reign of Henry VII.

[67]

lerned and virtuously dysposit as doctours of divinite, bachelers, opposers or masters of art, beyng prestes of habilite to procede to be doctours and to preche the worde of God' as fellows, at the salary of £8 the year. They were to be called the four priests of the Duke of Gloucester's foundation. These priests had various pious duties with particular attention to the honouring of Saints Anthony, Ninian and George. Their prayers were to benefit Richard and his relations and those of his entourage who had died at Barnet and Tewkesbury.

First the iiij prestes shell pray satisfactorie for the prosperuse astates of Richard the sayde duke of Gloucette and dame Anne his wife, and of Edwarde ther first begoten son erle of Salisbery with all sych yssue as God schalle sende betwixe tham, and of all ther soulis after ther decessis: also thay schalle pray for the goode and prosperuse astates of oure soveryne lorde kynge Edwarde the fourth, oure sovereyne lady quene Elizabet fundaresse of the sayde college, of the prince and all the kynges childer: and for the good astate of dame Cecile duchess of York moder to the kynge our sayde sovereyne lorde and to the sayde duke of Gloucetre: also for the soule of the ryght hygh and myghty prince of blessed memorie Richarde duke of Yorke fader to oure sovereyne lorde the kynge and to the sayde duke of Gloucetre: and for the soules of Edmunde erle of Rutlande, dame Anne duches of Excet[r], brother and sister of the sayde duke of Gloucetre and alle his other bredern and sistern: also for Richarde erle of Cambridge and all other of the sayde duke of Gloucetre noble progenitours: also for the saules of John Veir and dame Elizabeth his wife with the soules of the specialle benefactours of the saide college, sir John Pylkyngton, sir John Huddelston knyghtes, William Hopton sqwyer, Thomas Barowe clerke and William Tunstall: and for the soules of Thomas Par, John Milewater, Christofre Wursley, Thomas Huddelston, John Harper and all other gentilmen and yomen servanders and lovers of the saide duke of Gloucetre, the wiche were slayn in his service at the batelles of Bernett, Tukysbery or at any other feldes or jorneys, and for all cristen soulis.[49]

Early in 1478 the King's second son Richard Duke of York and newly created Duke of Norfolk, was married to the heiress Anne Mowbray. The Duke of Gloucester was present, and as well as helping to lead the new Duchess into the wedding feast he distributed alms beforehand.

[68]

The fourteenth day of January, the high and excellent Princesse came to the place of estate, in the Kings great chamber at Westminster, and there, according to her high and excellent estate, had a void after the forme and estate of this famous realme of England; accompanyed with many great estates and degrees, dukes and earles, and barons, and with great abundance of ladies and gentlewomen; and the Princesse before rehearsed was led by the right noble Count, Rivers. And on the morne, on Thursday the fifteenth day of the same moneth, this high Princesse before rehearsed came out of the Queenes chamber at Westminster, and so proceeded through the Kings great chamber, and into the White Hall, and so proceeded into Saint Stephens Chappell, being attended by great estates and many ladyes and gentlewomen, my lord the noble Count of Lincolne ledd her on the right hand, and upon the second hand the noble Count Rivers. And at her entry into the chappell before rehearsed, which was richly garnished with tappetts of azure culler, inramplished with flower de luces of gould curiously wrought; and also a little space within the dore of the same chappell, there was an imperiall of cloth of gould, in manner of a canopie; and under the saide canopie was the King, the Queene, and my Lord the Prince, and the right high and excellent Princesse and Queene of right, Cicelie Mother to the Kinge, the Lady Elizabeth, the Lady Mary, the Lady Cicely, daughters to the King our Soveraigne Lord; and there was my said Lady received by Doctour Goldwell, Bishopp of Norwiche. And when hee had received her in at the chappell dore, intending to proceed to her wedding, Doctor Cooke spake, and said that the high and mighty Prince Richard Duke of Yorke ought not to be wedded to that high and excellent Princesse, for that they were within degrees of marriage; the one at the fourth, the other at the third; for which cause hee defended the espousalls, without that there were a speciall lycence from the Pope, and dispensacion from the Pope for the said neerenes of blood.

Then Doctour Gunthrope, Deane of the Kings Chappell shewed an ample bull of authority, that they might proceede to the contracte and matrimony before rehersed. Thereupon the said Bishoppe of Norwiche proceeded to the marriage, and asked who should give the Princesse to the church and to him; and the King gave her, and so proceeded to the high altar to masse.

Then was there great number of gould and silver cast amongest the comone people, brought in basons of gold, by the high and mighty Prince the Duke of Gloucester; and after were accomplished the appurtenaunces of the said marriage; and after, spices and wyne, as appertayneth to matrimoniall feastes.

[69]

From the Chappell of Saint Stephen, led the said Princesse of this feast, the Duke of Gloucester upon the right hand, and upon the second hand the Duke of Buckingham; and so proceeding to the Kings greate chamber; and there, the second estate at the bord was the Bishopp, that did the appurtenaunces before rehearsed. On the second hand, the third estate at the bord sate the Dutchesse of Buckingham, and the Dutchesse of Norfolke mother to the Princesse of the feast. And then, at the first side table, satt the Marquis of Dorsett; the length of the same table accomplished with ladyes and gentlewomen; and, at the other end, my Lady of Richmond, and many ladyes and gentlewomen; and all the Parliament chamber, of ould tyme called Saint Edwards chamber, on both sides tables, and there satt ladyes and gentlewomen. And after the second course, Minstrells, as appertayneth to such high estate. And then Kings of Armes and Herauldes, thankeing her highness for her largesse; and then the Kings of Armes and Herauldes, to their cry, as appertayneth.[50]

At the same time that the Duke of Gloucester was helping to celebrate his nephew's marriage, his brother the Duke of Clarence was imprisoned in the Tower. Clarence was a perpetually dissatisfied person. He had recently been disappointed in a desire to marry the heiress of the Duke of Burgundy (his wife Isabel had died in childbirth in December 1476), he seems to have engaged in plots against his brother, he took the law into his own hands and tried, condemned and executed a servant for the murder of his wife, and finally he deliberately appealed to the King's Council over the heads of the judges in a case of sorcery involving two members of his household. This was the last straw for his brother Edward, and the Duke was arrested. He was tried for treason, found guilty and later died in the Tower on 18 February 1478. Richard was later accused of plotting his death, but no contemporary thus accused him, and a later and hostile witness says he protested against it.

The circumstances that happened in the ensuing Parliament my mind quite shudders to enlarge upon, for then was to be witnessed a sad strife carried on before these two brethren of such high estate. For not a single person uttered a word against the duke, except the king; not one individual made answer to the king except the duke. Some parties were introduced, however, as to whom it was greatly doubted by many, whether they filled

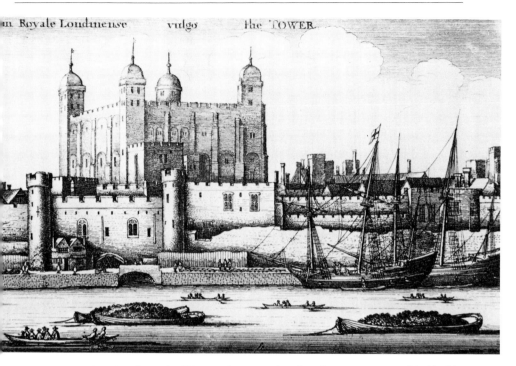

The Tower of London from the Thames in 1640, showing the water gate and behind it, rising above the walls, the fore-buildings next to the White Tower, the old royal apartments.

the office of accusers rather, or of witnesses: these two offices not being exactly suited to the same person in the same cause. The duke met all the charges made against him with a denial, and offered, if he could only obtain a hearing, to defend his cause with his own hand. But why delay in using many words? Parliament, being of opinion that the informations which they had heard were established, passed sentence upon him of condemnation, the same being pronounced by the mouth of Henry, duke of Buckingham, who was appointed Seneschal of England for the occasion. After this, execution was delayed for a considerable time; until the Speaker of the Commons, coming to the upper house with his fellows, made a fresh request that the matter might be brought to a conclusion. In consequence of this, in a few days after, the execution, whatever its nature may have been, took place, (and would that it had ended these troubles!) in the Tower

[71]

of London, it being the year of our Lord, 1478, and the eighteenth of the reign of king Edward.[51]

Thus she [Elizabeth Woodville] concluded that her offspring by the king would never come to the throne, unless the duke of Clarence were removed; and of this she easily persuaded the king. The queen's alarm was intensified by the comeliness of the duke of Clarence, which would make him appear worthy of the crown: besides he possessed such mastery of popular eloquence that nothing upon which he set his heart seemed difficult for him to achieve. Accordingly whether the charge was fabricated, or a real plot revealed, the duke of Clarence was accused of conspiring the king's death by means of spells and magicians. When the charge had been considered before a court, he was condemned and put to death. The mode of execution preferred in this case was, that he should die by being plunged into a jar of sweet wine. At that time Richard duke of Gloucester was so overcome with grief for his brother, that he could not dissimulate so well, but that he was overheard to say that he would one day avenge his brother's death. Thenceforth he came very rarely to court. He kept himself within his own lands and set out to acquire the loyalty of his people through favours and justice. The good reputation of his private life and public activities powerfully attracted the esteem of strangers. Such was his renown in warfare, that whenever a difficult and dangerous policy had to be undertaken, it would be entrusted to his discretion and his generalship. By these arts Richard acquired the favour of the people, and avoided the jealousy of the queen from whom he lived far separated.[52]

Ther be assignyd certen Lords to go with the body of the Dukys of Clarence to Teuxbury, where he shall be beryid; the Kyng intendis to do right worshipfully for his sowle.[53]

Richard and his Council (in common with other great men) operated as an agency for arbitration in disputes, making awards and encouraging peaceful agreement. One such dispute was that between Richard Clervaux and Rowland Place over land boundaries, their pews in church, retainers and rights of game, settled before Richard at Middleham Castle on 12 April 1478 'tendirring the peas and welle of the contre where the said parties inhabite and also gladly willyng gode concorde, rest, frendly suite to be had fro hensfurth between

[72]

Elizabeth Woodville, wife to Edward IV.

[73]

the sayd parties'.★ Another dispute concerned the parishioners of
Snaith who claimed that the Abbey of Selby was responsible for
providing their church with vestments, books and chalice. The
Duke's award of 15 March 1481 ordered the Abbey to provide these
objects by Easter but that the parish should find them in future.

And also that the said Abbot and convent fynde yerely for ever at their
charge Also all such lights of waxe and lampes as haith ben accustumed
theym to fynde hertofor in the said chirch. Also the said Duc by thadvise of
his counsell abovesaid ordineth awardeth and demeth that the said Abbot
and convent personz of the said chirch of Snath shal frely use and exercise
from hensforth their jurisdiccions and libertes their withoute let or
perturbacion of the said parishons for ever, and theirfor the said Abbot
shall withdrawe at his charge and discontynue all maner suets and accions
by hym or the convent or any other in his or their names ayenst the said
parishons or any of theym in any court commenced, And also that the said
parishons shal never from hensforth entermete or deale with any thing
belongyng to the jurisdiccions and libertes aforesaid oder than shalbe
lawfully according to their custome and duety, and withdrawe at thier
charge and discontynue all maner suets and accions by theym or any oder in
their name against the said Abbot and convent their officers and servants in
any court commenced. And over this the said Duc by thadvise above said
for the perpetual memory and thappeasinge of the premisses, awardeth and
demeth this ordinance to be putt in writyng indented and decreed by the
most Reverende fader in god tharchbishop of york Primate of England
betuyx this and cristynmesse next commyng At the charges and costs of the
said Abbot and conuent. Yeven under the signet of the said Duc the place
day and yere above said.[54]

★A.J. Pollard, 'Richard Clervaux of Croft: a North Riding Squire in the 15th
Century', *Yorkshire Archaeological Journal*, Vol. 50 (1978), p. 162.

A typical duty of Richard's position in the North as a 'good lord' was to act as executor. Sir John Pilkington came from a family of great influence in Yorkshire and Lancashire.

In the name of God, amen. I, Sir John Pylkyngton, knyght, of hole mynde, all if I be greved with secknes; at Skipton, the xxviij daye of June, mcccclxxviij. My body to be beried, at the pleasir of God and oure Lady, in my chauntery in the kirk of Wakefeld. . . . Item I will that my son Edward beforwith after my dethe be had to my lorde of Gloucestre and my lorde Chambrelane, hertly beseching thame as they will in my name sesuch [beseech] the king is goode grace that myn executors may have the wardeshipp and mariege of my said son and my lande, paying to the king v^c marcs; which shalbe delivered to thame in money: and then I will besuch my lorde of Gloucestre that my said son Edward may be in the house of my lorde Chambrelane, to he be of the age of xvj yere, and then to be put at the kingis pleasir: and at Giles Lyngard and Henry Dyneley may waite apon hym in the mean season. Item it is my will that all the revenus growing of my lands, over the fynding of my said sone, shalbe kepped w^t my lorde Chambrelane, to by for my said sone a mariege with land. . . . I lowly and hertly besuche my lorde of Gloucestre and my lorde Chambrelane, that they will, at the reverence of God, by myn executores; w^t them Will. Calverley and Robert Chaloner. I will that my lorde of Gloucestre have an emeraunt sett in golde, for which my said lorde wolde have geven me c marcs [£66. 13s. 4d.]; and that my lorde Chambrelan shall have a bedd of arrasse with angels of golde; and that William Calverley and Robert Chaloner shall have aither of theme c s., and their costes when they ryde and labour for performyng of this my will.[55]

Richard's major religious foundation in the North was his college at Middleham designed to provide perpetual prayers for himself and his family. Elaborate statutes were drawn up in 1478 providing for its establishment of a dean, six priests, and choristers, and laying down the religious services to be observed. Careful attention was paid to the veneration of Richard's particular saints as well as to the musical and academic ability of the members of the college. The college was also intended ultimately to benefit the parish of Middleham financially, and remove from it the burden of maintaining its parish church.

[75]

Richard, Duc of Gloucestre, grete Chamberleyn, Constable and Admiral of Englond, Lord of Glomorgan, Morgannok, Bergevenny, Richemond and Middelham, to all Christen people to whome thes presents shall come, greeting in our Lord everlasting. – Know ye that where it haith pleasid Almighty God, Creatour and Redemer of all mankynd, of His most bounteuouse and manyfold graces to enhabile, enhaunce and exalte me His most simple creature, nakidly borne into this wretched world, destitute of possessions, goods and enheretaments, to the grete astate, honor and dignite that He haith called me now unto, to be named, knowed, reputed and called Richard Duc of Gloucestre, and of His infynyte goodnesse not oonly to endewe me with grete possessions and of giftys of His divyne grace, bot also to preserve, kep and deliver me of many grete jeoperd', parells and hurts, for the which and other the manyfold benyfits of His bounteuouse grace and goodnesse to me, without any my desert or cause in sundry behalves shewed and geven, I, daily and ourly according to my deuty remembring the premisses, and in recognicion that all such goodnes cometh of Hyme, an finally determyned, into the lovyng and thankyng of His Deite, and in the honour of His Blissed moder our Lady Seint Marie, socour and refuge of all synners repentant, and in the honor of the holy virgyn Saint Alkyld, – of part of such goods as He haith sent me, to stablisshe, make and founde a Collage within my Town of Middelham at the parrishe church there, in the which shall be a deane, sex prests, foure clerks, sex queresters, and a clerk sacristan, to do divyne service there daily, to pray for the good astates of the King our Soverayn Lord and the Quene, and for the gude astates of my lady and moder Duchesse of York, and of me, my wiff, my son of Salesbury, and such other issue as shal pleas God to send me, whiles I liffe; and for the soules of my said soverayn lord the King, the Quene, and of me, my wiff, and myn issue after our decesses, and specially for the soules of my Lord and fader Richard Duc of York, of my bretheren and susters, and oyer my progenitours and successors, and all Christen soules, in part of satisfaccion of suche things as at the dredfull day of dome I shal answere for. The same my Collage to be called and named for ever the Collage of Richard Duc of Gloucestre, of Middelham, and to be ordained, stablisshed, and made followingly . . .

Also, that no deans of my saide College, that for the tyme shalbe after the said Sir William Beverley now deane of the same, in any wise be by me and myne heirez named, . . . enlesse he be one of the said sex prests, if eny of theme in literral connynge, gude disposicion, and in worldely pollicie may be fondon able; and in defect of such emong theme I wol that oon of the

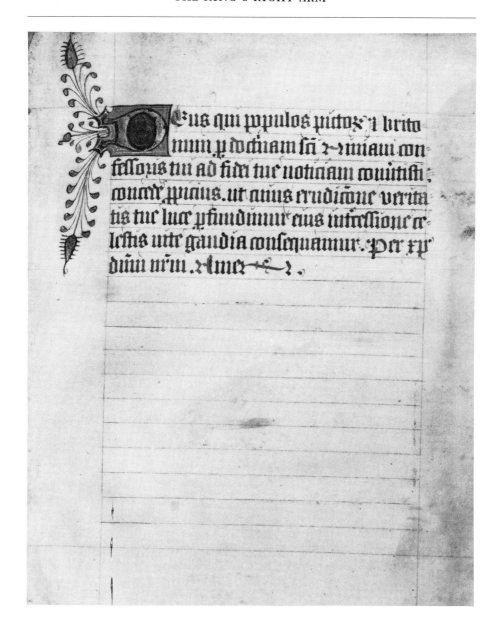

Richard III's Book of Hours: the collect for St Ninian. This collect was added to the book for Richard's use, St Ninian being the evangelist of the Picts and the saint of the Western March where Richard was Warden.

foure prests of my foundacion in the Quene College of Cambrige, abil in connyng, disposicion, and pollicie, as is affore rehersid, be, and for lak of such, that a graduate, at the lest Master of Arte or Bachelor of Law, of the Universite of Cambridge forsaide, be . . . ordened to be deane of the same; and also that none of the saide sex prests and fowre clerks so to be named prests or clerks . . . affore that they . . . be foundon sufficiently lierned, not onely in understanding and litterature, bot also in singing playne song, priked song, faburden, and descant of two mynymes at the lest, or that one of the saide foure clerks be a player upon the organes, and daily to play as oft as it shalbe requisite and appoynted; . . .

Also, that one of the saide foure clerks that shalbe electe by me and myne heires, in forme afforsaide admitted, be a man sufficiently lerned in practise of singing, aswel in playne song, priked song, faburdon, countr' [counterpoint], descant of all mesures used in any Cathedrall church or Collage, the same to teche the said sex queresters his connyng, and he to be named the maister and techer of theme, for the which teching, labor, besynesse and attendance abowte the same, I wol that he have of the said revenues by the hands of the said deane, for tyme being, over the said ten marks of his wages of oon of clerks, yerely five marks; . . . and that none of theme longer abide as querestors than ther brests serve theme to sing in childes voce, over the space of half a yere at most.

Also, I do statute, make, and ordeyne that eny deane, that for the tyme herafter shalbe of my said Collage, shalbe resident and continually abiding upon the same, and kep continuall houshold ther, and that the said sex prests shal bord theme with hyme, and pay everich of theme wekely for ther boord sextene pennex; and also the said foure clerks and the clerk sacristane in like wise, and everich of theme to pay wekely twolf pennes, during the tyme that thei be not married; and if eny of theme happen to be maried and dwel within my towne ther, then he to be at his libertee and chose in that behalve, and ellys alweys ther at bourd payng wekely as is afforsaid . . . that none of the said prests or clerks bring any straunger to dyne or soupe with theme within my said College, withoute the licence of the deane; . . . that than he so asking licence pay for his stranger every mele two pennes: provided always that if eny of them bring ony of ther frends, alies, kynnesmen, or other straunger to see the church or College, or make hyme or theme chere, that than I woll that the said straunger so comyng be curtesly welcomed and served with brede and ale, so that it be not ofte nor daly used.

Also, I statute, and ordeyne that the said deane, prests, and clerks shal distinctly, nother to [neither too] hastely ne to tariyngly, bot mesurable and devoutely, kep divine service daily in my saide Collage, be note after the use of Salesbury, . . . And assone as prime and houres is saide, the messe of our Lady to be song dayly, with priked song and organes, with the maister, clerkes and queresters, except by there ordinall they sey of our Lady, and except the Friday wokely, which day I woll that the saide master, clerks, and queresters the messe of Jhesu after prime and hours saide be song . . .

Also, I statute, make, and ordeyne that if eny prest, clerk, or oder ministre of the same College use at eny tyme in ire eny inhonest or slaunderous words ayenst his felow, his superior or inferior, of the same College, he shal pay of his wagys at evere tyme two pennez. If he draw violently a knyff, he shal pay of his saide wage at evere tyme so doing four penys, and if he draw blode he shal pay of his saide wage as moch as the deane, with one of the saide sex prests, shal resonable deme hyme to pay to be convectid in, to ye reparacion of the saide College. . . .

Also, I statute, make, and ordeyne that the deane forsaide have al maner tethes and offeryngs within my castell of Middelham, as of all oder place within the parissh of the church of Middelham, in eny wise appertynyng, withoute let or interrupcion of the deane of the chapell of my saide Castell, or eny other ministre of the same . . .

Also, I wol that suche saints as that I have devocion unto, be servid in the church throughoutly as double fest, aswel thos that be not by the ordinall of Sarum as thos that be, that is to say, Seint John Baptiste and Seint John the Evangeliste, Seint Peter and Seint Pall, Seint Simon and Jude, Seint Mihael, Seinte Anne, Seint Elizabeth, Seint Fabian and Seint Sebastian, Seint Antony, Seint Christofer, Seint Dyonyse, Seint Blaise, Seint Thomas, Seint Albane, Seint Gilys, Seint Eustace, and Seint Erasmus, Seint Loy, Seint Leonard, and Seint Martyn, Seint William of York, Seint Wulfrey of Rippon, Seint Kateryn, Seint Margarete, Seinte Barbara, Seint Martha, Seint Venefride, Seint Ursula, Seint Dorathe, Seint Radagunde, Seint Agnes, Seint Agathe, Seint Apolyne, Seint Cithe, Seint Clare, Seint Marie Magdalene: provided neverlesse that if eny fest of the forsaide Saints have noo fest or day in the kalender, or of theme self be double fest, that then the deane for the tyme being during my liffe shal take in this partie with myne adviace such good direccion as shalbe thoght most according to theeffect of this myne ordinance, which direccion so to be take, I wol be observid after my decese for ever.

Also, I wol that Seint George and Seint Nynyane be served as principal fests, whenso that ther daies fallys, and also Seint Cuthbert day in Lent, and Seint Antony day that fallys in Janiver', be served as principall in like wise.

. . . providid alweys that thenhabitance of my saide towne of Middelham for the tyme being be contributeres unto the same charges, in as ample maner and forme as they have bene in tyme past, unto such tyme as I, myne heires or myne assignes have made and accomplisshed such things both in enlargeyng or new makyng the church and churchyerd and mansions for and in the saide College: which so maide and accomplishide other be me, myne heires or assignes, I woll that the saide inhabitannce shal be discharged of the same contribucion, and then the saide deane so being to receve of the revenneux forsade the sowme of twenty pownd afforsaide, and in no wise affore. IN WITNESS wherof unto thies presentes I have sett my seal. YEVENE ye fourt day of the moneth of July, in the yere of our soverayne Lord King Edward fourt after the Conquest of Yngland eghteynd.[56]

During his years in the north Richard did a great deal for the well-being of the citizens of York. He supported them in their efforts to have illegal fish garths destroyed (weirs which restricted navigation and also the number of fish available to commoners), and petitioned his brother in 1476 not to withdraw the city's Charter of Liberties.

Ultimo die Decembris anno xvj regni Edwardi iiij [1476]

....

The saide day and tyme by the forsaide Maire and Counsaile it was holie agreed and assented that the Duk of Gloucestre shall for his grete labour of now late made unto the kinges goode grace for the conservacion of the liberties of this Citie, that he shalbe presented at his commyng to the citie with vj swannes and vj pikes.[57]

The Duc of Gloucestre Constable and Admirall of England

Right trusty and welbelovyd, we grete you wele and asserten you that accordyng to your desires late by your servaunt to us broght touching reformacion of Goldalegarth or eny other, we have moved the kynges grace in the same and therapon his said grace hathe commaunded us at our next home commyng to take a vewe and oversight of the said garthes and weeres

[80]

The Donne Triptych, by Hans Memling, dating from c.1477–80. The donor, Sir John Donne and his wife Elizabeth (sister of William Lord Hastings) and their eldest child Anne are shown in the centre panel. Sir John was knighted at Tewkesbury, and both he and his wife wear Yorkist collars of suns and roses, with pendants of the white lion of March, the badge of Edward IV. National Gallery, London.

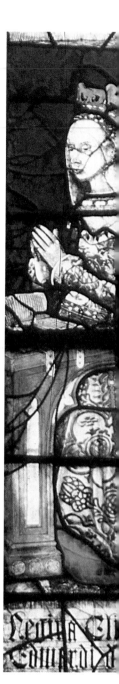

Portraits of Edward IV, Elizabeth Woodville and the
Prince of Wales from the 'Royal Windows' of
Canterbury Cathedral.

coyso ts
a regis

Edwardus princeps Wallie
primus filius Edwardi quarti

Crosby Hall, interior of the great hall, owned by Sir John Crosby. Richard rented the Hall as his London house while Duke of Gloucester.

and suche of thame as have not ben alowed afore justices of ayre, to see at they be pulled downe, the which or eny other thing that we may do to the wele of your said cite we shall put us in our uttermoste devour and gode will by Godes grace, who kepe you. Yeven under our signet at London the xv day of Novembre [1477].

To oure Right trusty and welbelovyd the maire and aldermen of the cite of Yorke.[58]

York Castle from the south. By F. Place, 1699.

Richard does in fact seem always to have shown great respect for the liberties of the city of York. When Thomas Redeheid, a servant of his household Treasurer, assaulted a citizen of York, he sent him in the custody of one of his household knights to be punished by the city.

xij^mo die Aprilis ante nonam, [12 April 1482]

At the which day cam into the counsell chaimbre the right wirshupful Sir Rauf Assheton knyght in the name and by the high comaundement of the right high and myghti prince the duc of Gloucestre, and ther and than

[81]

shewed howe that his highness was doon to understand that where on Thomas Redeheid, servaunt to the tresorer unto his said highnes, of old rancour and evilwill did countenaunce on Roland Pudsey cocitesyn of the cite of Yorke within the household of his said grace and hym showerid for the offence doon within this cite his said grace sent in to the said maiour and his brethern by the said Sir Rauf the said Thomas Redeheid to corect and punyssh hym for his said offence and uppon that commit to prison.[59]

In 1480 an invasion by the Scots was anticipated and Richard was made Lieutenant in the North (he was already Warden of the West Marches of Scotland), a grant repeated in June 1482 when he commanded an army against Scotland. He took Berwick on 24 August 1482 and marched on Edinburgh, laying waste as he went, and took the city. When Parliament met in January the following year Gloucester was rewarded by a grant to him and to his heirs male of the Wardenship of the West Marches and to hold all lands bordering England which he could take from the Scots as a hereditary County Palatine.

Edward etc Where we by endenture bearing date at our Tower of London the 20th day of February the 19th year of our reign retained towards us our right trusty and right entirely beloved brother Richard duke of Gloucester to be our Captain and Warden of the Castle and town of Carlisle and of the West Marches towards Scotland from the said 20th day unto the end and term of ten years next following. For the which cause our said brother shall take of us yearly in grete that is to say in time of peace or truce 1,200 marks and in time of war £1,000. Whereof after thafferant he shall be evenly paid from quarter to quarter at the beginning of every quarter yearly during the said terms by the hands of the Treasurer and Chamberlains of our Exchequer for the time being as in the said indenture more plainly is contained. We wol therefore and charge you that of all that if our said brother is behind unpaid of the said sums from the said 20th day of February hiderto and so from quarter to quarter and year to year during the said term of ten years, ye content and pay unto him or to his attorney or assignee in that behalve after the form, tenor and effect of the said indentures, receiving towards you of our said brother or his said attorney or assignee his letters of acquittance from time to time certifying the said payments which and these our letters shall be your sufficient warrant and discharge against us at all times. Given under our Privy Seal at our Manor of Greenwich 24th day of June, the 20th year of our reign, [1480][60]

Boar badge found at Middleham. Probably a livery badge to be associated with Richard III.

For Richard Duke of Gloucester, Lieutenant General against the Scots

The King; to all to whom these matters appertain, greeting. Although a truce of abstinence of war between Us and James, King of Scotland were shortly concluded and began, as was contained more fully in previous transactions, yet the same King of Scotland, treating Us with inveterate hostility and obdurate malice, despising the honour of our name and very nobility, broke the Treaty propounded by himself and thus violated his own word, decided to wage war in word and deed against us, and invade our realm by sudden armed attack; We therefore meaning to oppose his malice and such great injury, trusting with full powers our illustrious brother, Richard Duke of Gloucester, in whom not only for his nearness and fidelity of relationship, but for his proved skill in military matters and his other virtues, we name, depute and ordain him our Lieutenant General in our absence, to fight, overcome and expel the said King of Scotland our chief enemy and his subjects, adherents and allies, however great the fight may

[83]

be, giving and allowing to our same Brother, our Lieutenant, our power and full authority to summon and levy in order to serve us, all and singular our subjects and liegemen both of our Marches towards Scotland and in the Counties adjoining those Marches (of whatever state, rank or condition they are); to support us by all assistance in war against the aforesaid King of Scots our enemy, as far as our brother wishes to undertake in person and to command, train and govern the same subjects and liegemen in such manner summoned and levied as interests him personally; and to carry on a bitter struggle using all means which may be necessary and opportune both for invading the said Kingdom of Scotland and for defending our Realm of England and the aforesaid Marches, under his own supervision, just as we would do if acting in person.

To all and singular subjects and liegemen of our Marches and aforesaid Counties, both the Wardens of these Marches and all others whomsoever (of what rank and condition they are) in pursuance of this proclamation, we

Boar of Richard III, carved in the soffit of an oriel window at Barnard Castle County Durham. The castle was owned by Richard in right of his wife Anne.

grant our full support to all that our aforesaid Lieutenant may do in the execution of his duty, while assisting, aiding and obeying him in diligence as may be requisite on our behalf or on that of them

In testimony of which thing we give these letters patent in support.

By the King at Westminster, the 12th day of June [1482][61]

ROLL OF ACCOUNTS, EASTER, 22 EDWARD IV

To Sir John Elryngton, knight, the King's Treasurer at War, by the hands of Richard, Duke of Gloucester; viz. for the wages of 1700 fighting men, retained by the said Duke to accompany him in the war against the Scotch; viz. from the 11th August until the end of fourteen days then next following, £595.

To Peter Curteys, Keeper of the King's great wardrobe, for the purchase of divers stuffs and making thereof, at the King's command, for the Duke of Albany, for the journey of the said Duke, who accompanied the Duke of Gloucester in his expedition to the kingdom of Scotland, receiving the money from Thomas Shelley, merchant of London, £50.

To Richard Boteler, sent, by the King, to the town of Berwick, with 800*l.* in money counted, to be delivered to the King's Treasurer at War then being there; also sent upon other affairs concerning the preservation of the said town for the Duke of Gloucester and other nobility collected there on the part of the Lord the King; paid him for costs and expenses sustained for the purpose aforesaid during the space of five weeks, £12 19*s.* 4*d.*

....

To the Duke of Gloucester, in full payment of 2000 marks due from the King to the same Duke, at the feast of the Nativity of Saint John the Baptist, according to the form of a certain indenture thereon made between the King and the said Duke; paid by the hands of Thomas Lynham, £164 15*s.*

To Sir John Elryngton, knight, the King's Treasurer at War, in part payment of the wages of 20,000 men at arms, going upon a certain expedition with the Duke of Gloucester against the Scots; paid to his own hands, £4504 11*s.* 8½*d.*

[85]

To the same Treasurer, as a reward given to divers soldiers, as well in the retinue of the Duke of Gloucester as in the retinue of the Earl of Northumberland and others, for their expenses in going from the town of Berwick to their own homes; viz. by the hands of the aforesaid Duke, £350, and by the hands of the aforesaid Earl, £94 13s. 6d., and by the hands of John Broun, of the King's household, 16s., £345 9s 6d.

....

To Master William Hobbes, the King's physician and surgeon, sent by the King to the North to attend upon the Duke of Gloucester, in the King's service against the Scotch, with eight surgeons in his retinue, paid for their wages for one month, receiving for himself per day, 2s., and for each of the other seven surgeons aforesaid, 12d. per day, and for the other of the aforesaid persons, 6d. per day, by the hands of Simon Cole and Alexander Slye, £13 6s.

To John Clerk, the King's apothecary, for divers medicines, "ciripp, alexaundrines, botellis, electuary," and other necessaries, provided and purchased of the same, delivered, by the King's command, to the Duke of Gloucester, by the hands of Thomas Lynham, his servant, of the King's gift, for the use of the said Duke in his service against the Scotch; paid by his own hands, £13 16s. 9½d.

To Richard, Duke of Gloucester, by command of the King and the Lords of his Council, in money sent him by Henry Sambroke, one of the grooms of the King's chamber, to pay the wages of divers fighting men upon the western sea, proceeding against the Scotch, according to the discretion of the said Duke; paid to the hands of the said Henry, £133 6s. 8d.[62]

EDWARD IV. TO POPE SIXTUS IV.

Have resolved to state what was achieved this summer in Scotland, that the truth may be known.

Thank God, the giver of all good gifts, for the support received from our most loving brother, whose success is so proven that he alone would suffice to chastise the whole kingdom of Scotland. This year we appointed our very dear brother Richard Duke of Gloucester to command the same army which we ourselves intended to have led last year, had not adverse turmoil hindered us.

[86]

Wrote to your Holiness heretofore about James King of Scots; how he set at nought peace, truces, matrimonial alliances and other agreements made between the kingdoms, without provocation. When, as customary with borderers upon the rupture of truces, excursions were made last year by the troops on either side, the enemy was not satisfied with having been both the first and second cause of the disturbance, but impudently boasted in his letters, even to the Apostolic see, of having destroyed certain strongholds of ours, and put an army, 200,000 strong, to shameful flight. In fact, the army which our brother lately led into Scotland, traversing the heart of that kingdom without hindrance, arrived at the royal city of Edinburgh, and found the King with the other chief lords of the kingdom shut up in a most strongly fortified castle, nowise thinking of arms, of war, of resistance, but

Seated boar badge, found in London. Possibly a hat badge.

[87]

giving up that right fair and opulent city into the power of the English, who, had not their compassion exceeded all human cupidity, would have instantly doomed the same to plunder and the flames. The noble band of victors, however, spared the supplicant and prostrate citizens, the churches, and not only the widows, orphans, and minors, but all persons found there unarmed. To this favour there contributed the intercession of the Duke of Albany, who of late years having been undeservedly banished by his brother the King of Scots, and now by the power of our army restored to his estates and titles, was of opinion that his return would be the more welcome if our soldiers, for his sake, modified the contributions levied by them on the country.

The chief advantage of the whole expedition is the reconquest of the town and castle of Berwick, which one and twenty years ago, before our coronation, went over to the Scots; but previously it was in the uninterrupted possession of our forefathers, whose just title having descended to us, we were bound to recover what was ours. A small chosen band therefore received the surrender of the town immediately on sitting down before it, though the same was entirely surrounded with impregnable walls. The citadel, however, because of its well chosen position and state of defence, was not taken until the rest of the army had returned; when, not without some slaughter and bloodshed, it was reduced.

It now remains for your Holiness to complete the work by monitions; for we would that these two nations should be as united in heart and soul as they are by neighbourhood, soil, and language; which end, should it be sought by our adversaries, we shall always be found prone and placable, and now especially as the Duke of Albany so influences their policy, that the Scots will henceforth, we hope, observe treaties with us more steadily than is their wont.

From London, 8th kalends of September. [25 August 1482]
Signed: "Your devoted son, Edward R."[63]

[88]

Where it hath been late appoynted and agreed, betwene the Kyng oure Soverayne Lorde, and his entierly belovyd Brothre Richard Duc of Gloucestre, that the same Duc shuld have to hym and his heires masles of his body comyng, the Wardeynshipp of the West marches of Englond, for ageynst Scotland, and the Office therof, with all Libertees, Fraunchises, and other Profites and Commoditees to the same apperteynyng, in as large wise, as any Wardeyn of the seid Marches hath had and resonably used to have in tyme past; for th'ocupation and exercisying of the which Wardeynshipp and Office, oure seid Soverayn Lord shuld cause the same Duc, to be made sure to hym and to his seid heires masles, by auctorite of Parlement, of certain Castelles, Lordships, Manoirs, Londes, Tenementes, Rents, Reversions, Services and other Hereditamentes and thynges, as after in this Acte shall ensue. And for asmoche as oure seid Soverayn Lorde, and the Lordes Spirituelles and Temporelles, and the Comyns, in this present Parliament assembled, understand and considre, that the seid Duc, beyng Wardeyn of the seid Westmarches, late by his manyfold and diligent labours and devoirs, hath subdued grete part of the Westbordures of Scotlande, adjoynyng to Englond, by the space of xxx miles and more, therby at this tyme not enhanbite with Scotts, and hath gete and acheved diverse parcelles therof to be under the obbeisaunce of oure said Soverayne Lorde, not oonly to the grete rest and ease of th'enhabitauntes of the seid Westmerches, but also to the grete suerty and ease of the North parties of Englond, and moche more thereof he entendith, and with Goddis grace is like to gete and subdue herafter; and the seid Westmerches the more suerly to be defended and kept ayenst the Scotts, if the seid appoyntements and agrements be perfourmed and accomplisshed.

Therfore oure same Soverayne Lorde, by th'assent of the Lordes Spirituells and Temporelles, and the Comons, in this present Parliament assembled, and by auctorite of the same, graunteth, enacteth and stablissheth, that the seid Duc shall have to hym and to his heires masles of his body comyng, the seid Wardeynship of the seid Westmerches of Englond, for aneynst Scotland, and the Office therof, with all the Liberties, Fraunchises, and other Profites and Commoditees to the same apperteynyng, or the which shall or mowe growe in eny wise by reason of the same, in as large wise, as any Wardeyn of the seid Marches hath hadde

Opposite: Boar of Richard III from the obverse of his seal as Lord of Glamorgan, still in use when he was King.

[89]

Richard's signature on a leaf of his copy of a late fourteenth century collection of French chronicles. The miniature shows a fight outside Meaux.

and reasonably used to have in tyme past. And that for occupying of the seid Office of Wardeynshipp, by the seid Duc and his seide heires to be don, the same Duc by the same auctorite, shall have and enjoye to hym and to his seid heires masles of his body comyng, the things in this Acte hereafter comprised;

....

to be had and holden to the said Duc, and his seid Heires masles of his body commyng, of the Kyng and his Heires, Kyngs of Englond, by a Knyghtes fee for all manere of services. And also the seid Duc shall have to hym and his seid heires, as well the makyng and ordeynyng of the Sheref of the seid Countee of Cumberland, as the makyng and ordeynyng of the Escheatour of the same Countee, fro yere to yere and tyme to tyme. And also that the same Duc shall have to hym and his heires in fee symple, the Contreys and grounde in Scotlande, called Liddalesdale, Esdale, Ewsdale, Anandirdale, Waltopdale, Cliddesdale, and the Westmerches of Scotlande, whereof grete part is nowe in the Scotts handes, and all suche Castelles, Lordships, Maners, Londes, Tenementes and other Hereditamentes whatsoever they be, within the same Dales and Bordures or any of theim, the which the said Duc or his seid heires hath, or shall hereafter, with Goddes grace, gete and atcheve. And that the same Duc and his heires for ever, shall have as large Power, Auctorite, Jurisdiction, Libertee and Fraunchise in all things, and all Profites and Commoditees, within the same Dales and every suche parcell therof, as he or his heires shall or hath so gete and atcheved, as the Bishopp of Duresme hath within the Bisshoprike of Duresme.[64]

Sir John Crosby and his wife Agnes from St Helen's Church, Bishopgate. A grocer of London, he was the builder of Crosby Hall where Richard lived while in London as Duke.

[92]

BROTHER AND UNCLE OF KINGS

While Richard of Gloucester was in the North, King Edward IV died suddenly and unexpectedly.

. . . the king, neither worn out with old age nor yet seized with any known kind of malady, the cure of which would not have appeared easy in the case of a person of more humble rank, took to his bed. This happened about the feast of Easter; and, on the ninth day of April, he rendered up his spirit to his Creator, at his palace at Westminster, it being the year of our Lord, 1483, and the twenty-third of his reign.[65]

For asmuche as the lorde Awdeley and the lorde Barkeley nowe erly in this mornyng by thasent of the Kynges Councell sent unto the Mayre for to shewe and gyf knowledge howe that the Kynge is past oute of this present lyfe this last nyght, whom God pardon & bryng hym to his blys, Amen.

For the whiche the forsaid lordes by the will and avise of the Councell aforsaid willed the Mayre for the savegarde of the Citie and in kepyng of the Peas, to do call & haue byfor hym the Wardens of all felishippes & Craftes, and also the Cunstables, and to gyf them in commaundment & charge to se the peas be kepte euery to their power, And not to provoke, do or cause any debate or stryfe with any straunger or any other parson, on parell that may fall, but to theire power to resist, And to be assistant & helpyng the Mayre & shirriffes & eueryche of them ayenst alle & euery such parson entendyng or brekyng the Kynges peas. And that euery parson therfor to be redy in harnes if nede shulde so requyre & c. Whereuppon the Mayre this fornone had before hym the Wardens & Cunstables, & to them gafe the charge aforsaid, and the Wardens to shewe it furth to theire compenyes and euery constable in his parisshe & warde &c. Whiche commaundment and charge the Wardens have gyven to oure compeny this daye &c.[66]

Opposite: Edward IV, a portrait painted about 1515.

[93]

The body of the King was displayed at Westminster for ten to twelve hours and then followed eight days of services and ceremonies, concluding with the burial in his new collegiate chapel of Windsor on 18 April. During these days, behind the scenes of religious ceremony, the factions of the dead King's court declared their loyalties and ambitions in their plans to escort Edward V from Ludlow to London, and to arrange the future government of the boy King and his kingdom.

For while the councillors of the king, now deceased, were present with the queen at Westminster, and were naming a certain day, on which the eldest son of king Edward, (who at this time was in Wales), should repair to London for the ceremonial of his coronation, there were various contentions among some of them, what number of men should be deemed a sufficient escort for a prince of such tender years, to accompany him upon his journey. Some were for limiting a greater, some a smaller number, while others again, leaving it to the inclination of him who was above all laws, would have it to consist of whatever number his faithful subjects should think fit to summon. Still, the ground of these differences was the same in each case; it being the most ardent desire of all who were present, that this prince should succeed his father in all his glory. The more prudent members of the council, however, were of opinion that the guardianship of so youthful a person, until he should reach the years of maturity ought to be utterly forbidden to his uncles and brothers by the mother's side. This, however, they were of opinion, could not be so easily brought about, if it should be allowed those of the queen's relatives who held the chief places about the prince, to bring him up for the solemnization of the coronation, without an escort of a moderate number of horse. The advice of the lord Hastings, the Captain of Calais, at last prevailed; who declared that he himself would fly thither with all speed, rather than await the arrival of the new king, if he did not come attended by a moderate escort. For he was afraid lest, if the supreme power should fall into the hands of the queen's relations, they would exact a most signal vengeance for the injuries which had been formerly inflicted on them by that same lord; in consequence of which, there had long existed extreme ill-will between the said lord Hastings and them. The queen most beneficently tried to extinguish every spark of murmuring and disturbance, and wrote to her son, requesting him, on his road to London not to exceed an escort of two thousand men.

The same number was also approved of by the before-named lord; for, as it would appear, he felt fully assured that the dukes of Gloucester and Buckingham, in whom he placed the greatest confidence, would not bring a smaller number with them.

. . . all were most anxiously awaiting the day of the new king's coronation, which was to be the first Lord's day in the month of May, which fell this year on the fourth day of the said month. In the meantime, the duke of Gloucester wrote the most soothing letters in order to console the queen, with promises that he would shortly arrive, and assurances of all duty, fealty, and due obedience to his king and lord Edward the Fifth, the eldest son of the deceased king, his brother, and of the queen. Accordingly, on his arrival at York with a becoming retinue, each person being arrayed in mourning, he performed a solemn funeral service for the king, the same being accompanied with plenteous tears. Constraining all the nobility of those parts to take the oath of fealty to the late king's son, he himself was the first of all to take the oath.[67]

The two main narrative sources for this period, Dominic Mancini and the Croyland Chronicler, differ over the details of the means by which the Dukes of Gloucester and Buckingham gained control of the young King Edward V and sent his maternal relatives and closest supporters, Anthony, Earl Rivers, Richard Grey, the King's half brother, and Sir Thomas Vaughan, to prison in Richard's northern castles.

Mancini described the events in the following words:

While in London these events were happening, in the country the duke of Gloucester allied himself with the duke of Buckingham, complaining to the latter of the insult done him by the ignoble family of the queen. Buckingham, since he was of the highest nobility, was disposed to sympathize with another noble: more especially because he had his own reasons for detesting the queen's kin: for, when he was younger, he had been forced to marry the queen's sister, whom he scorned to wed on account of her humble origin. Therefore, having exchanged views and united their resources, both dukes wrote to the young king in Wales, to ascertain from him on what day and by what route he intended to enter the capital, so coming from the country they could alter their course and join him, that in their company his entry to the city might be more magnificent. The king assented to them, and did as they requested. When therefore he

[95]

had approached the twelfth milestone from the city, he halted at a certain village to await there his uncle. As his uncle drew near the spot, the young king ordered nearly all his attendants, of whom he had brought a large number from Wales, to proceed to the hamlets closer to the city, so that the village might be more convenient to receive his uncle. The king awaited with a few of his household, and, to deserve well of his paternal uncle by extreme reverence, he even sent his maternal uncle, whom we said was called Lord Rivers, to meet him. Rivers on coming to Gloucester was graciously received in a very strong place belonging to the duke, and after passing a great part of the night in conviviality, they both retired to bed. At dawn on the following day, when everything was prepared for the journey, Richard, after secretly giving curt orders to this effect, seized Rivers and his companions and imprisoned them in that place. Then with a large body of soldiers, and in company with the duke of Buckingham, he hastened at full gallop towards the young king. At the same time, by having the roads watched, the two dukes guarded against any one informing the young king of these happenings before their arrival.

Wherefore they reached the young king ignorant of the arrest and deprived of his soldiers, and immediately saluted him as their sovereign. Then they exhibited a mournful countenance, while expressing profound grief at the death of the king's father whose demise they imputed to his ministers as being such that they had but little regard for his honour, since they were accounted the companions and servants of his vices, and had ruined his health. Wherefore, lest they should play the same old game with the son, the dukes said that these ministers should be removed from the king's side; because such a child would be incapable of governing so great a realm by means of puny men. Besides Gloucester himself accused them of conspiring his death and of preparing ambushes both in the capital and on the road, which had been revealed to him by their accomplices. Indeed he said it was common knowledge that they had attempted to deprive him of the office of regent conferred on him by his brother. Finally, he decided that these ministers should be utterly removed for the sake of his own security, lest he fell into the hands of desperate men, who from their previous licence would be ready to dare anything. He said that he himself, whom the king's father had approved, could better discharge all the duties of government, not only because of his experience of affairs, but also on account of his popularity. He would neglect nothing pertaining to the duty of a loyal subject and diligent protector. The youth, possessing the likeness of his father's noble spirit besides talent and remarkable learning, replied

The Guildhall, London. The scene of the Duke of Buckingham's speech to the citizens explaining Richard's title to the throne on 24 June 1483, and proposing that he should be King. A reconstruction by Terry Ball.

The full achievement of arms of King Richard III, from the carving by Richard Epsom, Crosby Hall, London.

to this saying that he merely had those ministers whom his father had given him; and relying on his father's prudence, he believed that good and faithful ones had been given him. He had seen nothing evil in them and wished to keep them unless otherwise proved to be evil. As for the government of the kingdom, he had complete confidence in the peers of the realm and the queen, so that this care but little concerned his former ministers. On hearing the queen's name the duke of Buckingham, who loathed her race, then answered, it was not the business of women but of men to govern kingdoms, and so if he cherished any confidence in her he had better relinquish it. Let him place all his hope in his barons, who excelled in nobility and power. Finally, the youth, perceiving their intention, surrendered himself to the care of his uncle, which was inevitable, for although the dukes cajoled him by moderation, yet they clearly showed that they were demanding rather than supplicating. Therefore on that same day the youth was taken to the very town where they had seized Lord Rivers. Of the king's attendants, or those who had come out to meet him, nearly all were ordered home. Richard, the queen's other son, who was quite young, and but a little before had come from London to the king, was arrested with him in the same village, and with his brother, Richard was handed over to the care of guards in the same town.[63]

The Croyland Chronicler wrote:

On reaching Northampton, where the duke of Buckingham joined him, there came thither for the purpose of paying their respects to him, Antony, earl of Rivers, the king's uncle, and Richard Grey, a most noble knight, and uterine brother to the king, together with several others who had been sent by the king, his nephew, to submit the conduct of everything to the will and discretion of his uncle, the duke of Gloucester. On their first arrival, they were received with an especially cheerful and joyous countenance, and, sitting at supper at the duke's table, passed the whole time in very pleasant conversation. At last, Henry, duke of Buckingham, also arrived there, and, as it was now late, they all retired to their respective lodgings.

When the morning, and as it afterwards turned out, a most disastrous one, had come, having taken counsel during the night, all the lords took their departure together, in order to present themselves before the new king at Stony Stratford, a town a few miles distant from Northampton; and now, lo and behold! when the two dukes had nearly arrived at the entrance of that town, they arrested the said earl of Rivers and his nephew Richard,

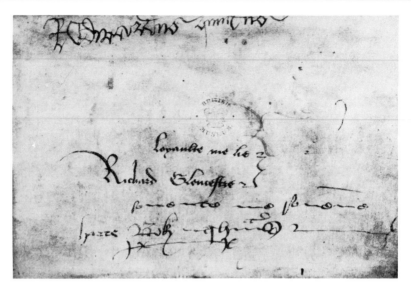

The signatures of Edward V, Richard of Gloucester with his motto *Loyaulte me lie*, and of the Duke of Buckingham with his motto *Souvente me souvene*. Possibly written in May 1483.

the king's brother, together with some others who had come with them, and commanded them to be led prisoners into the north of England. Immediately after, this circumstance being not yet known in the neighbouring town, where the king was understood to be, they suddenly rushed into the place where the youthful king was staying, and in like manner made prisoners of certain others of his servants who were in attendance on his person. One of these was Thomas Vaughan, an aged knight and chamberlain of the prince before-named.

The duke of Gloucester, however, who was the ringleader in this outbreak, did not omit or refuse to pay every mark of respect to the king, his nephew, in the way of uncovering the head, bending the knee, or other posture of the body required in a subject. He asserted that his only care was for the protection of his own person, as he knew for certain that there were men in attendance upon the king who had conspired against both his own honor and his very existence. Thus saying, he caused proclamation to be made, that all the king's attendants should instantly withdraw from the town, and not approach any place to which the king might chance to come, under penalty of death. These events took place at Stony Stratford on Wednesday, on the last day of April, in the year above-mentioned, being the same in which his father died.[69]

[98]

On the night of 30 April the Queen heard of the coup at Northampton. She immediately fled with her second son, the Duke of York, and her daughters into Westminster Abbey sanctuary. On 4 May Edward V and the Dukes of Gloucester and Buckingham entered London, proclaiming Woodville plots against them, and met with all the normal ceremonies of welcome from the Mayor and Aldermen of London and the City companies in their liveries.

These reports having reached London on the following night, queen Elizabeth betook herself, with all her children, to the sanctuary at Westminster. In the morning you might have seen there the adherents of both parties, some sincerely, others treacherously, on account of the uncertainty of events, siding with the one party or the other. For some collected their forces at Westminster in the queen's name, others at London under the shadow of the lord Hastings, and took up their position there.

In a few days after this, the before-named dukes escorted the new king to London, there to be received with regal pomp; and, having placed him in the bishop's palace at Saint Paul's compelled all the lords spiritual and temporal, and the mayor and aldermen of the city of London to take the oath of fealty to the king.[70]

For asmuche as by a Comen Councell it is agreed that certen parsones of euery feliship of the Citie in oon clothyng of murrey shallbe redie to attend on the Mayre on horsbak for to mete and receyue yn oure Kyng Edward the vth at suche tyme as by the Mayre shalbe commaunded &c., in Harnsey Parke. And that of oure felishipp there shall ryde the Nombre of xxx parsons, wherfor theis Parsons next undernamed ben therfor assigned to ryde.

Henry Davners	Wardens	Thomas Hore	Robert Weston
Hugh Brown		Raynolde Asshe	William Rollesley
William Pratt		John Elys	Raufe Ormeston
John Tate		Thomas Fabyan	William Weston
John Pykton		Richard Golofur	Richard Hartwell
Richard Twygg		John Mill	William Piers
Thomas Fuller		Thomas Bradbury	William Burwell
Cristofer Hawe		Thomas Quadryng	William Brown
Richard Lacon		William Rothewell	John Mynes
William Redy		Roger Basford	Thomas Berwik

[99]

Also it is agreed that euery of theis xxx parsones shall haue towar[d] his Costes for hors & harnes xiij s. iiij d. And that he to be redie to attend on the Mayre the daye therfor assygned on payn of xl s. to be payde to the Wardens for & to the behove of oure comen box. And no man departe to the Wardens be comen home again on the said payn &c.[71]

Bishopsgate, through which Edward V, escorted by the Dukes of Gloucester and Buckingham, probably entered London in May 1483; from the copper plate map of c.1550.

A council lasting several days was held to settle matters of immediate importance:

A council being now held for several days, a discussion took place in Parliament about removing the king to some place where fewer restrictions should be imposed upon him. Some mentioned the Hospital of Saint John, and some Westminster, but the duke of Buckingham suggested the Tower of London; which was at last agreed to by all, even those who had been originally opposed thereto. Upon this, the duke of Gloucester received the same high office of Protector of the kingdom, which had been formerly given to Humphrey, duke of Gloucester, during the minority of king Henry. He was accordingly invested with this authority, with the consent and good-will of all the lords, with power to order and forbid in every matter, just like another king, and according as the necessity of the case should demand. The feast of the Nativity of Saint John the Baptist being appointed as the day upon which the coronation of the king would take place without fail, all both hoped for and expected a season of prosperity for the kingdom. Still however, a circumstance which caused the greatest doubts was the detention of the king's relatives and servants in prison; besides the fact that the Protector did not, with a sufficient degree of considerateness, take measures for the preservation of the dignity and safety of the queen.[72]

On 3 June the result of the meeting of their representatives and lawyers with the Lord Protector, the Lord Chancellor and the King's Council at the Tower of London was reported to the Merchant Adventurers. The merchants had successfully secured the stopping of the collection of the customs charges of tonnage and poundage granted by Parliament to Edward IV for his life.

Where was shewed the conveyance & labour made for to be discharged of the Subsidie of tonnage & pondage. And as yisterdaye Mundaye at the Towre of London, we with other felishippes aventerers were at the said toure, havyng with vs oure lerned Councell, that is to saye Humfray Starkey, Recorder of London, Vavacer, seriaunt of lawe, Brown of the Temple & John Hawes of London, gentilman, were before the lorde protector & befor many other lordes & gentilles of the Kynges Councell. Where than the lorde Chaunceler in presens of the lorde Protectour and other aforsaid and by commaundment of the said lorde Protectour shewde howe by an acte of Parlement, Subsidie of tonnage & pondage was graunted & gyffyn to Kyng Edward the iiij^th duryng his lyfe naturall. Where and by reason of the deth of that said Kyng Edward the said Acte is determynyd & nowe as voyde & of non effecte. Wherfore & accordyng to oure labour & desire afor made, the said lorde Chaunceler Requyred the lorde Tresorer to gyve commaundment unto alle suche his officers Collectours & surveyours of the forsaid Subsidie to surces thexcersysyng & takyng of suche subsidie, and to suffur euery Marchaunt denysyn frely to haue up his goodes and Merchauntdises at his libertie with outen any interupcion, Clayme, enterces therof to haue for any subsidie of right nowe due vnto the Kyng, the whiche as by reason of his lawe, ne by any other is not, or can be founde to hym due &c. Wherfore of that charge nowe quytt & discharged &c.[73]

On 9 June Simon Stallworth wrote to William Stonor in Oxfordshire with news from London. Stallworth was well placed to hear the news as he was in the household of John Russell, Bishop of Lincoln, recently appointed the new Lord Chancellor in place of Thomas Rotherham, Archbishop of York. Rotherham had been disgraced for his over-eager support of Queen Elizabeth Woodville. The eldest son of the Queen by her first marriage, the Marquis of Dorset, was in hiding and his goods seized but he was never caught and escaped to Brittany.

Master Stoner. After dew recommendacions I recommend me to youe. As for tydynges seyns I wrote to youe we her none newe. The Quene kepys stylle Westminstre my lorde of Yorke my lorde of Salysbury with othyr mo wyche wyll nott departe as yytte. Wher so evyr kanne be founde any godyse of my lorde Markues it is tayne. The Priore of Westminstre wasse and yytt is in agret trobyll for certeyne godys delyverd to hyme by my lorde Markques. My lorde Protector, my lorde of Bukyngham, with all othyr lordys as wele temporale as spirituale wer at Westminstre in the councelchamber from 10 to 2 butt there wass none that spake with the Qwene. There is gret besyness ageyns the Coronacione wyche schalbe this day fortnyght as we sey. When I trust ye wylbe at Londone and then schall ye knoue all the world. The kynge is at the Toure. My lady of Glocestre come to Londone on Thorsday laste. Also my lorde commendys hyme to youe and he gave me in commaundment to wryte to youe and prayes youe to

[102]

be god master to Edwarde Jhonsone of Thame. He wass with my lorde and suede to be mayde a denysone for fer of the payment of this subsedy and my lorde send to Jever of the clerke of the corone and sawe the commissione and schewyde to hyme that he scholde pay butt 6*s*. 8*d*. for hyme selfe and so wer he better to do then to be mayde denysone wyche wolde coste hyme the thyrde parte of hys goodes and as for suche as has trovylde with in the lordchype of Thame my lorde wilbe advysyd by you at your commyng for the reformacione yf ye take note or ye come, for he thynkes that thei schalbe punysched in examplee of other and Jhesu preserve youe. In haste frome Londone by the handys of your servande the 9 day of June.

Simon Stallworthe.

To the ryght honorabille Ser Willyam Stoner, Knyght.[74]

On 10 and 11 June Richard decided he needed troops from the North to assist him. He wrote to the City of York and Lord Nevill of Raby, and probably others. Given the time it would take them to arrive they cannot have been needed very urgently. Possibly they were to support him over the period of the coronation set for 24 June and the subsequent Parliament which was to confirm him as Lord Protector. It is also possible he realized that strong opposition to him was to come from Hastings and his associates.

Mem. the xv[th] day of Juyn, in the furst yer of Kyng Edward the Vth, Richard Ratclyff, Knyght, delyvered to John Newton, Mair of the Cite of York, a lettre from my lord of Gloucestre, the tenour of which insueth.

The Duce of Glocestre, broder and uncle of Kyngs, protectour, defender, gret Chamberleyn Constabill and Admirall of England.

Right trusty and welbelovyd, we grete you well, and as ye love the wele of us, and the wele and surtie of your oun selff, we hertely pray you to come unto us in London in all the diligence ye can possible, aftir the sight herof, with as mony as ye can make defensibly arraied, their to eide and assiste us ayanst the Quiene, hir blode adherentts and affinitie, which have entended and daly doith intend, to murder and utterly distroy us and our cousyn, the duc of Bukkyngham, and the old royall blode of this realme, and as it is now openly knowen, by their subtill and dampnabill wais forcasted the same, and also the finall distruccion and disheryson of you and all odir thenheritours and men of honer, as weile of the north parties as odir

[103]

contrees, that belongen us; as our trusty servaunt, this berer, shall mor at large shew you, to whom we pray you geve credence, and as evyr we may do for you in tym comyng faille not, but hast you to us hidir. Yovyn under our signet, at London, the xth day of Juyn.

To our right trusty and welbelovyd John Newton, Mair of York, and his Bredir, and the Commons of the same and every thame. The credence of the which lettre is that such felichip as the citie may make defensably arraid, as wele of hors as of fute, be on Wendynsday at eyn next cummyng at Powmfret, their attendyng upon my lord of Northumbreland, and so with hym to go up to London, thar to attend apon my said lords gude grace.

At the wich day, for as moch as my lord of Gloucestre gude grace hath writtyn to the Cite whow that the Qwhen and hyr adherannts intendyth to distrew hys gude grace and odir of the blod riall, it agreid that Thomas Wrangwysh, William Wells, Robert Hancok, John Hag, Ricardus Marston and William White, with cc [200] horsmen, defensably arayd, shall ryd upp to London to asyst my said lord gude grace, and to be at Pomfret at Wedynsday at nyght next cumyng, thar to atend apon my lord of Northumbreland, to go to my said lord of Gloucestre gude grace.[75]

To my Lorde Nevyll, in hast.

My Lorde Nevyll, I recommaunde me to you as hartely as I can; and as ever ye love me, and your awne weale and securty, and this Realme, that ye come to me with that ye may make, defensably arrayde, in all the hast that ys possyble, and that ye wyll yef credence to . . . . . Richarde Ratclyff, thys beerrer, whom I nowe do sende to you, enstructed with all my mynde and entent.

And, my lord, do me nowe gode servyce, as ye have always befor don, and I trust nowe so to remember you as shalbe the makyng of you and yours. And God sende you goode fortunes.

Wrytten att London, xj. day of Jun, with the hande of your hertely lovyng cousyn and master,

R. GLOUCESTER.[76]

Friday June 13. Three very different accounts survive of the dramatic events at the Tower of London which led to the execution of Lord Hastings and the arrest of several other persons including the Archbishop of York, the Bishop of Ely and Lord Stanley.

And in the mene tyme ther was dyvers imagenyd the deyth of the duke of Gloceter, and hit was asspiyd and the Lord Hastinges was takyn in the Towur and byhedyd forthwith, the xiij day of Iune Anno 1483. And the archbeschope of Yorke, the bischop of Ele, and Oleuer King the secoudare, with other moo, was arestyd the same day and put in preson in the Towur, . . .[77]

Having got into his power all the blood royal of the land, yet he considered that his prospects were not sufficiently secure, without the removal or imprisonment of those who had been the closest friends of his brother, and were expected to be loyal to his brother's offspring. In this class he thought to include Hastings, the king's chamberlain; Thomas Rotherham, whom shortly before he had relieved of his office: and the bishop of Ely. Now Hastings had been from an early age a loyal companion of Edward, and an active soldier, while Thomas, though of humble origin, had become, thanks to his talent, a man of note with King Edward, and had worked for many years in the chancery. As for the bishop of Ely, he was of great resource and daring, for he had been trained in party intrigue since King Henry's [VI] time; and being taken into Edward's favour after the annihilation of King Henry's party, he enjoyed great influence. Therefore the protector rushed headlong into crime, for fear that the ability and authority of these men might be detrimental to him: for he had sounded their loyalty through the duke of Buckingham, and learnt that sometimes they forgathered in each other's houses. One day these three and several others came to the Tower about ten o'clock to salute the protector, as was their custom. When they had been admitted to the innermost quarters, the protector, as prearranged, cried out that an ambush had been prepared for him, and they had come with hidden arms, that they might be first to open the attack. Thereupon the soldiers, who had been stationed there by their lord, rushed in with the duke of Buckingham, and cut down Hastings on the false pretext of treason; they arrested the others, whose life, it was presumed, was spared out of respect for religion and holy orders. Thus fell Hastings, killed not by those enemies he had always feared, but by a friend

[105]

whom he had never doubted. But whom will insane lust for power spare, if it dares violate the ties of kin and friendship? After this execution had been done in the citadel, the townsmen, who had heard the uproar but were uncertain of the cause, became panic-stricken, and each one seized his weapons. But, to calm the multitude, the duke instantly sent a herald to proclaim that a plot had been detected in the citadel, and Hastings, the originator of the plot, had paid the penalty; wherefore he bade them all be reassured. At first the ignorant crowd believed, although the real truth was on the lips of many, namely that the plot had been feigned by the duke so as to escape the odium of such a crime.[78]

In the meanwhile, the lord Hastings, who seemed to wish in every way to serve the two dukes and to be desirous of earning their favour, was extremely elated at these changes to which the affairs of this world are so subject, and was in the habit of saying that hitherto nothing whatever had been done except the transferring of the government of the kingdom from two of the queen's blood to two more powerful persons of the king's; and this, too, effected without any slaughter, or indeed causing as much blood to be shed as would be produced by a cut finger. In the course, however, of a very few days after the utterance of these words, this extreme joy of his was supplanted by sorrow. For, the day previously, the Protector had, with singular adroitness, divided the council, so that one part met in the morning at Westminster, and the other at the Tower of London, where the king was. The lord Hastings, on the thirteenth day of the month of June, being the sixth day of the week, on coming to the Tower to join the council, was, by order of the Protector, beheaded. Two distinguished prelates, also, Thomas, archbishop of York, and John, bishop of Ely, being, out of respect for their order, held exempt from capital punishment, were carried prisoners to different castles in Wales. The three strongest supporters of the new king being thus removed without judgment or justice, and all the rest of his faithful subjects fearing the like treatment, the two dukes did thenceforth just as they pleased.[79]

On the 16 June Queen Elizabeth allowed the Duke of York to leave Westminster Sanctuary to join his brother Edward V in the Tower. The two main chroniclers give different accounts of the episode.

He therefore resolved to get into his power the duke of York, who, as was said, had fled with the queen to sanctuary. For Gloucester foresaw that the duke of York would by legal right succeed to the throne if his brother were removed. To carry through his plan he fixed the date of the coronation; and, as the day drew near, he submitted to the council how improper it seemed that the king should be crowned in the absence of his brother, who on account of his nearness of kin and his station ought to play an important part in the ceremony. Wherefore, he said that, since this boy was held by his mother against his will in sanctuary, he should be liberated, because the sanctuary had been founded by their ancestors as a place of refuge, not of detention, and this boy wanted to be with his brother. Therefore with the consent of the council he surrounded the sanctuary with troops. When the queen saw herself besieged and preparation for violence, she surrendered her son, trusting in the word of the cardinal of Canterbury, that the boy should be restored after the coronation. Indeed, the cardinal was suspecting no guile, and had persuaded the queen to do this, seeking as much to prevent a violation of the sanctuary as to mitigate by his good services the fierce resolve of the duke.[80]

On the Monday following, they came with a great multitude by water to Westminster, armed with swords and staves, and compelled the cardinal lord archbishop of Canterbury, with many others, to enter the sanctuary, in order to appeal to the good feelings of the queen and prompt her to allow her son Richard, duke of York, to come forth and proceed to the Tower, that he might comfort the king his brother. In words, assenting with many thanks to this proposal, she accordingly sent the boy, who was conducted by the lord cardinal to the king in the said Tower of London.[81]

The Palace of Westminster, with Westminster Abbey behind it, from the Thames. From Anthony van den Wyngaerde's map of 1540.

On the same day, Richard postponed Edward V's coronation to 9 November and postponed the parliament called for 25 June. Rumours began to circulate as to his intentions.

When Richard felt secure from all those dangers that at first he feared, he took off the mourning clothes that he had always worn since his brother's death, and putting on purple raiment he often rode through the capital surrounded by a thousand attendants. He publicly showed himself so as to receive the attention and applause of the people as yet under the name of protector; but each day he entertained to dinner at his private dwellings an increasingly large number of men. When he exhibited himself through the streets of the city he was scarcely watched by anybody, rather did they curse him with a fate worthy of his crimes, since no one now doubted at what he was aiming.[82]

In York on 19 June the tenor of Richard's letter of 10 June was proclaimed, and the imminent departure of men south to the support of the Duke announced. On the same day in London the Mayor and Aldermen were making plans to keep the peace and organising a watch. On 21 June Simon Stallworth wrote to Sir William Stonor of the expected arrival of the Northerners, although he had an excessive idea of their numbers. He also had many other interesting details to pass on.

The Duke of Gloucester's Proclamation

19 June 1483.

Richard, Brodyr and Unkill of Kyngs, Duce of Gloucestre, Protectour, Defendour, gret Chamberleyn, Constabill, and Admirall of England, streitly chargs and commands that all maner of men, in their best defensabill araie, incontenent aftir this proclamacon maid, do rise and on up to London to his highnes, in the compeny of his cosyn, the Erle of Northumberland, the lord Nevill and odir men of wirship, by his highnes appontyd, ther to aide and assist hym to the subdewyng, correctyng and punysshyng of the Whene, here blode, and othir hyr adherents, which haith intendyd, and dayly doith entend, to murther and utterly distroi his roiall person, his cosyn the duke of Bukkyngham, and other of old roiall blode of this realme, and also the nobill men of their companyes, and as it is notably knaun, by mony subtill and dampnabill ways forcastyd the same,

[108]

and also the speciall distruccion and disheryson of theym, and of all other thenheritorz and men of haneour, as weill of theis north parties as of other contrees that belongen tham, and therfor in all deligence prepare yourself and come up as ye love their honourz, weles and surties, and the surties of yourself and the common weil of this said realme.[83]

20 June. Quarter Day Court of the Mercers' Company.

Where it was shewde the mynde of the Mayre & Aldermen that is howe a Warden of a felishipp & oon that hath of the same felishipp ben Warden, stonde in Chepe to haue the ouersight of the Wache, as the cource shall com aboute of vij felishippes therfor assigned. Whiche be, Goldsmythes, Mercers, Skynners, grocers, fysshemongers, Haberdysshers and Ledersellers, but euery daye we must haue stondyng in Chepe x men clenly besene in harnes, & to be there from vij of the Clok till xj at none, and to be there agayn at oon of the Clok & to byde there still unto vj of the Clok at nyght. And thus dayly as we haue don so for to contynue unto that we have contrary commaundment &c.[84]

Worschipfulle Sir, I commend me to you and for tydynges I holde you happy that ye ar oute of the prese for with huse is myche trobulle and every manne dowtes other. As on Fryday last was the lorde Chamberleyne heddede sone apone Noone. On Monday last was at Westminstre gret plenty of harnest mene ther was the dylyveraunce of the Dewke of Yorke to my lorde Cardenale; my lorde Chaunceler and other many lordes temporale and with hym mette my lorde of Bukyngham in the myddes of the Halle of Westminstre, my lorde Protectour recevynge hyme at the Starre Chambere dore with many lovynge wordys and so departede with my lorde Cardenale to the Toure where he is, blessid be Jhesu Mery. The lorde Liele [Lisle] is come to my Lorde Protectour and awates apone hyme. Yt is thoughte ther schalbe 20 thousand of my Lorde Protectour and my lorde of Bukyngham menne in Londone this weike to what intent I knowe note but to kep the peas. My lorde haithe myche besynes & more thenne he is content with alle. Yf any other ways wolde be tayne the lorde Arsbyschoppe of Yorke, the Bysheppe of Ely ar yit in the Toure with Master Olyver Kynge. I suppose they schall come oute Nevertheless. Ther ar mene in ther placese for sure kepynge and I suppose that ther schall be sente menne of my lord Protector's to theis lordys placez in the countre. They ar not lyke to come oute off warde yytt. As for Foster he is in holde and mene fer hys lyffe. Mastres Chore [Shore] is in prisone; what schall

[109]

happyne hyr I knowe nott. I pray you pardone me of mor wrytynge, I ame so seke that I may nott wel hold my pene and Jhesu preserve you. From Londone the 21 day of June by the handys of your servand,

All the lord chamberleyne mene be come   Simon Stallworthe.
my lordys of Bokynghame mene.

To the ryght worshipfulle Ser William Stoner, Knyght.[85]

On Sunday 22 June sermons were preached at St Paul's Cross and elsewhere in favour of the Duke of Gloucester becoming King. Accounts (mostly after 1485) of the stories put about in these sermons are confused: the bastardy of Edward IV's issue was alleged on various grounds, and even the bastardy of Edward IV himself. What these later chroniclers and the contemporary Mancini agree upon is that Edward IV's children were to be bypassed, the crown to go to Richard, he being the legitimate heir and like his father in looks. Only the well-informed Croyland chronicler, who mentioned no sermons, knew that the main issue and revelation was a pre-contract between Edward IV and Eleanor Butler which invalidated his marriage to Elizabeth Woodville.

After that he took a special opportunity of publicly showing his hand; since he so corrupted preachers of the divine word, that in their sermons to the people they did not blush to say, in the face of decency and all religion, that the progeny of King Edward should be instantly eradicated, for neither had he been a legitimate king, nor could his issue be so. Edward, said they, was conceived in adultery and in every way was unlike the late duke of York, whose son he was falsely said to be, but Richard, duke of Gloucester, who altogether resembled his father, was to come to the throne as the legitimate successor.[86]

On 24 June, Midsummer Day, the Duke of Buckingham addressed the leading men of London on the subject of Richard's title to the throne. There is no good contemporary account of this event, Mancini being very confused, but the later London Chroniclers are all definite that it happened.

On 25 June Earl Rivers, Richard Grey and Sir Thomas Vaughan were executed at Pontefract.

Pontefract Castle, by Alexander Kierinck, c.1630. The scene of the executions of Rivers, Grey and Vaughan.

Shortly after, the lords previously described were cruelly put to death at Pontefract, being lamented by nearly everyone, and innocent of the deed with which they were charged. The Earl of Northumberland, their chief judge, then proceeded to London.[87]

These multitudes of people, accordingly, making a descent from the north to the south, under the especial conduct and guidance of Sir Richard Ratcliffe; on their arrival at the town of Pomfret, by command of the said Richard Ratcliffe, and without any form of trial being observed, Antony, earl of Rivers, Richard Grey, his nephew, and Thomas Vaughan, an aged knight, were, in presence of these people, beheaded. This was the second innocent blood which was shed on the occasion of this sudden change.[88]

Baynards Castle about 1649, with behind it the tower of the church of St Andrew by the Wardrobe. In 1483 Baynards was owned by Richard's mother, Cicely Duchess of York, and it was here that Richard was offered the crown.

KING BY THE GRACE OF GOD

On 26 June at Baynard's Castle, a bill of petition was presented to Richard by lords and commons, setting out his precise title to the throne, (this bill was later included in the text of the Act of Parliament which confirmed Richard's title in January 1484, see below). There he accepted the throne formally and was conducted to Westminster Hall where he sat in the marble chair of King's Bench and addressed the assembly. He began his reign on this day.

. . . Richard assumed the government of the kingdom, with the title of King, on the twentieth day of the aforesaid month of June; and on the same day, at the great Hall at Westminster, obtruded himself into the marble chair. . . . The colour for this act of usurpation, and his thus taking possession of the throne, was the following:- It was set forth, by way of prayer, in an address in a certain roll of parchment, that the sons of king Edward were bastards, on the ground that he had contracted a marriage with one lady Eleanor Boteler, before his marriage to queen Elizabeth; added to which, the blood of his other brother, George, duke of Clarence, had been attainted; so that, at the present time, no certain and uncorrupted lineal blood could be found of Richard duke of York, except in the person of the said Richard, duke of Gloucester. For which reason, he was entreated, at the end of the said roll, on part of the lords and commons of the realm, to assume his lawful rights. However, it was at the time rumoured that this address had been got up in the north, whence such vast numbers were flocking to London; although, at the same time, there was not a person but what very well knew who was the sole mover at London of such seditious and disgraceful proceedings.[89]

. . . the lord protectour took possescyon at westmynstyr In the grete halle, where he beyng sett In the kyngys Cheyer or place where alle kyngys take ffyrst possescion, The duke of Norffolk syttyng upon his Rigth hand that

[113]

beffore dayes was callid lord Howard, and upon his lyffth hand the duke of Suffolk he callid beffore hym the Jugys Commaundyng theym in Rigth streygth maner that they Justly & duly shuld mynystir his lawe withowth delay or ffavour, Afftyr which commandement soo to theym govyn and othyr Ceremonyes there ffynysshid, he than good In to the abbay, where at the chirch dore he was mett wyth procescion, and by the abbot or hys depute there delyverd to hym the Ceptre of Seynt Edward, he then yood unto the Shryne and there offyrd . . .⁹⁰

After the Protector had taken upon him the royal estate, preheminence and kingdome of this realm, as is aforesaid in the historie of King Edward the fift, he the next day folowying with a great traine, went on foote to Westminsterhall, and there when he had placed himselfe in the Court of Kings Benche, he declared to the audience that he would take upon him the crowne ther in that place where the king himselfe sitteth, and ministreth the lawe, because he considered that it was the chiefest duty of a king to minister the lawes. Then with as pleasaunt an oracion as he coulde, he went aboute to wynne the hartes of the nobles the merchauntes and artificers, and in conclusion all kinde of men, but speciall the lawyers of this realme. And finally to the entent that no man should hate him for feare, and that his deceytfull clemency might get him the good will of the people, when he had declared the discommoditie of discord, and the commoditie of concord and unitie, he made an open proclamacion, that he did put out of his minde all enemities, and that he there did pardon all offences committed against him. And to the extent that he might shew a proof thereof, he commaunded that one Fogge, whom he had deadly hated shouldbe brought before him, who being brought out of the Sanctuarie for thether had he fled for feare of him. In the sight of the people he tooke him by the hand, which thing the common people rejoysed at and praysed: But wise men tooke it for a vanitie. And in his retourne homewarde whomsoever he met, he saluted; for a mind that knoweth itselfe guiltie is in a manner dejected to a servile flattery.⁹¹

Opposite: Richard of Gloucester being offered the crown at Baynards Castle, 26 June 1483. Painting by Sigismund Goetze at the Royal Exchange.

Moorgate, London, through which Richard probably went to review his northern troops in June 1483. Based on the copper plate map of c.1550.

Richard ordered the setting aside of the oath of allegiance to Edward V and made known to Calais how he was king:

That othe notwithstanding, now every good true englissheman is bounde upon knowlage had of the said verray true title, to depart from the first othe so ignorantly gyven to him to whome it apperteyned not and thereupon to make his outhe of newe, and owe his service and fidelite to him that good lawe, reason and the concorde assent of the lordes & Comons of the Royaulme have ordeigned to Reigne upon the people, whiche is oure said soverayne lord king Richard the iij^{de}, brothere to the said king Edward the iiijth late decessed, whome god pardone. Whose sure & true title is evidently shewed & declared in a bille of peticione whiche the lordes spirituelx & temporelx and the commons of this land solemplye porrected unto the kinges highnes at London the xxvj^{ti} day of Juyne, Whereupon the kinges said highnes notably assisted by welle nere alle the lordes spirituelle & temporelle of this Royaulme went the same day unto his palais of Westminstre, and there in suche Roialle honorable appareilled within the gret halle there toke possessione and declared his mynde that the same day he wold begyne to Reigne upon his people, and from thens rode solemply to the Cathedralle Cherche of London and was resseyved there with processione, with grete congratulacione and acclamacion of alle the people in every place and by the weye that the king was in that day. The Copie of the whiche bille the king wille to be sent unto Calais and there to be redd and understanded togeder with thise presentes, desiring righte effectuously alle maner persones of the said thre iurisdiccions what astate, degre or Condicione that they be of, and also them of Guysnes & Hammes to make theire feithes & othes to him as to thaire soverayne lord, like as the lordes spirituelx & temporelx and many other noble mene in gret nombre being in England frely & of goode hert have done for their partes.[92]

The Northern supporters of Richard duly arrived and encamped north of the City. Richard visited them in the open fields between Moorfields and Holywell Priory, and then conducted them through the streets of London to a service in St Paul's, the streets lined with the men of the City's livery companies in armour. Both Mancini and the more prosaic Acts of Court of the Mercers' Company (only concerned to record the Mercers' role in events) had inflated ideas of the numbers of Northerners.

[117]

Meanwhile as the day appointed for the coronation approached, Richard summoned troops to the number of six thousand into the city from his own estates and from those of the duke of Buckingham. He was afraid lest any uproar should be fomented against him at his coronation, when there would be a very great concourse of people. He himself went out to meet the soldiers before they entered the city; and, when they were drawn up in a circle on a very great field, he passed with bared head around their ranks and thanked them; then accompanied by the troops he returned to the city.[93]

3 July. General Court of the Mercers' Company.

Forasmuch as therle of Northumberlande & therle of Westmorland with many other knyghtes, esquyers, gentilles & comens now comen oute of the North, to the nomber x M[1] men or mo, unto the Coronacion of Kyng Richard the iij[th] &c. And that the said Kyng pourposyng to ryde oute into the Felde betwene London and Halywell, where as the forsaid ij Erles with their compeny according to the Kynges commaundment there doth hove & abide for that the Kynges desire is to se all the said Compeny holle in theire arrey &c. And so to com yn alle together at Besshopgate thoroue the Citie to Poules &c.

For the whiche the Mayre commaunded that the Wardens of euery felishipp with all the clenly besene men in hernes, that euery man can make withyn his said felishipp shuld be redy & at Leden Hall with the Mayre & Aldremen at ferthist by xij of the Clok at none. And so to be sett in a raye from Besshopgate to Leden Hall & so to Poules &c.[94]

A few days after this, in a ceremony prepared very hastily, but none the less splendid, Richard of Gloucester was crowned King.

Then was hasty provicion made ffor his Coronacion Soo that upon the vj[th] daye of Julii he & Quene Anne his wyfe were at oon messe Solempnely Crownyd, and afftyr was the ffeest accustumyd wyth alle Cyrcumstauncys thereunto belongyng kept In westmynstir halle.[95]

The daye and yere aforesaid the King and the Queene comyng oute of the Whitehall unto Westmynster hall to the Kinges Benche and from thense the King and the Queene shall goo upon ray clothe bare foted into Saint Edwardes Shrine and all the noble lordes goinge with him every lorde in his degre acording as hereafter is writin. From there was going before the King first Trompettes and clarions and then harouldes of armes with the Kinges cote armour upon theim and after them the Crose with a riall procescion. First come the prestes with gray ameces then after folowe Abbotes and Byshops with myteres on there hedes and their croysys in their handes and the Bishop of Rochester bare the crose before the Cardenall and after them came the Erle of Northumberland with the pointles swourde naked in his hande, and my lord Standly bare the mase of Constableshippe the Erell of

John Estney, Abbot of Westminster 1474–98, shown on his brass of 1498 in his Mass vestments. As Abbot, Estney played a major part in the coronation ceremony of Richard III.

[119]

Kent bare the seconde swourde on the right hande of the Kinge naked, and my lorde Lovell bare the iij swourde on the left hande, than come the Duke of Suffolke with the Septure in his hand and the Erell of Lyncoln bare the crose with the ball, the Erell of Surrey bare the iiijth swurde of Estate before the King in the skabarde, then came the Duke of Norfolk bearing the Kinges crowne by twine his handes and anone after him came Kinge Richard the iij^{de} in his robes of purpill velvet and over his hede a clothe of Estate the barons of the V portes did it beare and on every syde of the Kinge a bishop going, the Byshop of Bathe and the Byshop of Durham then comme the Duke of Bokyngham bearing the Kinges trayne with a white staf in his hande as highe Steward of England than came before the Queene boeth erelles and barons. The Erell of Hontington bare the Quenes septre, the Lorde Vicont Lisle bare the rodde with the doffe and the Erell of Wilsher bare the Quenes crowne before her. Then comme the Queene betwene ij busshops in hir robes of a swtte like the Kinges and over hir hede a clothe of estate borne by the barons of the V portes and on every corner of the said clothe a bell of golde and on her hede a rych serkelet of golde with many preciouse perles and stones sett therin, and my lady of Richemond heyre to the Duk of Somerset bare the Queenes trayne, and than comme after theim the Duches of Suffolk in her robes of estate and on her hede a cronell of golde and then came the Duches of Norfolke lykewyse with other ladyes to the nombre of xx, and after them came boeth knightes and squiers and many typstawes and so they went fowrthe of the pallyce into the churche of the westende and so untill they comme unto Saint Edwardes Shrine to the seates of estate, and anone the King and the Queen satt downe in their seates and anone as this was done there came up before the Kinge and the Queene boeth pristes and clerkes singing the Leten and other priksong with greate realtie, and anone as that was done the King and Queene came downe to the high Alter and there they hade greate observance and service and in the meane while the King and the Queene departed from their robes and stode naked from the medle upwarde and anone the bishops anointed boethe the King and the Queene, and after that this was done the King and the Queene changed their robes into clothe of golde and than the Cardenall of Caunterburye and all the byshopes crowned boeth the King and the Queen with greate solempnite and anone they song Te Deum and the organes went and the Cardenall sensed the King and the Queene and anone they put on the King Seinte Edwardes Coppe and the bishopes toke the Kinge the Septre in his right hande and the crosse with the ball in his lyfte hande, the Queen bare the sceptere in her

[120]

ryght hand and the rodde with the dowve in her left hand and when that was done the Cardenall went to the masse and the King and Queene went to their settes again, and anon come up before the King two bishopes and kneled with theyre croiseres in there handes downe before him a litill while and so they arose and went up and kiste the Kinge one after a nother, and when they hade so done anone they stode beside the King than came up the Duke of Bokingham and stode on the right hande of the Kinge and the Duk of Norfolke stonding on the lefte syde and before the Kinge the Erell of Surrey with a swourd in his hande and there standing all the masse tyme, and on every syde of the Quene standing all the masse tyme a bishop, the Bishop of Exeter and the Bishop of Norwich and on ether syde a ladye knelinge and on the right hande of the Quene sitting the Duches of Suffolke in her estate and on the left side of the Queene sytting my lady of Richemonde. Then kneling behinde the Queenes fete the Duches of Norfolke with other ladys kneling with her, and so they satte still untill the paxe was geven, and whan it was geven anon the King and the Queene came downe from their seattes unto the highe aulter and there kneling anon the Cardenall terned him aboute with the holye Sacrament betwixte his hondes and there he departed the oste betwine the Kinge and Queene and so the King and the Queene went up unto Saint Edwardes Shrine, and there the

The crown of Queen Edith and the crown of St Edward. The mediaeval coronation crowns with which Richard and Anne were crowned in 1483.

[121]

Kinge offered and lefte Saint Edwardes Crowne with other many reliques and after that the lordes sett the Kinges owne Crowne upon his hede and so the King and the lordes retorne home warde every lorde in his degre according save only these pointes. The King bare the crose with the ball in his right hande and the sceptre in his lyfte hande, and the Duke of Norfolke bare the cape of maintenaunce before the King, and the Queene bare the sceptre in her right hande and the rode with the dove in her lefte honde and these bene the deverseties and so they went forthe untill the tyme they comme unto the highe deske at Westmynster halle, and when they were come thether anone the Kinge and the Queene toke their chambres and the clothes of estate left still in the hale and in the meane while that the King and the Queene were in their chambres came riding in to the halle the Duke of Norfolke as Erle marshall and his horse traped in clothe of golde downe to the grounde and so he rode aboute voiding the people saving only the kinges servaunts and the Duke of Bokingham and anone the Duke of Norfolke called unto him the marshall saing unto him that the King woulde have his lordes to sitt downe at iiij bordes in the great hall, and at iiij of the cloke the King and the Queen came unto the highe deske, and there the Kinge satt downe to his diner in the middes of the bowrde, and so on the lefte hande of the Kinge setting the Queene nighe hande to the bordes ende and on the right hande of the Queene stode my lady of Surrey and on the lefte hand my lady of Nothingham holding the clothe of pleasance or estate over her hede whan she dide eate and drinke and on the right hande of the King sytting the Byshop of Durham in the Cardenalles stede and anone the lordes and ladyes avoided down in the hale and wear sett every lorde in his degre and my lady of Suffolk setting in her estate and the Duches of Norfolke and my lady of Richmonde at a nother messe and so forthe all the ladyes at a borde syttynge all upon one side in the middle of the hall and at a nother borde sitting the Chancelar of England with other diverse bishops sitting with him and at the seconde borde satt the erelles and at the barons borde sitting the judges and other certein worshipfull men of the lawe the Lord Mayre sate at the table next the Cubborde the barrons of the portes sate at the table behind the lordes and anone every man avoided down into the hale and were sett every man to his degre and anone after came in the first course before the King and for the dressers the Duke of Norfolke Erle Marshall of Englande, Controller Sir Thomas Percy, Treasorer Sir William Hoppton, Chambrelein my lord Lovell, Steward my lorde of Surrye with a whyte staffe in his hand and master Fywater Sewer and so comyng forthe the first cowrse one dishe of goulde and another of silver so the Kinge was servid all with covered messe and my Lorde of Awdlye Karver unto the King and my Lord Scrope Copbearer, and my Lord Maior of London kepte the Kinges cobarde and when dinner was endyd served the King with a cope of silver and gilte or golde with sweet wyne and the Quene with another and when he hade done he toke the cope for his labor, and my lorde Lovell stode before the King all the diner tyme, and ij Squiers for the bodye leing under the borde all the diner at the Kinges fete, and my lorde Scrope of Upsale Copeberer then the Quene being servid in gylte plate and the Bishop of Durham servid also in sylver all iij with covered mese and at the second course came riding into the hale the Kinges Champion Sir Robert Dimmoke and his horse traped with white silke and redde downe to the grounde and so he come riding before the Kinge making his obeisance, and anone torned him aboute and an heralde proclaymed declaring in all the halle if there by any man that will saye the contrary why that King Richarde shulde not pretend and have the crowne, and anone every man helde their peace for a while and when he hade all said anone all the hale cried King Richard and anone as they hade so said the Champion cast down his gauntlett and so he dide thrise in the hale ones before the King and ons in the mydes of the hale and another tyme in the hale dore, and so he retorned up again before the King making his obbaycans, and anone one of the lordes brought him a cope wythe wine coverid, and so he toke it in his hande and dranke, and whan he hade done he cast owte the remenant of the wyne and covered the cope again and torned his horse and rode thoroughe the hall with the cupe in his right hande and that he hade for his labor. Then after this come before the King xviij haroldes out of a stage in the hall and iiij of theim wore crownes and anone one of them spake certein wordes unto the King proclaimyng his style and when they hade done anone the remenant cried King alarges and so they did iij tymes in the hale and went to their standing again and as to the thirde course it was so lat that there might no service be servide of the same saving only wafers and Ipocrase and anone after this come into the hale grete lightes of waxe torches and torchetes and when they were comme into the hale anone the lordes arose up and went up to the King making there obeisance and when this was done anone the King and the Quyne rose up from the bourd and whent unto their chambres and anone and anone all the people departid and went their wais.[96]

I become true and feithfulle liegeman unto my soverain lord Richard iij[de] by the grace of god king of England etc and to his heires kinges of England,

[123]

& to him and theim my feithe and trouthe shal bere during my lif naturalle, and with him and in his cause and quarelle at alle tymes shal take his parte and be redy to leve and dy ayenst alle erthly creatures and utterly endevor me to the Resistence and subpressing of his ennemyes, Rebelles and traytors if I shal any knowe, to the uttermost of my power, and no thing courte that in any wise may be hurting to his noble & royal persone, so god me helpe and thise holy evaungeliers.[97]

Immediately after his Coronation Richard deposited in Westminster Abbey the precious ampulla containing the holy oil of St Thomas with which he had been anointed. It had been given into his keeping the night before the ceremony by the monks of the Abbey.

R R [sign manual of the king]

This indenture made the vijth day of the moneth of Juyll the first yere of the regne of the most high and excellent cristen prynce Richard, by the grace of God, kyng of Inglond and of France and lord of Irlond the thirde, bitwene the same most excellent cristen kyng on that one partie and John, by the sufferaunce of God, abbot of the monastery of Seint Petir of Westminster and the covent of the same place on that other partie. Witnesseth that the said abbot and covent have receyved the day of makyng of this present endenture at the commaundement and wille of the forsaid most high and excellent cristen prynce and kyng, by the handes and deliveraunce of the right reverend fathers in God, Richard, by the sufferaunce of God, bisshop of Seint Asse [Asaph], and maister Thomas Langton, electe bisshop of Seint David, an egle of gold garnysshed with perles and precious stones in which is closed the precious relique called the ampulle, which the forsaid abbot and covent graunte and promyt by this present endenture to delivere ageyne to the said kynges highnesse whensoever it shall please hym to aske it. And the same most excellent cristen prynce and kyng ordeyneth and willeth that the same precious relique to abide and remayne after his decesse within the forsaid monastery among the regalies now beyng in the said monastery for evermore. In witnesse whereof aswele the signet of the forsaid most excellent cristen prynce and kyng as the commone seale of the said abbot and covent to thise present indentures chaungeably been sette. Yeven the day and yere abovesaid.[98]

After this Richard set out on a progress through the country to show himself to his people. After several days at Greenwich and Windsor he went via Reading to Oxford, where he heard disputations on moral philosophy at Magdalen College, and so via Woodstock to Minster Lovell, the home of his friend and Lord Chamberlain, Francis Lovell. Here he despatched a signed letter to John Russell Bishop of Lincoln, his Chancellor, concerning a mysterious 'enterprise'. It has been suggested that reference is being made to a forthcoming trial of persons unnamed for the murder of Richard's nephews. This has never been confirmed, and it has been recently and plausibly suggested that it refers to a conspiracy in London uncovered at about this time.*

Right Reverend Fader in God, right trusti and welbiloved, We grete you wele. And where as We undrestande that certaine personnes of such as of late had taken upon thaym the fact of an entrepruise as We doubte nat ye have herd, bee attached, and in warde. We desire and wol you that ye doo make our lettres of commission to such personnes as by you and our counsaill shalbee advised forto sitte upon thaym and to procede to the due execucion of our lawes in that behalve. Faille ye nat hereof as our perfacte trust is in you. Yeven undre our signet at this Manoir of Mynster Lovel the xxixth day of Juyll.[99]

* Rosemary Horrox, 'Richard III and London', *The Ricardian* 1984. Vol. 6, p. 325 and note 11.

From Minster Lovell Richard went on to Gloucester, which he reached on the 2nd of August. Here he granted a charter of liberties to the city whose name he had borne.

Richard, by the grace of God King of England and France and lord of Ireland, to all to whom the present letters come, greetings. We have inspected letters patent of our brother, the lord Edward IV, late King of England, made in these words . . .

Furthermore, because of the special affection which we bear towards the said town of Gloucester and its bailiffs and burgesses, and considering the good and faithful actions of the said bailiffs and burgesses in causes of

particular importance to us, and wishing to provide for their immunity, protection and peace, we, of our special favour and from certain knowledge and free impulse, have remitted and released for us, our heirs and successors, to the burgesses, their heirs and successors, £45, parcel of the £65 owed for the farm of the town or borough of Gloucester.

Furthermore of our fuller favour we grant to the said burgesses that on the Monday after the feast of St. Michael the Archangel next they may choose from among themselves a suitable mayor, who is to make an oath in the presence of the bailiffs and four of the more law-abiding and prudent burgesses of the town that he will perform the duties that pertain to the office of mayor in the said town.

Furthermore of our fuller favour we grant to the burgesses that, by whatever name or names they are styled in the grants made to them or their ancestors or predecessors by our forefathers or predecessors, from now on the mayor and burgesses are one corporate body by the name of 'the mayor and burgesses of the town of Gloucester' and by that name are able in person and capable in law of acquiring lands and tenements, to hold to them and their successors in fee and perpetuity and by whatever form of tenure from whatever persons or person who wish to grant the same to them; and they may hold all lands, tenements, possessions and heredita-ments which the said burgesses or their predecessors have held at any time; and they and their successors by name of the mayor and burgesses of the town of Gloucester may plead and be impleaded, make answer or cause to answer, in any kind of actions, real or personal, before us and our heirs in Chancery, before our justices of King's Bench, Barons of the Exchequer, the steward and marshal of our household or before any other justices in any kind of court in the realm of England.

Also, we grant that the mayor and his successors in the office shall have a sword carried before him within the town and its liberties, in the same manner as is the custom in other cities and towns in the realm of England.

We now moreover, of our especial grace, by the wording of these presents ratify and confirm to the said burgesses, their heirs, and successors the said gifts, grants, confirmations, liberties, privileges, franchises, acquittances, immunities, articles and customs and everything

Opposite: Gloucester Cross from the east. Previously standing in the centre of the city, the Cross was dismantled in 1751. A statue of Richard III was one of the eight displayed on it, and was possibly erected in recognition of his granting of the Charter in 1483.

[127]

else contained and specified in the said charters and letters, as the said charters and letters bear witness in due form. Furthermore we wish to show the said burgesses fuller favour in this regard.

We have granted to the said burgesses, their heirs, and successors, and by this charter have confirmed for us and our heirs and successors, that they may fully enjoy and use forever, without let or hindrance from us or our heirs or our justiciars, escheators, sheriffs, coroners, or other bailiffs or ministers whatever, any of the gifts, grants, confirmations, orders, liberties, privileges, franchises, acquittances, immunities, articles, or customs or anything else contained in the said charters or letters that have not been used up to the present time.

....

In witness thereof we have made these letters patent, witnessed by me at Westminster, 2 September in the first year of our reign.[100]

While on his progress, foreign affairs were not neglected. There was a somewhat frivolous exchange of letters with the dying Louis XI of France. In more serious vein, an ambassador was sent to Castile urging a new meeting in place of the one made impossible by the death of Edward IV.

My lord and cousin,—I have seen the letters that you have written to me by your herald Blanc Sanglier, and thank you for the news of which you have apprised me. And if I can do you any service I will do it with very good will, for I desire to have your friendship. And farewell, my lord and cousin. Written at Montilz lez Tours, the 21st day of July.

LEWIS.
Villechartre.

My lord, my cousin, I have seen the letters you have sent me by Buckingham herald, whereby I understand that you wish to have my amity, of which I am very glad, in good form and manner; for I do not mean to break such truces as have hitherto been concluded between the late king of most noble memory, my brother deceased, and you, for the term of the same. Nevertheless, the merchants of this my kingdom of England, seeing the great occasions given them by your subjects by taking vessels and merchandise and otherwise, doubt greatly to adventure themselves to go to Bourdeaux and elsewhere in your obeisance, until they may be assured on

The illuminated initial of the charter granted by Richard III to the Company of Wax Chandlers of London in 1484. Above the royal arms with the boar supporters is the motto *Loyaulte me lie*.

Margaret of York, Duchess of Burgundy, at prayer in 1475. From a religious treatise written for Margaret at Ghent by David Aubert.

your part that they may surely and safely exercise the feat of their said merchandise in all the places of your said obeisance, according to the right of the said truces. Upon which matter, in order that my said subjects and merchants be not deceived under the shadow of the same, I pray you that by my servant, this bearer, one of the grooms of my stable, you will let me know by writing your full intention, and at the same time if you desire anything that I can do for you, that I may do it with good will. And farewell, my lord my cousin.

Written in my castle of Leicester, the 18th day of August.

My lord my cousin, I commend me to you as much as I can. I have written to my servant Blanc Sanglier, now being with you, to make provision of certain wines of the growth of Burgundy and la Haute France, for myself and the queen my consort. I therefore pray you, my lord my cousin, that you will give order to your officers and subjects to suffer him to procure the said wines, and freely conduct them and pass into this my realm of England, without any disturbance or contradiction, and you will do me in this a very singular pleasure. And if there be anything which I can do for you, on your informing me I will accomplish it very willingly with the aid of God, who, my lord my cousin, have you in His holy keeping.

Written in my castle of Nottingham, the 20th day of August.[101]

Instruccions gevene by the king to Barnard de la Forssa to be shewed & opened to the kinges Cousyns, the King & Quene of Castelle. First after the presentacion of the kinges lettres to his said Cousyns with recommendacions in suche case accustumed, he shalle shewe & remembre the said king of the tendre love trust and effeccion that the king oure brothere now decessed whome god pardone had & bare towardes his said Cousyns. Latting them wit that his highnes is and evere entendethe to be of like disposicione towardes them in alle thinges that he may conveniently doo to theire honnor and pleasure.

And in likewise by alle meanes convenient the said Barnard shalle shewe that the king trusteth that his said Cousyns wolbe of like benevalence and disposicion towardes him.

And where in the yere last passed the kinges said brothere sent his Ambassiate to his said Cousyns for diverse maters then not fully concluded, and amonges othere for thentreteignyng of the peas, ligue & amyte passed & concluded betwixt his highnes and Henry late king of Castelle, against whiche many attemptates have be and daily be committed.

[129]

Wherof if due reformacion were not had the said peax, ligue & amite cowd not long contynue. It was therefore appoynted and concluded with his said Cousyns to have adiette [a meeting] in Spayne at Midsomer then next folowing or afor, to the whiche the kinges said Brothere was fully agreed. But for asmoche as it pleased almighti god to call him out of this miserable worlde unto his mercy afore the tyme appoyntd for the said diette, Aftere whiche decesse no gret maters mighte conveniently be appointed afore the king Coronacion and ordering of his Realme.

The said Barnard shalle for that and other causes suche as shalle best serve after his discrecion, excuse the tarying of comyssioners that shuld have come to that diette, and by the auctorite & powere to the said Barnard comitted by the kinges comission, agree & appoynted with the kinges said Cousyns or theire Commissioners to a new day of meeting for reformacion of the said attemptates suche as shalle pleas the kinges Cousyns aforesaid. And that the said Barnard aftere thappoyntementes of a day of meting soo agreed in alle goodly haste acertain the king and his Counselle of the same to thentent that Comissioners may be sent thidere sufficiently instructe and auctorized for due reformacion of the said attemptates to be had & made of theire partie.[102]

During this summer Richard made depositions for the government of Ireland. Most notably he decided to make his son Lieutenant of Ireland, thereby giving the country a definite status and direct link to the crown. William Lacy was sent to the powerful Earl of Kildare, who was to be deputy to the Lieutenant. The Bishop of Annaghdown was sent to the Earl of Desmond, the other great Earl of Ireland (whose power at this time could not however compare to Kildare's). The instructions to Annaghdown contain the famous and cryptic reference to the death of Desmond's father having been contrived by the same persons who had destroyed the Duke of Clarence and others near to Richard. The King concluded by urging Desmond to observe all the means of benevolent and just government, both for his own credit and the King's.

Appointment of the King's firstborn son Edward as Lieutenant of Ireland for three years, with all liberties, rights, powers, authorities, fees, profits, commodities and emoluments as George, late duke of Clarence, had by letters patent of Edward IV, provided that he shall not meddle with the disposition of vacant archbishoprics, bishoprics, abbeys and priories of the

King's patronage and shall not put lands acquired to other uses than the defence of that land and this by the advice of the King and council.

July 19th 1483, Westminster   By the King[103]

Edward, by the grace of God first-born son of the most serene prince Richard, by the grace of God King of England and France and Lord of Ireland, Duke of Cornwall Earl of Salisbury etc; to all to whom etc. greeting. As the same most excellent prince my father and lord, the most dread Richard, by the grace of God King of England and France and Lord of Ireland, by his letters patent given at Westminster on the nineteenth day of July in the first year of his reign ordained us, the aforesaid Edward, his lieutenant of his said land of Ireland, to have, occupy and exercise the said office for the term of three years next following and to occupy it fully giving and granting to us, the same Edward, by virtue of the aforesaid letters patent, the power to make ordain and appoint our deputy under us in the aforesaid land to have the rule & guidance of that land in our absence. Know that we, the aforementioned Edward, by virtue of the aforesaid letters patent to have made, ordained and deputed, and by these presents have appointed our beloved Gerald, Earl of Kildare, our deputy in the aforesaid office within the aforesaid land, to have, occupy and exercise the same office to him, Gerald, in our absence, from the last day of the month of August next, for one year then next following, and from then for as long as it pleases us and our said father, giving and granting by virtue of these presents, to our same deputy, full power and authority to do, exercise and execute each and everything contained and specified in the said letters patent of my lord father which properly belong to the said office or lieutenant of the land aforesaid, as fully and completely as we, the aforesaid Edward, by virtue and force of the said letters patent of the said king my lord can do or could have done if we were present in person. Specially saving to ourselves, however, the granting of the offices of the major officers of that land, that is to say: the office of Chancellor, Treasurer, the two Chief Justices, the Chief Baron of the Exchequer, the Master of the mint of that land, and the ordering of anything concerning the mint and its officers. And because we do not have my seal at hand, we have secured the placing of the privy seal of the said most dread lord my father on these presents.[104]

[131]

Instruccions yeven by the king oure soverayne lord to his trusty welbeloved Maister William Lacy sent from his highnes unto his said lande of Irland.

The said Maister William Lacy shal take with him certain the kinges lettres missives under his signet directe aswelle to the Counsaille there in generalle as to the particuler persones of the same, and by vertue of thaim he shal shewe & open by wey of Credence suche things as folowen, devidyng the maters according to the personages that he shal speke unto. Item the said Maister William shal shewe that the king after the stablisshing of this his Realme of England principally afore othere thinges entendethe for the wele of this lande of Irland to set & advise such good Rule and politique guydyng there as any of his noble progenitors have done or entended in tymes past to Reduce it. Item he shal shewe that the king hathe ordeyned for the wele of his lande of Irland the righte highe and mighti prince Edward, his first begotene sone, to be lieutenant of his said lande of Irland fro the xix day of July last past during the termes of thre yere next folowing etc. Item he shal shewe that Therle of Kildare is ordeyned & made deputie lieutenant to Edward, his said first begotene sonne, during a yere following, to begynne at the last day of August next commyng and so lenger to contynue at the kinges pleasure, Receyvyng for wages and fees Rately as it shal be Requisite for the same. And the cause is why that the king wolle alwey be at his libertee, to thentent the Relief of that lande by his immediat auctorite whensoever he may have furst leiser thereunto. Item that inconsideracione of the good fame and noble disposicione that Thomas Fitzgerard Erle of Kildare is Reported to be of, and namely for that he hathe endeavoured him self by his noble corage wele and feithefully to occupie as lieutenant to Richard, late duc of York, The king hathe ordeyned the said Thomas Fitzgerard to be deputie of the said mighti prince Edward now lieutenant during the kinges said pleasure. Item because the disposicione of the said Erle of Kildare aught furst to be understande afore any shewe or openyng to be made to other of the Counsaille there, considering that the gret part of al the direccions to be takyne in this behalve Resteth upon his assent in taking upon the said deputacione, therfore the said Maister William Lacy shal practise to have speche with him afore any othere. Item in delivering the kinges particular lettres directe to the said Erle, and in shewing to him his credence apart he shal say that the king oure soverayne lord hathe the said Erle for his gret merites in special favor & tendrenesse, trusting right moche upone his saddenes and trouthe. And for that he hathe abled him to be deputie to the said mighti prince his first begotene son as it shal appere by a Commissione made to him as deputie. Item the said Maister William shal delivere the said Erle upon his agrement to take the charge upon him aswelle the Commissione whiche the king hathe made to my lord prince as that my said lord prince hath made to him, whiche both Commissions the said Maister William shal have with him.

Item upon thacceptacion of the said Commissions and office the said Maister William shalle insist that the said Erle come or send in al possible hast to the king in England to endent with his grace as it shalle nowe be best accorded betwene thaim, havyng Respecte aswelle to the ease of this tymes as to othere presidentes passed afore . . .[105]

Instruccions geven by the kinges grace to his Counsellor the Bisshoppe of Enachden [Annaghdown] to be shewed on his behalf to his Cousyn, Therle of Dessemond, and other nobles & gentiles of his land of Irland.

Furst where the said Bisshop hathe enfourmed his said grace of the good toward disposicion and herty desire that the said Erle hathe forto doo him pleasur & service to his power as feithfully and humbly as any other of the kinges subgiettes, the said Bisshoppe shalle on the kinges behalve thanke him. Shewing that, aswele for the noblesse of bloode, as remembring the manyfold notable service and kyndnesse by therles fadre unto the famous prince the duc of York, the kinges Fader, at diverse seasons of grete necessite in thoos parties to his gret ieopardies and charges doon, causethe the kinges grace to accepte and Reteigne him in the tendre favor of the same, trusting of his contynuaunce.

Also he shalle shewe that albeit the Fadre of the said Erle, the king than being of yong Age, was extorciously slayne & murdered by colour of the lawes within Irland by certain persones than havyng the governaunce and Rule there, ayenst alle manhode Reason & good conscience, Yet notwithstanding that the semblable chaunce was & hapned sithen within this Royaulme of England, aswele of his Brother the duc of Clarence, As other his nighe kynnesmen and gret Frendes, the kinges grace alweys contynuethe and hathe inward compassion of the dethe of his said Fadre, And is content that his said Cousyne, now Erle, by alle ordinate meanes and due course of the lawes when it shalle lust him at any tyme hereafter to sue or attempt for the punysshement thereof.

Also the kinges grace wolle that the said Bisshop have auctorite forto take in the kinges name of the said Erle his othe of liegeaunce as other lordes have doon here within this his Royaulme after the fourme here ensuyng. . . .

[133]

Also the said Bisshop shalle shewe unto the said Erle the kinges gret pleasure touching his dealing or entring into any mariage with any blood without thadvise and knowlage of his grace, considered that the same with alle celerite entendethe forto ordeigne and provide in that behalve for his said Cousyn in suche wise and of suche noble blode as shalle Redounde to his welle & honnor and of alle his Frendes & kynnesmen, trusting that the said Erle wolle remembre the same and utterly applie him thereunto. Also the said Bisshop upon perfite understanding that the said Erle shalbe of hoole entencion and promise to his powair to perfourme the premisses. And over that utterly to dispose for many consideracions concernyng the kinges highe pleasur and entent, forto Renounce the wering and usage of the Irisshe arraye and fromthensfurthe to geve and applie him self to use the maner of thapparelle for his persone after the Englisshe guyse, and after the fasshon that the kinges grace sendethe unto him by the said Bisshop, aswele of gownes doublettes hosen and bonettes, and soo folowingly in tyme commyng, as the caas or chaunge of the said fasshion shalle require, that than the said Bisshop shalle deliver unto his said Cousyne in most convenient place and honnorable presence the kinges lyvree, that is to wite a Color of gold of his devise and other apparelle forsaid for his persone. Also above alle other thinges he shalle shewe unto the said Erle that the kinges grace in noo wise wolle oure hooly modre the Churche to be wronged, deroged or preiudiced neither in liberties, Fraunchies, grauntes, Custumes or any other spirituelle emolumentes belonging to the same, but that his said Cousyn shalle mayntene, assiste & support it in every behalve as iustice & righte requireth. And over that to see that no manner Robberys, spoliacions, oppressions or extorcions be suffred to be committed amongst any of the kinges subgiettes of thoos parties, of what Astate degree or condicion so ever they be, and in caas any happen to be, to see theim so offending utterly to be punysshed according with the kinges lawes. And that the said Erle shalle be alle weyes & means of pollycie see and provide that by the passage of the commune highe wayes there, the kinges subgiettes may be assured to goo and passe without robbing and unlawffulle letting. So that the said Erle, according to the kinges gret trust, and also to his gracious demeanyng here in this Royaulme of England may appere and be named a veray Justicer, aswele for his propre honnor & wele, as for the Common wele of those parties etc.[106]

[134]

His progress was seen as a success by at least one of his companions: Thomas Langton, Bishop of St David's, and later to be Richard's Bishop of Salisbury and Henry VII's Bishop of Winchester. He was a famous educationalist and a much loved patron. He responded with enthusiasm to Richard's actions and personality.

I trust to God sune, by Michelmasse, the Kyng shal be at London. He contents the people wher he goys best that ever did prince; for many a poor man that hath suffred wrong many days have be relevyd and helpyd by hym and his commands in his progresse. And in many grete citeis and townis wer grete summis of mony gif hym which he hath refusyd. On my trouth I lykyd never the condicions of ony prince so wel as his; God hathe sent hym to us for the wele of us al . . .

Richard III, Anne Neville and their son Edward of Middleham, from the Rous Roll. Anne is in her coronation robes and wears a crown, at her feet a muzzled Neville bear; she is being presented with two crowns to represent her two marriages. Richard is surrounded by the crests of St Edward, France, Gascony and Guienne, England, Ireland and Wales, with his white boar at his feet. Edward holds the gold rod of the Prince of Wales with which he was invested at York.

The problem of retainers, particularly within towns, and the wearing of liveries showing the affiliation of the wearer to a particular lord or gentleman, was one on which Richard wrote frequently. His letter to Southampton is an impressive example.

Richard etc, To oure trusty and welbeloved the Maire Shireffes of oure Towne of Suthampton that now be or hereaftere for the tyme shallbe greting. Forsomoche as it is fulle according and righte welethy that the commonaltee of every Citee or Towne be hoole and of one wille and agrement in alle causes concernyng the same, and that noone occasione be suffred to entre or lefte to contynue amongst them that in any wise mighte sowne to the contrarie, We considering that Reteyndres taking and using of lyveres at the desires of foreyne persones heretofore amongst diverse of the commons in suche Townes incorporate & othere hathe caused oftentymes gret divisione & goperdie [jeopardy] unto theire Rulers & governors of the same, Whiche we entende fromhensfurthe to be advoided. And therefore wolle & streitly charge you that ye ne suffre hereaftere any maner persone amongst you within oure Towne there nor Suberbes therof forto be outwardly reteyned with any persone of whatsoever astate or degree he be, nor to receive or were any livree of clothing Bagien or othere signe contrarie to oure lawes and the statutes ordeigned & made in that behalve, but onely oures. Latting you wit we ne wolle suffre oure derrest sone the prince to deale or entermeate within you nor youre Fraunchises in any suche causes abovespecified nor within any Citee or Towne incorporate of this oure Realme. And if any wolle presume to take upone him so to doo we eftsones charge you, that ye furthwith doo him or theim so offending to be comitted to sure warde & prisone, there to remayne withoutene baille or maynprise to suche tyme as ye shalle understande oure ferthere pleasure in that behalve without failling as ye desire to eschue oure highe displeasure. Yevene etc at Pountfret the xxij[th] day of Septembre.[108]

In minor gifts to religious establishments in the first few months of his reign Richard remembered Coverham in Yorkshire, close to his own Middleham Castle, and Barnards Castle parish church in County Durham.

To Geffrey Franke Receivor of Middelham

Righte trusty & welbeloved etc. And forsomoche as we of oure grace especialle have graunted unto oure trusty & welbelovede in god Thabbot & Convent of Coverham xx li [£20] of money towardes the belding of theire Churche and reperacione of othere thinges necessarie within thaire place, to be takene of thissues proffites & Revenues commyng & growing of oure lordshippe of Middelham, We therefore wolle & charge you to content & pay unto the said Abbot & Convent the said somme of xx li according to our graunt abovesaid Receiving of theim suffisaunt lettres of acquitaunce specifieng the payment that ye shalle soo make by the which and by thise oure lettres we wolle that ye have thereof due allowaunce in youre accompt at alle tymes. Yevene etc the xxij[th] day of Septembre Anno primo etc[109]

Richard, To the Receivor of oure lordshippe of Barnardes Castelle that now is or that hereaftere for the tyme shalbe greting.

Forasmoche as we of oure grace especialle have yevene & graunted towardes the building of the Churche of oure blissed lady within oure said lordshippe the summe of xl li [£40] We therefore wolle and charge you that of thissues & Revenues commyng & growing of the same oure lordshippe that shalbe due unto us at the Feste of seint Martyn in yeme next commyng, ye content & pay unto the Wardeyns of the said Churche the summe of xx li, and at the same Fest in the yere then next folowing othere xx li without delaye. And thise oure lettres shalbe youre warraunt & sufficient discharge in that behalve. By the whiche we wolle ye have due allouance thereof before oure Auditors there at youre accomptes. Yevene etc the xj[th] day of Octobre Anno primo[110]

From Gloucester Richard went on to Warwick and then to Coventry, Leicester and Nottingham. At Nottingham, on 24 August, he created his son Edward Prince of Wales.

The king to the archbishops etc. greeting. The clarity and charity of the sun's light is so great that when it is poured on the other heavenly bodies the sun shines with no less light and splendour, nor does it suffer any diminution of its strength, rather it is pleased to be seen, to shine as a king in the midst of his nobles and to adorn the greater and lesser stars in the whole court of heaven with his outstanding light. Which without doubt we should take as an example seeing the vocation to which we are called, that is, by the favour of the almighty to govern and be set at the head of all the mortals of this realm. We have turned the gaze of our inward eye to the greatness of this noble state and of its members, having great care that, in the great anxieties which press upon us, those who are necessary to support us should not now seem to be lacking. And since among the provinces subject to us none requires separate and immediate rule under us as much as the principality of Wales, because of its remote position and because of the language and customs of the people, remote from those of other areas, and the county of Chester which almost adjoins and borders it. We therefore, following the footsteps of our ancestors and with the assent and advice of the said prelates, dukes and barons of our realm of England, have determined to honour our dearest first born son Edward, whose outstanding qualities, with which he is singularly endowed for his age, give great and, by the favour of God, undoubted hope of future uprightness, as prince and earl, with grants preogatives and insignia and we have made and created, and do make and create, him Prince of Wales and Earl of Chester. And we have given and granted and do give and grant to the same Edward the name style title state dignity and honour of the same principality and earldom and by this our present charter we confirm them and have placed him at the head of the said principality and earldom, as in the same charter, to have the charge of those parts and govern them and defend them. And we invest him as the custom is by the girding on of the sword, the handing over and setting of the garland on his head, and of the gold ring on his finger, and of the gold staff in his hand, to have and hold to him and his heirs, kings of England, for ever. Wherefore we will and firmly decree for us and our heirs that the said Edward our son shall have the name style title dignity and honour of the principality of Wales and the earldom of Chester aforesaid to him and his heirs Kings of England as aforesaid for ever. With these witnesses etc. Given etc.[111]

The progress continued to York, reached on 29 August. Here the King and his wife and son were splendidly received, and the King decided to invest his son with his principality of Wales. He sent to the Great Wardrobe in London for robes and banners for the ceremony.

Being now desirous, with all speed, to show in the north, where in former years he had chiefly resided, the high and kingly station which he had by these means acquired, he entered the royal city of London, and passing through Windsor, Oxford, and Coventry, at length arrived at York. Here, on a day appointed for repeating his coronation in the metropolitan church, he also presented his only son Edward, whom, on the same day, he had elevated to the rank of Prince of Wales, with the insignia of the golden wand, and the wreath upon the head; while, at the same time, he gave most gorgeous and sumptuous feasts and banquets, for the purpose of gaining the affections of the people.[112]

By the king

We wolle & charge you to deliver unto the bringere hereof for us thise parcelles folowing that it to say First one doublet of purpille satyne lyned with holand clothe and entrelyned with Buske, one doublet of Tawney sattyne lyned in likewise, ij short gownes of Cremsyne clothe of gold that one with droppis & that othere with nettes lyned with grene velvet, one cloke with a cape of violet ingraned the bothe lyned with blak velvet, oone Stomagere of purpille sattyne, one Stomachere of Tawney sattyne, oone gowne of grene velvet lyned with Tawney sattayne, one yerde & iij quartres corse of sike medled with gold & asmoche blak corse of silke for oure spurres, ij yerdes & halff & iij naylles of white cloth of gold for a Cryneire for a Barde, fyve yerdes of black velvet for lynyng of a gowne of grene sattyne, one plakcard made of part of the said ij yerdes and oon halff and ij nayles of white cloth of gold lyned with bukeram, iij paire of Sporres short alle gilt, ij paire of spurres long white parcelle gilt, ij yerdes of blak bokeram for amending of the lynyng of diverse trappors, oone Banere of Sarcenet of oure lady, one Banere of the Trinite, one banere of Seinte George, one banere of Seint Edward, one of seint Cuthbert, one of oure awne Armes alle sarcenet, iij Cotes of Armes betyne with fyne gold for oure owne persone, fyve Cote Armors for heraultes lyned with bukeram, xl trumpet baners of sarcenet, DCCxl penselles of Bokeram, CCCl penselles of Tarteryn, iiij Standerdes of sarcenet with bores, xiij M^l [thirteen thousand] Quynysans

[139]

of fustyane with bores. And thise oure lettres etc Yevene etc at York the last
day of August the first yere of oure Reigne.
To Piers Curteys[113]

Memorandum. On the 29th day of the month of August, on the feast of the
Beheading of St John the Baptist, in the year of our Lord 1483, Richard III,
King of England and France came to the City of York. With him were the
Queen and the Prince, and many other magnates, both spiritual and
temporal, including five Bishops, those of Durham, Worcester, St Asaph,
Carlisle and St Davids, the erls of Northumberland, Surrey and Lincoln,
Lords Lovell, FitzHugh, Stanley, Strange, Lisle and Graystoke and many
others. After being received by the civic authorities in solemn procession at
the chapel of St James outside the walls, they were honourably received
into the City, and passed through displays and decorations to the
Metropolitan Church of St Peter. Here the King was honourably received
at the west door by the Dean and Canons and other ministers of the said
church, all vested in blue silk copes, sprinkled with holy water and censed.
On an ornamental footstool at the font he said a Paternoster, the Succentor
of the Vicars saying the responses to the De Trinitate, that is "Honor
virtus", this being finished by the Choir before the steps of the High Altar.
Here a pause was made for about the space of a Paternoster and an Ave. The
Dean then began the prayer "Et ne nos inducas" for the King. This being
done the Dean and Canons then withdrew into their stalls with the other
ministers and Amen finished on the organ. The psalm Te Deum followed,
begun by the officiating prelate, and finished by the choir and the organ, at
once the antiphon De Trinitate was sung by the Succentor, that is "Gratias
tibi Deus", with a versicle and a prayer to the Trinity. The procession then
went to the palace of the Lord Archbishop.

On the feast of the Nativity of the Blessed Virgin Mary, the King and the
Queen both crowned, went in procession to the aforesaid church, the
Prince and all the other Lords, both spiritual and temporal being in
attendance. The Bishop of Durham was the officiating prelate, and the
High Altar was ornamented with silver and gilt figures of the twelve
Apostles and many other relics given by the Lord King. These remained
there until the sixth hour. After Mass they all returned to the Palace, and

Opposite: Sir John Cheney from his monument in Salisbury Cathedral. He was Master of
the Horse to Edward IV, one of the leaders of the autumn 1483 revolt against Richard III,
and became Lord Cheney under Henry VII.

there before dinner, he [i.e. Edward] was created Prince by the Lord King, in the presence of all. And so they sat, crowned, for four hours, there being present the Dean, Robert Both, the Canons, that is Treasurer Portyngton, Archdeacon Potman of York and the Sub-Dean, and four other prebendaries, ten parsons and twelve Vicars with other ministers of the church.[114]

From York Richard made his way south again, reaching Lincoln on 11 October, via Pontefract and Gainsborough. Here he heard that a great rebellion had broken out in the southern counties, headed by his erstwhile ally, Henry Duke of Buckingham. This uprising was originally meant to restore Edward V to the throne, but when rumours of his death spread the Lancastrian claimant Henry Tudor was invited to join the rebellion.

At last, it was determined by the people in the vicinity of the city of London, throughout the counties of Kent, Essex, Sussex, Hampshire, Dorsetshire, Devonshire, Somersetshire, Wiltshire, and Berkshire, as well as some others of the southern counties of the kingdom, to avenge their

grievances before-stated; upon which public proclamation was made, that Henry, duke of Buckingham, who at this time was living at Brecknock in Wales, had repented of his former conduct, and would be the chief mover in this attempt, while a rumour was spread that the sons of king Edward before-named had died a violent death, but it was uncertain how. Accordingly, all those who had set on foot this insurrection, seeing that if they could find no one to take the lead in their designs, the ruin of all would speedily ensue, turned their thoughts to Henry, earl of Richmond, who had been for many years living in exile in Britany. To him a message was, accordingly, sent, by the duke of Buckingham, by advice of the lord bishop of Ely, who was then his prisoner at Brecknock, requesting him to hasten over to England as soon as he possibly could, for the purpose of marrying Elizabeth, the eldest daughter of the late king, and, at the same time, together with her, taking possession of the throne.

The whole design of this plot, however, by means of spies, became perfectly well known to king Richard, who, as he exerted himself in the promotion of all his views in no drowsy manner, but with the greatest activity and vigilance, contrived that, throughout Wales, as well as in all parts of the marches thereof, armed men should be set in readiness around the said duke, as soon as ever he had set a foot from his home, to pounce upon all his property; who, accordingly, encouraged by the prospect of the duke's wealth, which the king had, for that purpose, bestowed upon them, were in every way to obstruct his progress. The result was, that, on the side of the castle of Brecknock, which looks towards the interior of Wales, Thomas, the son of the late Sir Roger Vaughan, with the aid of his brethren and kinsmen, most carefully watched the whole of the surrounding country; while Humphrey Stafford partly destroyed the bridges and passes by which England was entered, and kept the other part closed by means of a strong force set there to guard the same.[115]

As seen, rumours of the deaths of Edward IV's sons played a large part in the origins of the Buckingham rebellion. These rumours have continued to reverberate ever since. It is undoubtedly true that the Princes had disappeared by October 1483. There are only two unequivocal records referring to them after the younger, Prince Richard, joined his brother in the Tower on 16 June. One is by Mancini, probably obtained from information given him by the Princes' doctor, John Argentine, later Provost of King's College, Cambridge. This may be dated between 16 June and mid-July, when

Mancini left London. The other record of their being seen occurs in the Great Chronicle. It is definitely dated before the end of the 1483 mayoral year on 29 September, and could well refer to the same period as the Mancini reference. There is no definite record of the Princes being seen after this, nor is there any definite record of their being murdered. All subsequent stories, including Thomas More's, merely record rumours.

But after Hastings was removed, all the attendants who had waited upon the king were debarred access to him. He and his brother were withdrawn into the inner apartments of the Tower proper, and day by day began to be seen more rarely behind the bars and windows, till at length they ceased to appear altogether. The physician Argentine, the last of his attendants whose services the king enjoyed, reported that the young king, like a victim

John Argentine, Doctor to Edward V in 1483, and one of the last people reported to have seen him alive. Later Doctor to Prince Arthur, and Provost of King's College Cambridge. Shown in cap and academic gown from his brass in King's College, 1507.

[143]

prepared for sacrifice, sought remission of his sins by daily confession and penance, because he believed that death was facing him. This context seems to require that I should not pass over in silence the talent of the youth. In word and deed he gave so many proofs of his liberal education, of polite, nay rather scholarly, attainments far beyond his age; all of these should be recounted, but require such labour, that I shall lawfully excuse myself the effort. There is one thing I shall not omit, and that is, his special knowledge of literature, which enabled him to discourse elegantly, to understand fully, and to declaim most excellently from any work whether in verse or prose that came into his hands, unless it were from among the more abstruse authors. He had such dignity in his whole person, and in his face such charm, that however much they might gaze he never wearied the eyes of beholders. I have seen many men burst forth into tears and lamentations when mention was made of him after his removal from men's sight; and already there was a suspicion that he had been done away with. Whether, however, he has been done away with, and by what manner of death, so far I have not at all discovered.[116]

And duryng this mayris yere, The childyr of kyng Edward were seen shotyng & playyng In the Gardyn of the Towyr by sundry tymys.[117]

On hearing the news of the rebellion Richard moved to Grantham, where he wrote to the Chancellor for the Great Seal, and expressed in the postscript added in his own hand his outrage at the desertion of the Duke of Buckingham. The letter was carried by his own Gloucester King of Arms.

By the King

Right Reverend Fadre in God, right trusty and welbeloved, We grete you wele. And in oure hertiest wyse thanke you for the manifold presentes that youre servantes on your behalve have presented unto us at this oure being here, whiche We assure you We toke and accepted with good hert and soo We have cause. And where as We by Goddes grace entende briefly to avaunce Us towards our rebelle and traytoure the Duc of Bukingham to resiste and withstonde his maliciouse purpose as lately by oure other lettres We certifyed you our mynde more at large. For whiche cause it behoveth us to have oure grete sele here, We being enformed that for suche infirmitees and diseases as ye susteyne ne may in youre persone to youre ease conveniently come unto us with the same. Wherfore we desire and nathelesse charge you that forthwith upon the sight of thies ye saufly doo the same oure grete sele to be sent unto us and suche of thofficers of our Chauncery as by youre wysedom shalbe thought necessary. Receyvyng thise oure lettres for youre sufficient discharge in that behalve. Yeven undre oure signet at oure Cite of Lincoln the xijth day of Octobre.

[In the King's hand:] We wolde most gladly ye camme yorselff yf ye may & yf ye may not We pray you not to fayle but to acomplyshe in all dyllygence oure sayde comaundement to sende oure seale incontenent apon the syght heroff as We trust you with suche as ye trust & the offycers perteinyng to attend with hyt prayng you to assertayne Us of your newes. Here loved be God ys all well & trewly determyned & for to resyste the malysse of hym that hadde best cawse to be trewe the duc of Bokyngham the most untrewe creature lyvyng whom with Godes grace we shall not be long tyll we wyll be in that partyes & subdewe hys malys. We assure you was never falss traytor better purvayde [provided] for, as berrerr [bearer], Gloucestre, shall shewe you.[118]

Letter from the King requesting the Lord Chancellor to send him the Great Seal which he needed in the emergency of the rebellion. Richard added a long emotional postscript in his own hand denouncing the treachery of the Duke of Buckingham.

[145]

Richard gathered troops rapidly, and marched out of Leicester, whence he had moved thirteen days after hearing of the rebellion. He issued a proclamation against the chief traitors.

Forasmuch as the King our Soverain Lorde, remembryng his solempne profession which he made at the tyme of his coronation to mercy and justice, and folowyng the same in dede; first beganne at mercy in gevyng unto all maner personnes his full and generall pardon, trustyng therby to have caused all his subgettes to have be surely determyned unto hym according to the duety of their ligeance; and eftson his Grace, in his owne person, as is well knowen, hath dressed himselfe to divers parties of this his reame for the indifferent admynystracion of justice to every person, havyng full confidence and trust that all oppressours and extortioners of his subjectes, orible adultres and bawdes, provokyng the high indignation and displeasure of God, shuld have be reconsiled and reduced to the wey of trouth and vertue, with the abiding in good disposition.

This yet notwithstanding Thomas Dorset, late Marques Dorset, which not feryng God, nor the perille of his soule, hath many and sundry maydes, wydowes and wifes dampnably and without shame devoured, defloured and defouled, holding the unshampfull and myschevous woman called Shore's wife in adultry, Sir William Noreys, Sir William Knevet, Sir Thomas Bourghchier of Barnes, Sir George Broun, Knyghtes, John Cheyne, John Noreis, Walter Hungerford, John Russh, and John Harecourt of Staunton, with other unto theym traytourly associat, without the Kinges auctorite have assembled and gadered his people by the comforte of his grete rebell and traytour the late Duc of Bukyngham, and Busshoppes of Ely and Salesbury, entending not oonly the destruccion of the riall person of oure seid Soveraign Lord and other his true subjectes, the brech of his peace, tranquillite, and commen wele of this his reame, but also in letting of vertue and the dampnable maintenaunce of vices and syn as they have done in tymes passed to the grete displeasur of God and evyll exemple of all cristen people.

Wherfor the Kinges Highnes of his tender and lovyng disposicion that he hath and bereth unto the commyn wele of this his reame, and puttyng downe and rubuking of vices, graunteth that no yoman nor commonner thus abused and blynded by thes tratours, adulters and bawedes, or eny of theym, shall not be hurte in their bodies ne goodes if they withdrawe them self fro their false company and medell no ferther with theym.

[146]

And over this oure seid Soveraigne Lorde graunteth that whoo so ever put hym in devoier and taketh the seid Duc and bringeth hym unto his Highness, shall have a M. in money or C. in land, and for every of the seid Busshopps and Marques a M. marke in money or C. marke in land, and for every of the seid Knyghtes D. marke in money or x ll in land in reward, and that nowe every true subjecte and lover of vertue and peace put his hand in resistyng the malicious entent of the seid traytours, and punysshing of the grete and dampnable vices of the seid traytours, adultrers and bawedes, so that by their true and feithfull assistens vertue may be lyfte up and praysed in the reame to the honour and pleasure of God, and vice utterly rebuked and dampned to the suertie and comfort of all the true and good commons of this reame. And over this the Kyng's Grace woll that it be knowen that all thoo that in any wise eyde, comforte or assist the seid Duc, Busshoppes, Marques or any other of the Kinges rebelles and traytours aforesaid after this proclamation other with goodes, vitelles or otherwise, be reputed and taken for his traytours.

Leicester   23 October[119]

As the King marched into the south and west it became obvious that the rebellion was a failure, partly due to bad organisation, and partly to floods caused by heavy rain which trapped Buckingham and his troops on the west side of the Severn. Buckingham, deserted by his men, was finally arrested and executed, and Richard dealt rapidly with other parts of the uprising.

In the meantime, the duke was staying at Webley, the house of Walter Devereux, lord Ferrers, together with the said bishop of Ely and his other advisers. Finding that he was placed in a position of extreme difficulty, and that he could in no direction find a safe mode of escape, he first changed his dress, and then secretly left his people; but was at last discovered in the cottage of a poor man, in consequence of a greater quantity of provisions than usual being carried thither. Upon this, he was led to the city of Salisbury, to which place the king had come with a very large army, on the day of the commemoration of All Souls; and, notwithstanding the fact that it was the Lord's day, the duke suffered capital punishment in the public market-place of that city.

On the following day, the king proceeded with all his army towards the western parts of the kingdom, where all his enemies had made a stand, with

[147]

the exception of those who had come from Kent, and were at Guilford, awaiting the issue of events. Proceeding onwards, he arrived at the city of Exeter; upon which, being struck with extreme terror at his approach, Peter Courteney, bishop of Exeter, as well as Thomas, marquis of Dorset, and various other nobles of the adjacent country, who had taken part in the rebellion, repaired to the sea-side; and those among them who could find ships in readiness, embarked, and at length arrived at the wished-for shores of Britany. Others, for a time trusting to the fidelity of friends, and concealing themselves in secret spots, afterwards betook themselves to the protection of holy places. One most noble knight of that city perished, Thomas Saint Leger by name, to save whose life very large sums of money were offered; but all in vain, for he underwent his sentence of capital punishment.[120]

After the collapse of the uprising it only remained for Richard to settle the remaining unrest by proclamation, and eventually by the attainder of Buckingham and his followers (see below).

Proclamation proclaimed in Kent. The king oure soverayne lord remembring that many and diverse of his true subgiettes of this his Countie of Kent have now late bene abused & blynded by Sir John Gilford, Sir Thomas Lewkenor, Sir William Hawte, knightes, Edward Ponynges, Richard Gilford, William Cheney, Thomas Fenys, William Brandone, John Wingfeld, Anthony Kene, Nicholas Gaynesford, John Isley, Rauff Tikhille, Anthony Broune, John Pympe, Robert Brent, Long Roger, Richard Pottere, Richard Fissher, Sir Markus Hussy, prest, and othere the kinges Rebelles & traitors whiche imagyned & utterly conspired the distruccione of the king oure said soverayne lordes most roialle persone the subversion of this his Royaulme & the common wele of the same, and many of his said subgiettes of this his Countie of Kent whene they knew & understode theire said conspired treasons lefte & forsoke them and as his true subgiettes sethens have wele & truely behaved theim. For the which the kinges grace standethe & wolbe to theim good & graciouse soverayne lord and willethe & desirethe alle his said true subgiettes to put them in theire effectuelle devors to take his said Rebelles & traitors, and graunteth that he or they that shalle happe to take the said Sir John Gilford, Sire Thomas Lewkenor, Sir William Hawte, William Cheyne, Richard Gilforde, or Reynold Pympe shalle have for eche of thaim CCC marcs or x

London Bridge from the Southwark bank of the Thames, From the drawing by Anthony van den Wyngaerde in 1540. The houses and shops can all be seen, as well as the gate house in the centre guarding the draw-bridge, and behind it the large chapel of St Thomas Becket.

li of land, and for everiche of the othere afore named C li or x marcs of land and gret thanke of the kinges grace. And over this the king wolle it be knowen that if any persone harboroughe, logge, Comfort socoure or kepe within his house or otherwise aide or resette wettingly any of the said Traitoures and disclose them not nor bring them to the king in alle goodly hast possible aftere this proclamacione that than he or they so harbouring, Aiding, comfortting, socouring, resetting or logging them or any of them hereaftere to be taken & reputed as the kinges Rebelles and traitors. And also that no man presume aftere this proclamacione to kepe any goodes or Catailles of the said Traitors but theim utter & showe to the kinges Commissioners in this his said Counte of Kent assigned & appointed. And they that so truely wille shewe it shallbe wele rewarded, and they that doo the contrarie shalbe punysshed accordinge to the lawe. And over this the kinges highnes is fully determyned to see due administracione of Justice thoroughe out this his Realme to be had, And to reforme punysshe &

[149]

subdue alle extorcions & oppressions in the same, And for that cause wolle that at his commyng now into this his said Countie Kent that every persone dwelling within the same that find him greved oppressed or unlawfully wronged do make a bille of his compleynt and put it to his hignes and he shalbe herd and without delay have suche convenient remydye as shalle accorde with his lawes, For his grace is utterly determyned alle his true subgiettes shalle leve in rest & quiete and peasibly enyoie theire landes lyvelodes & goodes according to the lawes of this his land whiche they be naturally borne to enherite. And therefore the king chargeth & commaundeth that no maner man of whatsoever condicion or degre he be robbe, hurt or spoille any of his said subgiettes in theire bodies or godes upone payne of dethe, And also that no maner man make, pike or contrive any quarelle to othere for any olde or new rancor, hate, malice or cause or offres make upon payne of dethe. Nor also take mannys mete, horsmete or any othere vitaille or stuff without he pay truly therefore to the ownere thereof upon peyne of losing of his horsse harneys, goodes and his body to prisone at the kinges wille. And over this that no maner man trouble or vexe any fermor or occupioure of any of the landes that apperteigned to the abovenamed Rebelles & traitors otherwise than by the kinges commaundement or auctorite, And that alle suche fermors and occupiers Reteyne & kepe stille in theire owne handes the revenues & money growene & to growe of the said landes unto the tyme they knowe the kinges pleasure in that behalve. And the king oure said soverayn lord chargethe streitly alle his officers mynystres & subgiettes within this his said Countie to Resiste & withstande all persones that wolle attempe any thing contrarie this proclamacion, and them take & suerly kepe in prisone unto they have from the kinges highnes otherwise in commaundement for theire delivere.[121]

In December Richard issued writs of summons to the peers of the realm for his first Parliament, to be held in the new year. His son Edward was among the peers summoned.

To Thomas cardinal archbishop of Canterbury.
Order to cause proclamation to be made for a parliament to be held at Westminster on 23rd January next with the clause premunientes. Dated Westminster 9 December.

Like writs to the bishops undermentioned under the same date.

....

To Edward the King's son, Prince of Wales, duke of Cornwall and earl of Chester. Summons to the said parliament.[122]

....

Richard developed the work of the royal council receiving the petitions of the poor who could not afford the usual processes of the law. He appointed a special clerk to deal with these matters. From this developed the Court of Requests.

December 27, 1483. Grant for life to the king's servitor John Haryngton, for his good service before the lords and others of the council and elsewhere and especially in the custody, registration and expedition of bills, requests and supplications of poor persons, of an annuity of £20 at the receipt of the Exchequer and the office of clerk of the council of the said requests and supplications, with all commodities.[123]

1484 opened auspiciously for Richard with Epiphany celebrations, at which he particularly honoured the citizens of London, and a visit to Kent, taking in Canterbury and some south coast ports. At Canterbury the citizens had collected for a gift to the King, which he refused, in the same way he had refused gifts on his earlier and interrupted progress after the coronation.

Tuesday 13 January. In the same Council was shown a certain gold cup, with a cover also of gold, garnished with pearls and other precious stones, which the Lord King Richard the Third on the feast of Epiphany last past [6 January], sitting crowned in the Whitehall at dinner, gave to the Mayor and Aldermen then present, to the use of the City, which the King desired to be used in the Chamber of Guildhall, etc.

This day it was declared in the same Common Council how the King, for the very great favour he bears towards this City, intended to bestow and make the borough of Southwark part of the liberty of the City, and also to give £10,000 towards the building of walls and ditches around the said borough.[124]

[151]

A royal feast in the 1480s.

For the Lord King on his first coming to Canterbury
And paid for a purse bought at London – 26s 8d, which purse with £33 6s
8d in gold, collected from the mayor and his brethren and thirty-six of the
better sort of persons of the city of Canterbury, was given and offered to the
Lord King and which the Lord King with gracious actions ordered to be
redelivered to the said persons from whom the said sum had been collected.

[152]

This being done the said purse was given to Doctor Langton, at that time Bishop of St Davids, on account of his many acts of kindness and favours to the citizens of Canterbury. Upon all these considerations the aforesaid mayor and his brethren presented the following gifts to the Lord King. Firstly paid to John Burton for four great fattened beefs – £7. And paid to the same John Burton for twenty fattened rams – 66s 8d. And paid for twenty capons of various prices given to the Lord King – 21s 10d. And paid for six capons given to the Bishop of St Davids and other bishops then with the King – 6s. And paid to John Stoubregge for two gold beads given to the Bishop of St Davids and the Bishop of 'Seynt Tasse' – 5s 4d.

Total £13 6s 6d.[125]

Richard's only Parliament opened on Friday 23 January 1484. Of primary importance to the King was the confirmation of his title in an act which incorporated the full text of the bill presented to him on 26 June 1483, which had asked him to take the throne. This bill set out how a pre-contract of marriage between Edward IV and Eleanor Butler and a subsequent clandestine marriage between Edward and Elizabeth Woodville made Edward V, his brother and sisters illegitimate under canon law.

Laws passed to benefit Richard's subjects included one declaring 'benevolences' (demands for free gifts of money which Edward IV had made use of) illegal. Another instructed that persons arrested on suspicion should be allowed bail and that their goods should not be seized before conviction. A sub-clause to an act imposing restrictions on imports by aliens exempted books, and allowed all aliens practising aspects of the book trade to work and live freely in England.

The recent rebellion was also dealt with in a mammoth act of attainder against more than one hundred persons headed by the Duke of Buckingham.

The Croyland Chronicler commented sourly upon the proceedings ratifying Richard's title, the numerous attainders and the subsequent parcelling out of the rebels' lands to Northern supporters of the King, 'the planting of the Northerners' in the South of England.

[153]

Where late heretofore, that is to say, before the consecracion, coronacion, and inthronizacion of oure Souveraign Lord the King Richard the Thirde, a rolle of perchement, conteignyng in writeing certeine articles of the tenour undre writen, on the behalve and in the name of the thre Estates of this Reame of Englond, that is to wite, of the lords spirituells and temporalls, and of the Commons, by many and diverse lords spirituells and temporalls, and other nobles and notable persones of the Commons in grete multitude, was presented and actualy delivered unto oure said Souveraine Lord the King, to th'entent and effect expressed at large in the same rolle; to the which rolle, and to the consideracions and instant peticion comprized in the same, our said Souveraine Lord, for the public wele and tranquillite of this land, benignely assented.

Nowe forasmoch as neither the said three Estats, neither the said personnes, which in thair name presented and delivered, as is abovesaid, the said rolle unto oure said Souverain Lord the King, were assembled in fourme of Parliament; by occasion whereof, diverse doubts, questions and ambiguitees, been moved and engendred in the myndes of diverse personnes, as it is said: Therfore, to the perpetuall memorie of the trouth, and declaration of th'same, bee it ordeigned, provided and stablisshed in this present Parliament, that the tenour of the said rolle, with all the contynue of the same, presented, as is abovesaid, and delivered to oure before said Souverain Lord the King, in the name, and on the behalve of the said three Estates out of Parliament, now by the same three Estates assembled in this present Parliament, and by auctorite of the same, bee ratifyed, enrolled, recorded, approved and auctorized, into removyng the occasion of doubtes and ambiguitees, and to all other lawfull effect that shall mowe thereof ensue; soo that all things said, affirmed, specifyed, desired and remembred in the said rolle, and in the tenour of the same underwritten, in the name of the said three Estates, to the effect expressed in the same rolle, bee of like effect, vertue and force, as if all the same things had ben soo said, affirmed, specifyed, desired and remembred in a full Parliament, and by auctorite of the same accepted and approved. The tenoure of the said rolle of parchement, whereof above is made mencione, foloweth and is such.

To the High and Myghty Prince Richard Duc of
Gloucester.

Please it youre Noble Grace to understande the consideracon, election, and petition underwritten of us the lords spiritual and temporal and commons of this reame of England, and thereunto agreably to geve your assent, to the common and public wele of this lande, to the comforte and gladnesse of all the people of the same.

Furst, we considre how that heretofore in tyme passed this lande many years stode in great prosperite, honoure, and tranquillite, which was caused, forsomuch as the kings then reignyng used and followed the advice and counsaill of certaine lords spirituelx and temporelx, and othre personnes of approved sadnesse, prudence, policie, and experience, dreading God, and havyng tendre zele and affection to indifferent ministration of justice, and to the comon and politique wele of the land; then our Lord God was dred, luffed loved, and honoured; then within the land was peace and tranquillite, and among neghbors concorde and charite; then the malice of outward enemyes was myghtily repressed and resisted, and the land honorably defended with many grete and glorious victories; then the entrecourse of merchandizes was largely used and exercised; by which things above remembred, the land was greatly enriched, soo that as wele the merchants and artificers as other poor people, laboryng for their lyvyng in diverse occupations, had competent gayne to the sustentation of thaym and their households, livyng without miserable and intolerable povertie. But afterward, whan that such as had the rule and governaunce of this land, deliting in adulation and flattery and lede by sensuality and concupiscence, folowed the counsaill of persons insolent, vicious, and of inordinate avarice, despising the counsaill of good, vertuous, and prudent personnes such as above be remembred, the prosperite of this lande dailie decreased, soo that felicite was turned into miserie, and prosperite into adversite, and the ordre of polecye, and of the law of God and man, confounded; whereby it is likely this reame to falle into extreme miserie and desolation, – which God defende, – without due provision of convenable remedie bee had in this behalfe in all godly hast.

Over this, amonges other thinges, more specially we consider howe that the tyme of the raigne of Kyng Edward IV., late decessed, after the ungracious pretensed marriage, as all England hath cause so say, made betwixt the said King Edward and Elizabeth sometyme wife to Sir John Grey, Knight, late nameing herself and many years heretofore Queene of England, the ordre of all politeque rule was perverted, the laws of God and of Gode's church, and also the lawes of nature and of Englond, and also the laudable customes and liberties of the same, wherein every Englishman is

[155]

inheritor, broken, subverted, and contempned, against all reason and justice, so that this land was ruled by self-will and pleasure, feare and drede, all manner of equitie and lawes layd apart and despised, whereof ensued many inconvenients and mischiefs, as murdres, estortions, and oppressions, namely, of poor and impotent people, soo that no man was sure of his lif, land, ne lyvelode, ne of his wif, doughter, ne servaunt, every good maiden and woman standing in drede to be ravished and defouled. And besides this, what discords, inward battailes, effusion of Christian men's blode, and namely, by the destruction of the noble blode of this londe, was had and comitted within the same, it is evident and notarie through all this reaume unto the grete sorrowe and heavynesse of all true Englishmen. And here also we considre howe that the said pretensed marriage, bitwixt the above named King Edward and Elizabeth Grey, was made of grete presumption, without the knowyng or assent of the lords of this lond, and alsoe by sorcerie and wichecrafte, committed by the said Elizabeth and her moder, Jaquett Duchess of Bedford, as the common opinion of the people and the publique voice and fame is through all this land; and hereafter, if and as the case shall require, shall bee proved suffyciently in tyme and place convenient. And here also we considre how that the said pretenced marriage was made privatly and secretly, with edition of banns, in a private chamber, a profane place, and not openly in the face of church, aftre the lawe of Godds churche, but contrarie thereunto, and the laudable custome of the Churche of England. And howe also, that at the tyme of contract of the same pretensed marriage, and bifore and longe tyme after, the said King Edward was and stoode marryed and trouth plyght to oone Dame Elianor Butteler, doughter of the old Earl of Shrewesbury, with whom the saide King Edward had made a precontracte of matrimonie, longe tyme bifore he made the said pretensed mariage with the said Elizabeth Grey in manner and fourme aforesaide. Which premises being true, as in veray trouth they been true, it appeareth and followeth evidently, that the said King Edward duryng his lyfe and the said Elizabeth lived togather sinfully and dampnably in adultery, against the lawe of God and his church; and therefore noe marvaile that the souverain lord and head of this londe, being of such ungodly disposicion, and provokyng the ire and indignation of oure Lorde God, such haynous mischiefs and inconvenients as is above remembered, were used and committed in the reame amongst the subjects. Also it appeareth evidently and followeth that all th issue and children of the said king beene bastards, and unable to inherite or to clayme anything by inheritance, by the lawe and custome of England.

[156]

Moreover we consider howe that aftreward, by the thre estates of this reame assembled in a parliament holden at Westminster the xvijth yere of the regne of the said King Edward the iiijth, he then being in possession of coroune and roiall estate, by an acte made in the same parliament, George Duc of Clarence, brother to the said King Edward now decessed, was convicted and attainted of high treason; and in the same acte is conteigned more at large. Because and by reason whereof all the issue of the said George was and is disabled and barred of all right and clayme that in any wise they might have or challenge by enheritance to the crowne and roiall dignitie of this reame, by the auncien lawe and custome of this same reame.

Over this we consider howe that ye be the undoubted sonne and heire of Richard late Duke of Yorke verray enheritour to the said crowne and dignitie roiall and as in ryght Kyng of Englond by way of enheritaunce and that at this time the premisses duely considered there is noon other person lyvyng but ye only, that by right may clayme the said coroune and dignitie roiall, by way of enheritaunce, and how that ye be born within this lande, by reason whereof, as we deme in our myndes, ye be more naturally enclyned to the prosperite and comen wele of the same: and all the three estates of the land have, and may have more certain knowledge of your birth and filiation above said. Wee considre also, the greate wytte, prudence, justice, princely courage, and the memorable and laudable acts in diverse battalls which we by experience knowe ye heretofore have done for the salvacion and defence of this same reame, and also the greate noblesse and excellence of your byrth and blode as of hym that is descended of the thre most royal houses in Christendom, that is to say, England, Fraunce, and Hispaine.

Wherefore these premises by us diligently considered, we desyring affectuously the peas, tranquilitie and wele publique of this lande, and the reducion of the same to the auncien honourable estate and prosperite, and havyng in your greate prudence, justice, princely courage and excellent virtue, singular confidence, have chosen in all that in us is and by this our wrytyng choise you, high and myghty Prynce into our Kyng and soveraine lorde &c., to whom we knowe for certayn it appartaneth of enheritaunce so to be choosen. And hereupon we humbly desire, pray, and require your said noble grace, that accordinge to this election of us the three estates of this lande, as by your true enheritaunce ye will accept and take upon you the said crowne and royall dignitie with all things thereunto annexed and apperteynyng as to you of right belongyng as well by enheritaunce as by lawfull election, and in caas ye do so we promitte to serve and to assiste your highnesse, as true and faithfull subjietz and liegemen and to lyve and dye

[157]

with you in this matter and every other just quarrel. For certainly we bee determined rather to aventure and comitte us to the perill of our lyfs and jopardye of deth, than to lyve in suche thraldome and bondage as we have lyved long tyme heretofore, oppressed and injured by new extorcions and imposicions, agenst the lawes of God and man, and the liberte, old police and lawes of this reame wherein every Englishman is inherited. Oure Lorde God Kyng of all Kyngs by whose infynyte goodnesse and eternall providence all thyngs been pryncypally gouverned in this worlde lighten your soule, and graunt you grace to do, as well in this matter as in all other, all that may be accordyng to his will and pleasure, and to the comen and publique wele of this land, so that after great cloudes, troubles, stormes, and tempests, the son of justice and of grace may shyne uppon us, to the comforte and gladnesse of all true Englishmen.

Albeit that the right, title, and estate, whiche oure souverain lorde the Kyng Richard III. hath to and in the crown and roiall dignite of this reame of England, with all thyngs thereunto annexed and apperteynyng, been juste and lawefull, as grounded upon the lawes of God and of nature, and also upon the auncien lawes and laudable customes of this said reame, and so taken and reputed by all suche personnes as ben lerned in the abovesaide laws and custumes. Yet, neverthelesse, forasmoche as it is considred that the moste parte of the people of this lande is not suffisiantly lerned in the abovesaid lawes and custumes whereby the trueth and right in this behalf of liklyhode may be hyd, and not clerely knowen to all the people and thereupon put in doubt and question: And over this howe that the courte of Parliament is of suche autorite, and the people of this lande of suche nature and disposicion, as experience teacheth that manifestation and declaration of any trueth or right made by the thre estats of this reame assembled in parliament, and by auctorite of the same maketh before all other thyng, moost faith and certaintie; and quietyng men's myndes, remoweth the occasion of all doubts and seditious language:

Therefore at the request, and by the assent of the three estates of this reame, that is to say, the lords spirituelx and temporalx and comens of this lande, assembled in this present parliament by auctorite of the same, bee it pronounced, decreed and declared, that oure saide souveraign lorde the kinge was and is veray and undoubted kyng of this reame of Englond; with all thyngs thereunto within this same reame, and without it annexed unite and apperteynyng, as well by right of consanguinite and enheritance as by lawful election, consecration and coronacion. And over this, that at the request, and by the assent and autorite abovesaide bee it ordeigned,

[158]

enacted and established that the said crowne and roiall dignite of this reame, and the inheritaunce of the same, and other thyngs thereunto within the same reame or without it annexed, unite, and now apperteigning, rest and abyde in the personne of oure said souveraign lord the kyng duryng his lyfe, and after his decesse in his heires of his body begotten. And in especiall, at the request and by the assent and auctorite abovesaid, bee it ordeigned, enacted, established, pronounced, decreed and declared that the high and excellent Prince Edward, sone of our said soveraign lorde the kyng, be hiire apparent of our saide souveraign lorde the kyng, to succeed to hym in the abovesayde crown and roiall dignitie, with all thyngs as is aforesaid thereunto unite annexed and apperteignyng, to have them after the decesse of our saide souveraign lorde the kyng to hym and to his heires of his body lawfully begotten.[126]

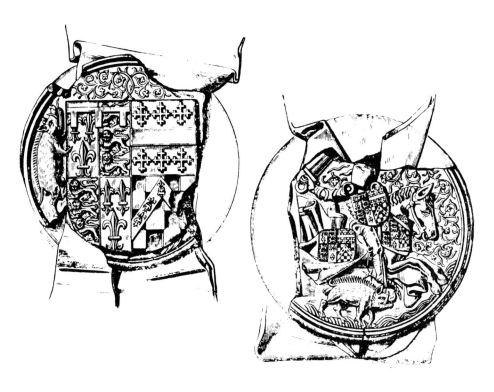

Seal of Richard III as Lord of Glamorgan, fixed to a charter of 1484, showing his use of his ducal seal after he became King.

[159]

The Subjects of this Realm shall not be charged by any Benevolence.

The King remembering how the commons of this his realm, by new and unlawful inventions, and inordinate covertise, against the law of this realm, have been put to great thraldom and importable charges and exactions, and in especial by a new imposition called Benevolence, whereby divers years the subjects and commons of this land, against their wills and freedoms, have paid great sums of money to their almost utter destruction. For divers and many worshipful men of this realm, by occasion thereof, were compelled by necessity to break up their households, and to live in great penury and wretchedness, their debts unpaid, and their children unpreferred, and such memorials as they had ordained to be done for the wealth of their souls were anentized and annulled, to the great displeasure of God, and the destruction of this realm. Therefore the King will it to be ordained, by the advice and assent of the Lords Spiritual and Temporal, and the Commons, of this present Parliament assembled, and by the authority of the same, that his subjects, and the commonalty of this his realm, from henceforth in no wise be charged by none such charge, exaction, or imposition, called a Benevolence, nor by such like charge; and that such exactions, called Benevolences, before this time taken, be taken for no example to make such or any like charge of any of his said subjects of this realm hereafter, but it shall be damned and adnulled for ever.[127]

Every Justice of Peace may let a Prisoner to Mainprise. No Officer shall seise the Goods of a Prisoner until he be attainted.

Forasmuch as divers persons have been daily arrested and imprisoned for suspection of felony, sometime of malice, and sometime of a light suspection, and so kept in prison without bail or mainprise, to their great vexation and trouble. Be it ordained and established by authority of this present Parliament, that every Justice of Peace in every shire, city or town, shall have authority and power, by his or their discretion, to let such prisoners and persons so arrested, to bail or mainprise, in like form as though the same prisoners or persons were indicated thereof of record before the same Justices to their Sessions; and that Justices of Peace have authority to inquire in their Sessions of all manner escapes of every person arrested and imprisoned for felony. And that no Sheriff, Under-Sheriff, nor Escheator, Bailiff of Franchise, nor any other person, take or seise the goods of any person arrested or imprisoned for suspicion of felony, before that the same person, so arrested or imprisoned, be convicted or attainted of such felony according to the law, or else the same goods otherwise lawfully forfeited; upon pain to forfeit the double value of the goods so taken, to him that is so hurt in that behalf, by action of debt to be pursued by like process, judgement and execution, as is commonly used in other actions of debt sued at the Common Law; and that no essoin or protection be allowed in any such action; nor that the defendant in any such action be admitted to wage or do his law.[128]

The Exemption of Books.

Provided always that this Act, or any part thereof, or any other Act made or to be made in this said Parliament, shall not extend to be in prejudice, disturbance, damage, or impediment to any artificer, or merchant stranger, of what nation or country he be or shall be of, for bringing into this realm, or selling by retail or otherwise, any books written or printed, or for inhabiting within this said realm for the same intent, or any scrivener, alluminor, reader, or printer of such books, which he hath or shall have to sell by way of merchandise, or for their dwelling within this said realm for the exercise of the said occupations, this Act or any part thereof notwithstanding.[129]

The Attainder of the Rebels.

Whereas in late days herebefore great troubles, commotions, assemblies of people, conspiracies, insurrections and heinous treasons have been committed and made within this realm by divers persons, unnatural subjects, rebels and traitors unto our sovereign lord King Richard III. and great multitude of people by them abused to consent and be partners of the same offences and heinous treasons, whereby both the king's highness and his peace, and also the politic rule and common weal of this his realm have been greatly inquieted and troubled; they intending thereby, as much as in them was, the universal subversion and destruction of the same, and also of the king's most royal person, the which troubles, commotions, and other offences abovenamed, by God's grace, and the great and laborious vigilance of our said sovereign lord, with the assistance of his true and faithful subjects, been now repressed. Wherein howbeit that his said highness for great considerations touching the weal of this his realm, having therewith respect to the abuse and deceit of the said multitude as before is rehearsed, moved with benignity and pity, and laying apart the great rigour of the law, hath granted to divers persons culpable in the said

[161]

offences his grace and pardon; yet nevertheless, such it is according to reason and all policy that such notary and heinous offences and treasons, in no wise utterly passe unpunished, which if it should so happen the example thereof might and should be a great occasion, cause, and boldness unto other hereafter to attempt and commit like offences and exorbitations, whereby great inconveniences might and were like to ensue, though God forbid. And also to the intent that benignity and pity be not so exalted that justice be set apart, nor that justice so proceed that benignity and pity have no place, but that a due moderation and temperament be observed in every behalf as appeareth to eschew the manyfold and irreparable jeopardies and the inconveniences that else might and be like to ensue.

Considering furthermore that those persons whose names be underwritten were great and singular movers, stirrers and doers of the said offences and heinous treasons; that is to say, Henry late Duke of Buckingham now late days standing and being in as great favour, tender trust, and affection with the king our sovereign lord, as ever subject was with his prince and liege lord, as was notarily and openly known by all this realm, not being content therewith, nor with the good and politique governance of his said sovereign lord, but replete with rancour and insatiable covetise; and also John Bishop of Ely, William Knyvet late of Bokenham Castle in the Shire of Norfolk, John Rush late of London, merchant, and Thomas Nandike late of Cambridge, necromancer, being with the said Duke at Brecknock in Wales the 18th October 1483, falsely conspired the death and destruction of the king and to depose him, and to execute their said purpose assembled at Brecknock as aforesaid with great number of people harnessed and arrayed in manner of war to give battle to the king and his true lords and subjects; and after various traitorous proclamations there made, proceeded thence to Weobley. And also the said duke on the 24th September by his several writings and messages by him sent, procured and moved Henry calling himself Earl of Richmond and Jasper late Earl of Pembroke being there in Brittany, great enemies of our said sovereign lord, to make a great navy and bring with them an army from Brittany; by reason where of the said Henry and Jasper and their adherents came from Brittany with a navy and army of strangers and landed. And

The first page of the popular military treatise *De Re Militari* by Vegetius, illuminated with the English royal arms and the griffin of the Earl of Salisbury. The presence of the griffin suggests that this manuscript was made for the use of Richard's son, who was created Earl of Salisbury in 1478.

[163]

over this, George Broun late of Beckworth, Surrey, (and others who are named), at the traitorous procurement and stirring of the said duke, the said 18th day of October in the year aforesaid at Maidstone as rebells and traitors intended &c. the king's death, and on that day and on the 20th of the same month at Rochester, and on the 22d at Gravesend, and on the 25th at Guildford, assembled, harnessed and arrayed in manner of war and made sundry proclamations against the king to execute their said traitorous purpose: and also at the traitorous motion of the said duke, William Noreys late of Yackendon, Berks, knight, Sir William Berkeley of Beverston, Sir Roger Tocote of Bromham, Richard Beauchamp Lord St. Amand, William Stonor, knight, (and others who are named), on the said 18th October, at Newbury co. Berks, and John Cheyney, (and others who are named), at Salisbury, compassed and imagined the king's death. The parties enumerated were therefore declared to be convicted and attainted of high treason, and their estates to be forfeited.[150]

I shall pass by the pompous celebration of the feast of the Nativity, and come to the Parliament, which began to sit about the twenty-second day of January. At this sitting, Parliament confirmed the title, by which the king had in the preceding summer, ascended the throne; and although that Lay Court found itself [at first] unable to give a definition of his rights, when the question of the marriage was discussed, still, in consequence of the fears entertained of the most persevering [of his adversaries], it presumed to do so, and did do so: while at the same time attainders were made of so many lords and men of high rank, besides peers and commoners, as well as three bishops, that we do not read of the like being issued by the Triumvirate even of Octavianus, Antony, and Lepidus. What immense estates and patrimonies were collected into this king's treasury in consequence of this measure! all of which he distributed among his northern adherents, whom he planted in every spot throughout his dominions, to the disgrace and lasting and loudly expressed sorrow of all the people in the south, who daily longed more and more for the hoped-for return of their ancient rulers, rather than the present tyranny of these people.[131]

[164]

In February an oath of allegiance was taken to Edward Prince of Wales as Richard's heir.

One day, at this period, in the month of February, shortly after mid-day, nearly all the lords of the realm, both spiritual and temporal, together with the higher knights and esquires of the king's household (among all of whom, John Howard, who had been lately created by the king duke of Norfolk, seemed at this time to hold the highest rank), met together at the special command of the king, in a certain lower room, near the passage which leads to the queen's apartments; and here, each subscribed his name to a kind of new oath, drawn up by some persons to me unknown, of adherence to Edward, the king's only son, as their supreme lord, in case anything should happen to his father.[132]

Another success for Richard during the sitting of his Parliament was the acceptance of his terms by Elizabeth Woodville, Queen of Edward IV. On 1 March she came out of sanctuary at Westminster with her daughters and Richard took a public oath to provide for them all.

During this last Parliament of the kingdom, and after frequent entreaties as well as threats had been made use of, queen Elizabeth, being strongly solicited so to do, sent all her daughters from the sanctuary at Westminster before-mentioned, to King Richard.[133]

Memorandum that I, Richard by the grace of god king of England and of Fraunce and lord of Irland, in the presens of you my lordes spirituelle & temporelle and you Maire & Aldermen of my Cite of London, promitte & swere, verbo Regio, & upon these holy evangelies of god by me personelly touched, that if the doughters of dam Elizabeth Gray, late calling her self Quene of England, that is to wit Elizabeth, Cecille, Anne, Kateryn and Briggitte wolle come unto me out of the Saintwarie of Westminstre and be guyded, Ruled & demeaned after me, than I shalle see that they shalbe in suertie of their lyffes and also not suffre any maner hurt by any maner persone or persones to theim or any of theim in their bodies and persones to be done by wey of Ravisshement or defouling contrarie their willes, nor theim or any of theim, emprisone within the Toure of London or other prisone, but that I shalle put theim in honest places of good name & fame, and theim honestly & curtesly shalle see to be foundene & entreated and to have alle thinges requisite & necessarye for their exibicione and findinges as my kynneswomen. And that I shalle do marie suche of theim as now bene mariable to gentilmen borne, and everiche of theim geve in mariage landes & tenementes to the yerely valewe of CC marc [200 marks = £133 6s. 8d.] for terme of their lyves, and in like wise to the other doughters when they come to lawfulle Age of mariage if they lyff, and suche gentilmen as shalle happe to marie with theim I shalle straitly charge from tyme to tyme lovyngly to love & entreate theim as their wiffes & my kynneswomen, As they wolle advoid and eschue my displeasure. And over this that I shalle yerely fromhensfurthe content & pay or cause to be contented & paied for thexibicione & finding of the said dame Elizabeth Gray during her naturelle liff at iiij termes of the yere, that is to wit at pasche, Midsomer, Michilmesse & Christenmesse to John Nesfelde, one of the squiers for my body, for his finding to attende upon her the summe of DCC marc [700 marks = £466 13s. 4d.] of lawfulle money of England by even porcions. And moreover I promitte to theim that if any surmyse or evylle report be made to me of theim or any of theim by any persone or persones that than I shalle not geve thereunto faithe ne credence nor therefore put theim to any maner ponysshement before that they or any of theim so accused may be at their lawfulle defence and answere. In witnesse whereof to this writing of my othe & promise aforsaid in your said presences made I have set my signemanuelle the first day of Marche the first yere of my Reigne.[134]

Goods paid for by the Exchequer on the King's order in the first two of months of 1484 included the items of plate the King had given as New Year's gifts, jewels and suits of Italian armour.

Richard etc. Whereas there is due by us unto our trusty and welbeloved Edmond Shawe, knight and Alderman of our City of London the sum of DCClxiiij li xvijs. vjd. [£764 17s. 6d.]. as well for certain plate by him ordeigned for our yeres gifts against Christmasse last past and for other jewells by him ordeigned and delivered to our own hands. We wol therefore and straightly charge you that towards his contentacion of the same without any delay or excuse ye content and pay the said Edmond Shawe in ready money of the furst money to be received of the profits which shall come to your hands in the terme of Pasche next coming the sum of D marks, parcell of the forsaid sum of DCClxiiij li xcijs. vjd., withouten prest or any other charge to be set upon him for the same in any manner wise. And these

[166]

our letters shall be to you warrant sufficient and discharge for the same. Given under our privy seal at our Palois of Westminster the xxij day of January the furst year of our reign. [1484]

Richard etc. Where we of late have bought of one Gillam de Bretayne merchant of Bretayne and Lewes de Grymaldes merchant of Jene (Genoa) Clxviij harneys complete for five marks the harneys so for us bought in our town of Sandwiche by our servant Robert Lilborne which harneys were delivered unto our Tower of London by the hands of our trusty servant John Stockes the sum of which harneys in all amounteth DLX li. [£560]. Whereof we have paid and contented unto the said Gillam CCxx li and so resteth due unto the said Lewes de Grymaldes CCCxl li. Whereof he hath not perceived of us any payment. We willing him to be contented and paid for the same wol and charge you that ye by way of assignment or otherwise content and pay to the said Lewes the forsaid CCCxl li in such place or places as by your sage discretions shall be thought most sure contentacion and payment for the said Lewes. And these our letters shall be unto you in this behalve warrant sufficient and discharge. Given unto our privy seal at our Palois of Westminster the vjth day of February the furst yere of our reign. [1484][135]

The first few months of 1484 saw Richard making arrangements for the marriage of Katherine, his illegitimate daughter, to William Herbert, Earl of Huntingdon, with generous financial provision for the couple. (Katherine is known to have been dead by 1487.)

THIS endenture, made at London the last day of Februare, the first yere of the raigne of our souverain lord King Richard Third, betwene oure said souverain lord on the oon partie, and the right noble Lord William Erle of Huntingdon on the other partie, witnesseth, that the said erle promiseth and graunteth to our said souverain lord, that before the fast of St. Michael next commying by God's grace he shall take to wiff Dame Katerine Plantagenet, doughter to oure saide souverain lord, and before the day of their marriage to make or cause to be made to his behouff a sure, sufficient, and lawfull estate of certain his manoirs, lordships, lands, and tenements in England to the yerely valeue of cc over all charges, to have and hold to him and the said Dame Katerine, and to their heires of their two bodies lawfully begotten remayndre to the right heires of the said erle, for the whiche oure said souverain lord graunteth to the said erle and to the said Dame Katerine

[167]

to make or cause to be made to theim before the said day of mariege a sure, suffisaunt, and lawfull estate of manoirs, lordships, lands, and tenements of the yerely value of a M. marc over all reprises to have to theim and to theire heires masles of their two bodyes lawfully begotten in maner and fourme folowinge, that is to wit, lordships, manoirs, lands, and tenements in possession at that day to the yerely value of vjc marc, and manoirs, lordships, lands, and tenements in reversion after the decesse of Thomas Stanley Knight, Lord Stanley, to the yerely value of iiijc marc; and in the mean season oure said souverain lord grauntith to the said erle and Dame Katerine an annuite of iiijc marc yerely to be had and perceyved to theim from Michelmasse last past during the lif of the said Lord Stanley of the revenues of the lordships of Newport, Brekenok, and Hay in Wales by the hands of the receyvours of theim for the time being, and overe this oure said souverain lord granteth to make and bere the cost and charge of the said mariage at the day of the solemnizing therof.

In witnesse whereof oure said souverain lord to that oon partie of these endentures remaynyng with the said erle hath set his signet, and to that other partie remaynyng with oure said soverain lord the said erle hath set his seal the day and yere abovesaid.[136]

William Erle of Huntingdon and Katheryn his wif have iontly an Annuytie of Clij li x s x d of the Revenues of al Castelles lordships etc in the Counties of Caermerden & Cardigane & of the lordship of Haverfordwest in the Southwales by the handes of the Receyvor[137]

William Erle of Huntingdon and Kateryn his wif. Commission to the fermors etc of the manoir & lordship of Cattepathe, late Edward Courteneys in Devone, the manoirs of Alewynshey and Kyngstone late Thomas Arundelle in Dorset, al landes and tenementes in saint Mary Clyst late Sir William Stonors, the manoirs of Shevyok, West Tawtone, Portloo, Port Pygham, Treverbyne, Trelugan, Tregamewre, Crofthoole, Northille, Landrene, late Erle of Devone in Cornewaille, the manoire of Corymalet in Somerset, with the fee ferme of xl li going out of the Castel of Caurs in the marche of Wales, to take him as owner of the same and to be ayding etc. Anno primo apud York in May.[138]

Richard and his Queen visited Cambridge from the 9th to the 11th of March. The town recorded the expenses of the visit. Before he left London Richard had given instructions that assistance be given to the building programme of King's College Chapel. Both he and the Queen also gave a generous grant of lands to Queens' College. The University responded by remembering them both in its prayers.

For a present given to the Lord the King, namely in fish, £6. 5s.

....

For the minstrels of the Lord King Richard the Third, this year, 7s.; and in rewards to the minstrels of the Lord the Prince, 7s.; and in rewards to the minstrels of the Queen, 6s. 8d.; and in rewards to the minstrels of the Duchess of York, 6s. 8d[139]

Maister Walter Feld hath a warrant directed to John Hayes to content and pay unto him, towardes the buylding of the Chirche within the Kinges College at Cambrigge, the some of iij^c li [£300] of the Revenues of the temporalties of the Bisshopriche of Excestre. Yeven at Westminstre the last day of Fevriere Anno ij^{do}.[140]

Master Andrew Doket, president & the felowes of the Quenes College, within the universitee of Cambrigge, the maner of Covesgrane in the Countie of Buckingham, and alle the landes & tenementes in Shelding-thorp, Market Deping, Bragham & Stowe in the Countie of Lincolne. Also the maner of Neuton in the Countie of Suffolk, the manor of Stanford in the Countie of Berkshire, the manor of bukby in the Countie of Northamptone. And also Cx li of an Annuyte to be takene in forme folowing that is to say lx li of the feeferme of the Towne of Aylesbury in the Countie of Bukingham, And l li [£50] residue of the feeferme of Ramesey in the Countie of Huntingdon.[141]

TO all the faithful in Christ who shall inspect these letters. The most reverend father in Christ, the Lord Thomas Rotherham, by the grace of God Archbishop of York, Primate of England, Legate of the Apostolic See, and Chancellor of the University of Cambridge, and the unanimous assembly of the Regents and Non-regents of the same University, greeting in the Saviour of all. Whereas the most renowned prince the King of

[169]

England and France, and Lord of Ireland, Richard, after the Conquest, the Third, has conferred very many benefits upon this his University of Cambridge, and especially has lately, liberally, and devoutly founded exhibition for four priests in the Queen's College. And now also the most serene Queen Anne, consort of the same lord the king (that most pious king consenting and greatly favouring), has augmented and endowed the same college with great rents. Whereas also, the same most fortunate king has, with the greatest kindness, bestowed and expended not a little money for the strength and ornament of the university, both in most graciously ratifying the privileges of the university, as also with most devout intention founding and erecting the buildings of the King's College, the unparalleled ornament of all England. These, and many designs considering in our minds, we, the aforesaid chancellor and the unanimous assembly of the masters of the said university, embracing with gratitude such great and royal munificence, and desiring as far as we can to bestow spiritual recompense, decree, that for all time to come whilst the same renowned prince shall continue in this life, on the second day of May, the mass of Salus Populi shall be celebrated by the whole congregation of regents and non-regents of the aforesaid university, for the happy state of the same most renowned prince and his dearest consort Anne. And after the aforesaid most renowned King Richard shall depart this life, we appoint and decree, that when that shall first come to our knowledge, exequies for the dead, and a mass of requiem, diligently and devoutly we will perform for the soul of the same most illustrious Prince Richard, and the souls of all the progenitors of the same. And that every of the premises granted and decreed may obtain strength and virtue, these our present letters concerning them we have caused to be sealed with the common seal of our university, and also with the seal of the chancellor affixed to fortify the same. [16 March 1484][142]

Richard continued to be concerned that his people should clearly understand by what title he held the crown. In April the London companies attended at Westminster to hear the title read to them, they also heard it explained in sermons at St Mary Spittal. At Warwick, John Rous recorded brief details of Richard's title in his 'Roll' with other laudatory remarks.

In primus paide ffor ij whiryes to convey the ffelauschipp to Westmester in Aperell anno Ricardi tercii primo at the which tyme the kyng tytylle and right was ther publyshid and shewid – ijs.[143]

The moost myghty prynce Rychard, by the grace of God kynge of Ynglond and of Fraunce and lord of Irelond, by verrey matrimony with owt dyscontynewans or any defylynge yn the lawe by eyre male, lineally dyscendyng from kynge Harre the second, all avarice set asyde, rewled hys subiettys in hys realme ful commendabylly, poneschynge offenders of hys lawes, specyally extorcioners and oppressors of hys comyns, and chereschynge tho that were vertues, by the whyche dyscrete guydynge he gat gret thank of God and love of all his subiettys ryche and pore and gret laud of the people of all othyr landys a bowt hym.[144]

The effigy on the tomb of Edward of Middleham at Sheriff Hutton.

[171]

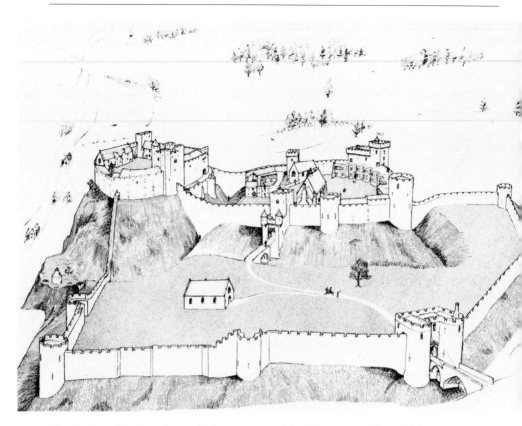

Nottingham Castle as it would have appeared in about 1500. Here Richard and Anne learned of the death of their son Edward, whence Richard referred to it as his Castle of Care, and here he awaited the invasion of Henry Tudor in the summer of 1485.

In April disaster struck. Richard's only legitimate son died and was buried at Sheriff Hutton. The Croyland Chronicler witnessed the grief of the King and Queen at Nottingham where the news reached them. The shock to the Queen may have caused the onset of the tuberculosis of which she possibly died six month later.

Local tradition at Nottingham records that Richard ever after called the Castle his 'Castle of Care', a phrase he could have taken from *The Vision of Piers Plowman* by William Langland.

Little is known of Richard's Prince of Wales except for a brief financial account of his household listing his clothes, his almsgiving and some of his entertainments 1483–4.

However, in a short time after, it was fully seen how vain are the thoughts of a man who desires to establish his interests without the aid of God. For, in the following month of April, on a day not very far distant from the anniversary of king Edward, this only son of his, in whom all the hopes of the royal succession, fortified with so many oaths, were centred, was seized with an illness of but short duration, and died at Middleham Castle, in the year of our Lord, 1484, being the first of the reign of the said king Richard. On hearing the news of this, at Nottingham, where they were then residing, you might have seen his father and mother in a state almost bordering on madness, by reason of their sudden grief.[145]

> 'Tis the Castle of Care; whoso cometh therein
> May mourn that he born was, in body or soul.
> There watcheth a wight, and Wrong is his name,
> The father of falsehood, and finder of ill.
> Adam and Eve he to evil incited,
> Gave counsel to Cain, how to kill his brother,
> And Judas beguiled with the Jews' silver,
> Who hung himself after, on branch of an elder.
> He letteth all love, and he lies to all those
> That trust in his treasure, whom soon he betrays.[146]

Warrant to Thauditors of Middelham to allowe Geoffrey Franke Receivor of the same in his accompotes the sum of £186 10s. That is to wit:

22s and 9d	for gre clothe for my lord prince and Maistre Nigulle by him bought
20d	for making of gownes of the same clothe
13s 4d	to the Gild of Alvertone
5s	for chesing of the king at Westwittone

26s 8d	to Seint Christofire gild at York
5s	for a fethere to my lord prince

22s 3d	for the lord Richard Costes from Middelham to Pountfret
46s 4d	for the lord Richard Berialle [the burial of Richard Grey; he was executed with his uncle Lord Rivers and Sir Thomas Vaughan in 1483 shortly before Richard III's coronation].
14s 1d	to Dyryk Shomakere for stuff foe my lord prince

6s 8d	for the chesing of the king of Middelham
15s	for my lord prince offering to oure lady of Gervaux, Coverham and Wynsladale [Wensleydale].

20d	for my lordes prince offering at Gervaux [Jervaulx].
2s 6d	for offering at Founteyns
4s	for his offering at Pountfret
48s 9d	to Jayne Colyns for offeringes and othere stuff by hire boughte

12d	to Martyn the fole [fool]

20d	for my lordes drynkyng at Rynghouses

13s 4d	for a prymmere for my lord [book of hours]
7s 10d	for blak Satane for Coveryng of it and of a Sawtere [psalter]

[174]

6s 8d	to Metcalff and Pacok for Rynnyng on fote by side my lord prince
100s	to Jane Colyns for hire hoole yere wages ending at Michelmesse

....

23s 4d	for thexpenses of my lord prince housholde from York to Pountfret

....

6s 5½d	for thexpenses of my lord prince Chariot from York to Pountfret and there
3s 4d	to a wiff besides Dancastre by the kinges commaundement

....

8s 2d	for thexpenses of my lord prince horsse at York
20s 1d	for bringing of stuff from Barnardes Castelle

....

£6 18s	for money paied to Sir Thomas Gowere by him laid out for thexpenses of the lord Ryvers

Yevene the 25 day of Septembre Ano primo [1483][147]

John de la Pole, Duke of Suffolk, and his wife Elizabeth, sister of Edward IV and Richard III, from Wingfield Church, Suffolk. Their son John, Earl of Lincoln, became Richard's heir on the death of his own son.

[175]

Matters of state always included the sea and the king's ships. Richard was particularly concerned that proper convoys of armed ships should protect fishing and trading vessels from the East coast to Iceland. In July 1484, while at Scarborough, a town to which he gave an impressive charter and which he clearly saw as an important port, worthy of royal encouragement, he made some further orders in the matter of convoys. About the same time he was also engaged in a sea battle against the Scots.

The Croyland Chronicler (no friend of any northerner) was impressed by Richard's victories over the Scots on land and sea and pleased to record the successful peace negotiations at Nottingham in September. Letters survive between the Kings of Scotland and England arranging the safe-conducts of the Scots ambassadors.

Shippes going to Island. Richard etc, To alle maner awners Maisters and Mariners of the Naveye of oure Counties of Norffolk & Suffolk, aswele fisshers or other, entending to departe into the parties of Island and to every of them greting. Forasmoche as we understande that certain of you entende hastely to departe towardes Island not purveied of waughters [wafters = conveyers] for youre suertie in that behalve, We for certain gret causes and consideracions us moving wolle & straitly charge you alle & every of you that ye ne noon of you severelly depart out of any of oure havens of this oure Realme towardes the said parties of Island without oure licence furst had soo to do. And thereupone that ye gadre and assemble youre selff in suche one of oure havens or poortes in oure said Counties of Norffolk & Suffolk as ye shalle thinke most convenient, Wele harneyssed & apparelled for youre owne suertie, and soo forto departe alle togidere toward Humbre to attende there upon oure shippes of Hulle as youre waughters, for the suertie of you alle. And that ye dessevre [separate] not without tempest of wedere compelle you bot that ye kepe you togedere, aswele going into the said parties as in youre Retorne into this oure Realme, without any wilfulle breche to the contrarie upon payn of forfaiture of youre shippes and goodes in the same. Yevene etc the xxiij day of Februarij Anno primo.[148]

Richard etc, To alle maner merchauntes fisshermene maister mariners and othre oure subgiettes now being in the parties of Island and to every of thayme greting. We late you wite that for diverse consideracions us

[176]

moveing we have appointed and commanded oure trusty servaunt, William Combreshalle, Captain of oure ship named the Elizabeth to departe withe the same towardes youe and to be youre Conveier and Wafter to suche place or places as he shalle thinke convenyent, aswele for youre sureties as for odre gret causes convernyng oure pleasure. Wherefor we wolle and straitly charge you all and every of youe that whensoever ye shalle fortune to mete with oure said servaunt ye dispose you to be ordred and guyded by him and in nowise to departe frome him unto suche tyme as the hole flete of you shall comme to gidres and mete withe othre of oure Armye now being upone the see, And that ye ne faile in any wise upone payne of forfaicting of youre Shippes and goodes. Yevene etc at Scardburghe the sept day Julye Anno Secundo.[149]

Besides this (although at the commencement of the second year of his reign, on giving some attention to maritime affairs, he had lost some ships, together with two captains of the greatest bravery, Sir Thomas Everingham and John Nesfeld, Esquire, above-mentioned, who were taken by the French near the town and castle of Scarborough), just at this period, by means of his skill in naval warfare, he had gained a victory in a surprising manner over the Scots; so much so, that although, in the same summer, they had sustained a great defeat from our people by land, they received no less a one in this. At this time, too, there fell into his hands, besides many of the English who were taken in battle, certain persons who had fled from Scotland, such as lord James Douglas, and many others of his fellow exiles. Upon this, the persons of the highest rank that could be found in that kingdom were sent as ambassadors to the king at his town and castle of Nottingham, on the seventh day of the month of September, and in a lengthy and eloquent address most earnestly entreated for peace and a cessation of warfare. A treaty being accordingly made between commissioners from either kingdom in full conformity with the king's wishes, as to those points which seemd to require especial consideration, the Parliament was dissolved, and the king returned to London in Michaelmas Term. This was in the year of our Lord, 1484.[150]

The king of Scottes lettre sent to the King.
Righte excellent hie and mighti prince and Righte traist and welbelovit Cousing. We commende us unto you in the maist hertly wise. Signifying unto youre Cousinage that we ar nowe advertisit . . . that youre Cousinage is wele applyt and inclynit to the god of trewes abstinence of werre betwix

[177]

Effigy of Ralph Fitzherbert at Norbury Church, showing the Yorkist collar of suns and roses with the boar badge of Richard III as a pendant.

you and us oure Realmes and lieges. And also that luf Amytie and specialle alliauncez of mariage was avisit appointit and concludit betwix youre blode and oures. Whereunto we ar in likewise inclinit. And according to youre empleasire and to shewe in that parte oure gud mynde to the commone gude of treux and abstinence of were, we have lymyt and ordand oure traist and welbelovit Cousinges and Consalores, Colme erle of Ergile, lord Cambelle, Lorne oure Chauncelere, a Reverend fader in god William, Bisshop of Abberdene, Robert lord Lile, Laurence lord Oliphant, Johnne of Drummond of Stobhalle and maister Archibald of Quhitelaw, Archideicon of Lothiane, oure Secretarie, with fulle powaire and Commissione to comme within youre Royaulme unto you to youre Towne of Notingham the vij day of Septembere next . . . And that youre sauf conduyt in the meantyme may be sent to the persones above expremit to the nombre of a C hors or within to come to youre toune above expremit Richte excellent hie and mighty prince and traist Cousing the blessit trinite have you in keping writen undre oure Signet at Edinburghe the xxj day of July.

James

[178]

The Kinges lettres of answere unto the same . . . Righte highe and mighty prince righte trusty and welbeloved Cousin we late your Cousinage wite that this youre loving and toward disposicion is to us righte agreable, trusting that by the mean of this youre Ambassade instructed in al the forsaid maters, as plenerly as the caas shal Require, and to do therein as largely in al pointes as ye were present in propre persone, according to that that is expressed in youre said lettres, suche good weyes shalbe taken betwix bothe Royaulmes whereby effusione of Cristen blood may be eschewed, love and tendrenesse growe daily, and encreace aswele betwix you and us, as the Inhabitauntes of bothe Royaulmes, whiche we take god in witnesse we as hertly have entended with good condicions, and soo shal hereafter, as any prince lyving can or may. And to thentent no thing faille necessary or behoveful to the spedy execucion of the premisses nor of youre partie ne of oures we have passed our lettres patentes of Saufconduyt undre oure gret seale . . .[151]

One of Richard's most notable and enduring achievements was the establishment of the Council of the North, essentially a continuation of his ducal council in the same area. It was to be the final arbiter of local disputes, and an ever available source of justice for the king's subjects. He drew up careful regulations to ensure its impartiality and diligence.

Thise Articles folowing be ordeyned and Stablisshed by the kinges grace to be used & executed by my lord of Lincolne and the lordes and other of his Counselle in the North parties for his suertie & welthe of thenhabitantes of the same.
Furst the king wolle that none lord ne other persone appoynted to be of his Counselle for favor, affeccione, hate, malace or mede, do ne speke in the Counselle otherwise then the kinges lawes & good conscience shalle require, but be indifferent and no wise parcelle, As ferre as his wit & reasone wolle geve him in alle maner maters that shalbe mynestred afore theym.
Item that if there be any mater in the said Counselle moved which toucheth any lord or other persone of the said Counselle, than the same lord or persone in no wise to syt or remayne in the said Counselle during the tyme of thexamynacion & ordering of the said mater enlesse he be called, and that he obeie & be ordured therein by the remenant of the said Counselle. Item that no maner mater of gret weghte or substaunce be ordered or

[179]

North west view of Sheriff Hutton Castle in 1824. Sheriff Hutton was a Neville castle, granted to Richard in 1471, and used by him when King as the seat of his Council of the North.

determyned within the said Counselle enlesse that two of thise that is to say with oure said Nepueu be at the same. And they to be Commissioners of oure peax thoroughout those parties.

Item that the said Counselle be hooly if it may be onys in the quarter of the yere at the leste at York to here, examyne & ordre alle billes of compleyntes & other there before theym to be shewed, and oftyner if the case require.

Item that the said Counselle have auctorite and power to ordre and direct alle riottes, forcible entres, distresse takinges, variaunces, debates & othere mysbehavors ayenst oure lawes & peas committed and done in the said parties. And if any suche be that they in no wise can thoroughly ordre, than to referre it unto us, and thereof certifie us in alle goodly hast thereafter.

Item the said Counselle in no wise determyn mater of land without thassent of the parties.

Item that oure said Counselle for gret Riottes done & committed in the gret lordshippes or otherwise by any persone, committe the said persone to warde to oon of oure Castelles nere where the said Riott is committed. For we wolle that alle oure Castelles be oure gaole, and if noo suche Castelle be nere, than the next common gaole.

[180]

Item we wolle that oure said Counselle, incontynent after that they have knowlage of any Assembles or gaderinges made contrarie oure lawes & peas, provide to resiste, withstande & ponysshe the same in the begynnyng according to their demerites without ferther deferring or putting it in respecte.

Item that alle lettres & writinges by oure said Counselle to be made for the due executing of the premisses be made in oure name, and the same to be endoced with the hande of oure Nepueu of Lincolne, undre neth by thise wordes, *per Consilium Regis.*

Item that oon suffisaunt persone by appoynted to make out the said lettres and writinges and the same put in Regestre from tyme to tyme, and on the same oure said Nepueu, and suche with him of oure said Counselle then being present, setto their handes and a seale to be provided fre for the sealing of the said lettres & writinges.

Item we wolle & streitly charge alle & singuler oure officers, true liegemen & subgiettes in thise northe parties to be at alle tymes obeieng to the commaundementes of oure said Counselle in oure name and duely to execute the same, as they and every of theym wolle eschue oure gret displeasur & indignacion.

Memorandum that the kinges grace afore his departing do name the lordes & other that shalbe of his Counselle in these parties to assiste and attende in that behalve upon his Nepueu of Lincolne.

Item Memorandum that the king name certen lierned men to be attending here, so that oon alweys at the lest be present, and at the meting at York to be alle there.

Item that the king graunt a Commissione to my lord of Lincolne and othere of the Counselle according to theffect of the premisses.[152]

[181]

Justice was a perennial 'perturbation' of Richard, both justice for ill-treated individuals and, perhaps more significantly, the administration of justice. The Year Books report one of his most famous acts, which was to call together all his justices and pose them three questions concerning specific cases, two involving official malpractice (misprision). His final words: 'to say "by my justices" and to say "by my law" is to say one and the same thing' are not merely specific to the case in hand but also give a more general idea of Richard's comprehension and commitment to his coronation oath to uphold the law and its proper procedures.

The lord the King called all the justices before him in the inner Star Chamber and asked of them three questions. This was the first question. If anyone brought a false writ and action against some man by which he was taken and imprisoned and kept in prison, shall there be any remedy in that case for the party or for the King etc.? And thereupon the lord the King notified the justices that there was a certain Thomas Gate against whom a certain Thomas Staunton etc. had judgment in the Chancery of the lord the King touching certain lands and tenements. And upon the same judgment Staunton had execution touching the aforesaid lands, and, contrary to the judgment and execution, the said Thomas Gate re-entered in the aforesaid lands, and seized and imprisoned etc. the aforesaid Staunton by colour of the said false and fictitious action. In answer to this the justices replied that no penalty follows upon the prosecution of a false action etc. because it is not known that it is a false action until it is determined, and then the King has the fine, etc. And as to the contempt of the judgment etc. the answer is 'yes' if the whole time the same Thomas Gate had notice of the judgment, and afterwards the Chancellor of England can constrain him by imprisonment etc.

The second question was this. If some justice of the Peace had taken a bill of indictment which had not been found by the jury, and enrolled it among other indictments 'well and truly found' etc. shall there be any punishment thereupon for such justice so doing? And this question was carefully argued among the justices separately and among themselves, . . . And all being agreed, the justices gave the King in his Council in the Star Chamber their answer to his question in this wise: that about such defaults enquiry ought to be made by a commission of at least twelve jurors, and thereupon the party, having been presented, accused and convicted, shall lose the

[182]

office and pay fine to the King according to the degree of the misprision etc.

The other question was that a certain John Barret of Bury Saint Edmunds was prosecuted in London by writ of debt, and the record of the whole process, to wit, the original three *capias* and the exigent and the outlawry at the Hustings was in the name of John Barret. And afterwards the attorney of the plaintiff in that plea, perceiving that those writs had been wrongly sued, came to Thomas Danby, the Keeper of the writs, and caused all the aforesaid writs to be erased, and they caused a William Barret to be outlawed; and because the whole record against John was destroyed and annulled, a new one against William was made etc. And before the King and his Council in the Star Chamber the statute of 8 Henry the Sixth, chapter 12, was viewed and read, and by that, according to William Huse, with the agreement of all the justices, the whole of that action was declared to be felony by these words: 'If any record, writ, return, process, panel etc, or part thereof be stolen, taken away, withdrawn or amended or avoided because of which some judgment be reversed etc.' And because it appeared that William Barret was outlawed rightly yet falsely, and fraudulently yet without error instead of John Barret, so it was impossible to correct that record by writ of error, and the whole record against John Barret was null and void by the erasure. And how much more false it is to destroy and annul the whole record than a part thereof. And the words of the statute are sufficient when it says 'who steals a record or part thereof etc. Wherefore etc.' And when the whole record is destroyed and withdrawn, it is not possible to correct it by writ of error, and the damage is greater than when a part is embezzled etc. And afterwards when the whole matter had been set forth to the King's Council learned in the law, it appeared as follows: five persons had consulted together to annul the aforesaid record, to wit, Henry Faunt who was the plaintiff against John Barret, Thirlwynd who was his attorney in that plea, J. Mundus who erased the original writ, Thomas Danby who was Keeper of the writs, and I.H. one of the clerks of the counter [a prison of the Sheriff] in London. And all these annulled the record but J. Mundus alone erased the original and he did nothing else nor was he consulted. And this erasure took place in London at Cliffords Inn in the parish of Saint Dunstan, and the three *capias* were likewise erased there with the assent of the said Thomas Danby, Henry Faunt the plaintiff and Thirlwynd the attorney. And all the rolls were erased at Westminster, to wit, the three *capias* and the exigent by assent of the said Thomas Danby, Henry Faunt and Thirlwynd. And a writ of exigent [having issued], he was afterwards outlawed at the Hustings in London, by the name of John

[183]

Barret. The said I.H. clerk of the counter at Westminster erased the exigent after he had been outlawed, and in place of this word 'John,' he sent and put in this word 'William' etc. And other abettors likewise caused this same word to be erased and 'William' etc. to be written in the roll at Westminster etc. And all this, done in the form and manner in which it was done, constitutes a felony etc. And part of that act and the chief act was done in London, to wit, the erasure of the original writ. . . .

And afterwards when the whole matter had been set forth [it was found that the erasure] of part thereof [had been made] in London and of another part at Westminster, and this erasure of the writ in London destroyed the record of the original writ, which appears to be felony. And all who had agreed etc. And because the lord the King was perturbed over the matter, Thomas Danby and the other three were indicted in the King's Bench of the misprision of that erasure in Middlesex, and, the King sitting there, they were accused, and they admitted the offence in particular and were convicted thereof etc. and were committed to prison until they had paid the fine etc. And afterwards J. Mundus who erased the original writ, was taken to Westminster Hall and led to the bar in the King's Bench and was committed to Newgate. And afterwards Huse [Chief Justice of King's Bench] Bryan [Chief Justice of Common Pleas] and Starkey [Chief Baron of the Exchequer] went to the Guildhall, London, and there the said Mundus was indicted of the aforesaid misprision, because, although it was felony yet misprision is involved in it etc. . . .

And afterwards all the justices assembled at the church of St. Andrew in Holborn, and there they all consulted together how those who had been convicted of misprision should pay the fine. And they were all agreed that in every case where anyone had been convicted of misprision, trespass or otherwise, when a fine or ransom shall be paid, the justices before whom he had been convicted shall take security and pledges for the fine etc. and afterwards, at their discretion, they (and not the lord the King either by himself in his chamber or otherwise before him, unless by his justices) shall assess the fine.

And this is the King's will to wit, to say 'by his justices' and 'by his law' is to say one and the same thing.[153]

[184]

An elaborate financial memorandum of Richard's showed concern for efficient and fast levying of his money and resources, the appointment of honest officials to the benefit of himself and his subjects, and the subjection of the accounts to the personal auditing of the King.

In a similar vein were his instructions to Sir Marmaduke Constable, Steward of the Honour of Tutbury.

A remembraunce made aswele for hasty levy of the kynges Revenues growing of alle his possessions & hereditamentes as for the profitable Astate and governaunce of the same possessions.

....

Also that the said Court of Eschequier be clerely dismyssed & discharged with any medling with any forayne lyvelode in taking of accomptes, As Wales, Duchies of Cornewaille, York, Norffolk, Erldoms of Chestre, Marche, Warrwik, Sarum, and of alle othre landes being in the kinges handes be reasone of forfaictor whiche is thoughte most behovefulle and profitable to be assigned to othre foreyne auditours for diverse causes ensueing etc . . .

Fiurst for more hasty levie of money. Also for more ease and lesse coste of the officers of suche lyvelode. Also for cause that the lordshippes may be yerely surveied by the Stiwardes auditors and Receivours in the tyme of accomptes of officers of the same for Reperacions wodesales and for othre direccions to be had amonge the tenantes with many mo causes necessarye etc.

And where that mony lordshippes, Manours, landes & tenementes perteynyng to the crowne bene committed to diverse persones for fermes in certeyne, by the whiche the kinges wodes and his courtes with othre casuelties bene wasted and lost to his gret hurt. And gret allowances had for reperacions of his Castelles and manors and they not forthy repaired as it is said. And also the said lordshippes ofte tyme set within the value. It is thoughte that a foreyne Auditor shuld be assigned for alle lordshippes Manors landes & tenementes belonging to the crowne and a Receivor for the same yerely to ride surveie receyve and remembre in every behalf that myghte be most for the kinges profite, And thereof yerely to make report of the astate and condicione of the same by the which the kinges grace shuld knowe alle the lordshippes that perteynethe to his crowne, whiche as nowe be unknowyne as it is said etc.

[185]

Also it is thoughte that suche certayne auditours as bene of gode, true and sadde disposicione and discrecione shuld be assigned to here and determyne thaccomptes of alle the kinges foreyne livelode as is above discharged fro theschequier, and to have so many auditours and no mo, but as may conveniently and diligently determyne the said livelode betwixt Michelmas and Candelmes, with Sadde and discrete examinacione of alle defaultes and hurtes of alle officers accomptable severaly in theire offices executing, wherein Thawditors of theschequier can never have so evydent knowlege for reformacione of the same.

Also that the Receivours of gode and true disposicione and also of havor of Richesse be assigned to the said lyvelode and they to se for reperacions of Castelles, Manors, milnes, parkes and othre, and in the Cirquyte of theire receipte they to se the wele of every lordshippe.

....

Also where that lordes, knightes and Esquiers, many of them not lettered bene made Stewardes of the kinges livelod in diverse counties, thay taking gret fynes and rewardes of the kinges tenantes to there propre use to the kinges hurt and poveresshinge of his said tenants, and also wanting cunnyng & discrecione to ordre and directe the said lyvelode lawfully with many moo inconvenientes. Therefore it is thoughte that lerned men in the lawe where most profitable to be Stiwardes of the said livelod for many causes concernyng the kinges profite and the wele of his tenantes.

....

Also it is thoughte that alle the forsaid auditours every yere at the fest of Michelmes next after the declaracione made of alle foreyne lyvelod by for the said persones by the king so assigned shuld delivere or doo to be delivered the bookes of accomptes of the same into the kinges eschequier afore the Barons there, after the first yere of the premises there to remayne of recorde so that the bookes of accomptes of the later yere be alway in the handes of the said auditours for theire presidence, the duchie of Lancastre the lordshippes of Glamorgane and Bergevenny alwey except etc.[154]

Instruccions yeven by the king unto Sir Marmaduc Constable knighte Steward of Thonnor of Tutbury.

....

Also the said Sir Marmaduc shalle see that noo lyveres ne conysaunce [liveries nor cognisance] be gevene within the said honnor contrarie to the lawe and to the statutes thereof made.

[186]

Also where heretofore diverse extorcions and opprissions have ben doone by the Countie baillieffes upon trust that they shuld contynue and not to be removed from their offices, The king wolle that fromhensfurthe, the said Sir Marmaduc put able and wele disposed persones in the said Bailliefwykes suche as been sufficient to answere the king of his duetie, and they to be chaunged from yere to yere, and that a proclamacion to be made at every gret court, that if any persone wolle come and compleyne of any of the said baillieffes that they shalbe herd, and due reformacion and punysshement be had according to the kinges laws and their demerites.

Also that the lieutenant, the Boweberer and Receivors of Wardes be suche persones as be of good demeanaunce ayenst the kinges wood and game and sworne to the same. And that they and every of theym wele and duely oversee the game and woddes in the parkes and waardes of the said honnor according to theire offices as they have bene accustumed aforetyme.
Also the said Sir Marmaduc to put into thoffice of Bailliefwykes that be accomptauntes good and suffisaunt persones, and suche as be Able to doo the king service, and to content the king of suche as they shalbe charged with alle upon their accomptes.[155]

Richard received the dedication of only one of William Caxton's books. This was, appropriately enough, a translation of Raymond Lull's *Order of Chivalry*, made by Caxton himself.

Here endeth the book of thordre of chyvalry whiche book is translated oute of Frensshe in to Englysshe at a requeste of a gentyl and noble esquyer by me William Caxton dwellynge at Westmynstre, besyde London, in the most best wyse that God hath suffred me, and accordynge to the copye that the sayd squyer delyuerd to me. Whiche book is not requysyte to every comyn man to haue, but to noble gentylmen that by their vertu entende to come & entre in to the noble ordre of chyvalry, the whiche in these late dayes hath ben used accordyng to this booke here to fore wreton but forgeten, and thexersytees of chyvalry not used, honoured, ne excercysed as hit hath ben in auncyent tyme, at whiche tyme the noble actes of the knyghtes of Englond that used chyvalry were renomed thurgh the unyuersal world. As for to speke to fore thyncarnacion of Jhesu Cryste where were there ever ony lyke to Brenius and Belynus that from the grete Brytayne now called Englond unto Rome & ferre beyonde conquered many Royammes and londes, whos noble actes remayne in thold hystoryes of the

[187]

Romayns. And syth the Incarnacion of oure lord, byhold that noble kyng of Brytayne kyng Arthur with al the noble knygtes of the round table, whos noble actes & noble chyvalry of his knyghtes occupye so many large volumes that is a world or as thyng incredyble to byleve. O ye knyghtes of Englond, where is the custome and usage of noble chyvalry that was used in tho dayes? What do ye now but go to the baynes (baths) & playe att dyse. And some not wel advysed use not honest and good rule ageyn alle ordre of knyghthode. Leve this. Leve it and rede the noble volumes of saynt Graal, of Lancelot, of Galaad, of Trystram, of Perse Forest, of Percyual, of Gawayn & many mo. Ther shalle ye see manhode, curtosye & gentylnesse. And loke in latter dayes of the noble actes syth the conquest, as in kyng Rychard dayes Cuer du Lyon, Edward the fyrste and the thyrd and his noble sones, Syre Robert Knolles, Syr Johan Hawkwode, Syr Iohan Chandos & Syre Gaultier Manny. Rede Froissart. And also behold that vyctoryous and noble kynge Harry the fyfthe and the capytayns under hym, his noble bretheren, therle of Salysbury, Montagu, and many other whoos names shyne gloryously by their vertuous noblesse & actes that they did in thonour of thordre of chyvalry. Allas what doo ye but slepe & take ease, and ar al disordred fro chyvalry. I wold demaunde a question, yf I shold not displease, how many knyghtes ben ther now in Englond that have thuse and theexercyse of a knyghte, that is to wete, that he knoweth his hors & his hors hym. That is to saye, he beynge redy at a poynt to have al thyng that longeth to a knyght, an hors that is accordyng and broken after his hand, his armures and harnoys mete and syttyng, & so forth, et cetera. I suppose and a due serche shold be made ther shold be many founden that lacke. The more pyte is. I wold it pleasyd oure soverayne lord that twyes or thryes in a yere, or at the lest ones, he wold do crye justes of pees, to thende that euery knyght shold have hors and harneys and also the use and craft of a knyght, and also to tornoye one ageynste one, or ii agenyst ii. And the best to have a prys, a dyamond or jewel, suche as shold please the prynce. This shold cause gentylmen to resorte to thauncyent customes of chyvalry to grete fame and renomee [renown]. And also to be alwey redy to serve theyr prynce whan he shalle calle them or have nede. Thenne late euery man that is come of noble blood and entendeth to come to the noble ordre of chyvalry, rede this lytyl book and doo therafter in kepyng the lore and commaundements therin comprysed. And thenne I doubte not he shall atteyne to thordre of chyvalry, et cetera. And thus thys lytyl book I presente to my redoubted, naturel and most dradde soverayne lord, kyng Rychard kyng of Englond and of Fraunce, to thende that he commaunde this book to be had and redde unto other yong lordes, knyghtes and gentylmen within this royame, that the noble ordre of chyvalrye be herafter better used & honoured than hit hath ben in late dayes passed. And herin he shalle do a noble & vertuouse dede. And I shalle pray almyghty God for his long lyf & prosperous welfare, & that he may have victory of al his enemyes, and after this short & transitory lyf to have everlastyng lyf in heven where as is joye and blysse, world without ende, Amen.[156]

There is not much doubt that Richard III was a man of genuine piety. He made considerable benefactions to religious institutions, as has been seen. He also took seriously the prince's duty of encouraging virtuous living, writing a circular to his bishops to this effect.

Reverend fadre in god righte trusty and welbeloved we grete you wele. Acertaynyng you that amonges othre our seculer besynesses and Cures, our principalle entent and fervent desire is to see vertue and clennesse of lyving to be avaunced, encresed and multiplied, and vices and alle othre thinges repugnant to vertue, provoking the highe indignacion and ferefulle displeasire of god, to be repressed and adnulled. And this perfitely folowed and put in execucion by persones of highe estate, preemynence and dignitie not oonly enducethe persones of lower degree to take thereof example, and to ensue the same, but also thereby the great and infinite goodnesse of god is made placable and graciously enclyned to thexaudicion of our peticions and prayers. And forasmoche as it is notarily knowen that in every Jurisdiccion aswele in your pastoralle Cure as othre, there be many aswele of the spirituelle partie, as of the temporalle delyring [departing] from the true weye of vertue and good lyving to the pernycious example of othre & lothsomnesse of every wele disposed personne. We therefore wol and desire you and, on goddes behalf inwardly exhort and Require you, that according to the charge of youre professione you wol see within thauctoritie of your Jurisdiccion alle suche persones, as set aparte vertue and promote the dampnable execucion of Synne and vices, to be reformed repressed and punysshed condignely after theire demerytes, not sparing for any love, favor, drede or affeccion, whethre thoffendors be spirituelle or temporelle. Wherin ye may be assured We shal yeve unto you our favor aide and assistence if the caas shal soo Require and see to the sharpe punysshement of the Repugnators and interruptors hereof if any suche be. And if ye wol diligently applie you to thexecucion and performyng of this

[189]

Clementissime dñe Jesu xp̄e vere dom̄s qui
a sinu patris omnipotentis sede mi[...]s t̄s in
medio terrata relaxare, peccatorū
relnuare.

-res afflictos captiuos redimere. in carcere
positos dissoluere. dispsos congregare. p̄-
nos in suam p̄tam reducere. contritos
corde mediari. tristes confortare. dolen-
tes t lugentes consolari. digñs me ab-
soluere de afflicōne temptacōne dolore in
firmitate t pauptate seu piculo in quib;
positus sum et consilium in dare. Et tu
dñie qui genus humanū cum p̄e
in concordia restituisti. ac illam p̄scripta
hereditatem a paradiso cuiu p̄prio p̄cōso
sanguine mercatus es t int homines
t angelos pacem fecisti. dignare int me
et inimicos meos stabilire t firmare con-
cordiam. grām et glīam tuam sup me
ostendere t effundere. ac omne illoz o
diuu quod contra me habent digñs
mitigare delmiare extinguere t ad in

[190]

matere ye shal not oonly do unto god righte acceptable pleasire, but over that we shall see suche persones spirituelle as ben undre your pastoral Cure non othrewise to be entreated or punysshed for their offenses but according to the ordenances and lawes of holy Churche. And if for the due execucion of the premisses any complaint or subgestione be made unto us of you, we shal remytte the determynacion thereof unto the Courtes of our Cousin tharchbisshop of Cantirbury, Cardinal, And thus proceding to thexecucion hereof ye shal doo unto yourself grete honor and unto us righte singlier pleasire. Yeven etc at Westminstre the xth day of Marche.[157]

A prayer composed for Richard sometime during his reign and added to his book of hours in a careful book-hand is in the tradition of fifteenth-century personal piety but has an intensity which is readily reinforced by a knowledge of the King's predicament:

Most merciful Lord Jesus Christ, very God, who was sent from the throne of Almighty God into the world to deliver the sinful from their transgressions, comfort the afflicted, ransom the captives, set free those in prison, bring together those who are scattered, lead travellers back to their native land, minister to the contrite in heart, comfort the sad, and to console those in grief and distress, deign to release me from the affliction, temptation, grief, sickness, necessity and danger in which I stand, and give me counsel. And you, Lord, who reconciled the race of man and the Father, who purchased with your own precious blood the confiscated inheritance of paradise and who made peace between men and the angels, deign to make and keep concord between me and my enemies. Show me and pour over me your grace and glory. Deign to assuage, turn aside, destroy, and bring to nothing the hatred they bear towards me, even as you extinguished the hatred and anger that Esau had for his brother Jacob. Stretch out your arm to me and spread your grace over me, and deign to deliver me from all the perplexities and sorrows in which I find myself, even as you delivered Abraham from the hands of the Chaldees, Isaac from sacrifice by the means of the ram, Jacob from the hands of his brother Esau, Joseph from the hands of his brothers, Noah from the waters of the flood by the means of the

Opposite: Richard III's Book of Hours: the first page of the prayer written for the King, showing its altered beginning. The preceding folio is missing and no satisfactory explanation for the alteration can be offered.

ark, Lot from the city of the Sodomites, your servants Moses and Aaron and the people of Israel from the hand of Pharaoh and the bondage of Egypt, and likewise Saul on Mount Gilboa, and King David from the power of Saul and from Goliath the giant. And even as you delivered Susanna from false witness and accusation and Judith from the hand of Holofernes, Daniel from the den of lions, and the three young men from the burning fiery furnace, Jonah from the belly of the whale, the child of the woman of Cana from the torment of devils, and Adam from the depths of hell, with your own precious blood. Also Peter from the sea and Paul from the chains. Therefore, Lord Jesus Christ, son of the living God, deign to free me, thy servant King Richard from every tribulation, sorrow and trouble in which I am placed and from all the plots of my enemies, and deign to send Michael the Archangel to my aid against them, and deign, Lord Jesus Christ, to bring to nothing the evil plans that they are making or wish to make against me, even as you brought to nothing the counsel of Achitofel to Absalom against King David. Deign to deliver me by your holy merits, your incarnation, your nativity, baptism, and your fasting, by the hunger and thirst, the cold and heat, by the labour and suffering, by the spit and abuse, by the blows and the nails, by the crown of thorns, the lance, the drink of vinegar and gall, by your most cruel and shameful death on the cross and the words which you spoke while on the cross. Firstly begging your Father, 'Lord Father, forgive them, for they know not what they do'. You said, Lord, to the thief hanging on the cross, 'Today, you shall be with me in Paradise'. You said Lord, to your mother, 'Mother, behold your son', and to the disciple, 'Behold your mother'. Lord, you said, 'Heloy, heloy, lamazabathani' which being interpreted means, 'God, my God, why have you forsaken me?' You said, Lord, 'I thirst', that is to say for the salvation of the blessed souls. Lord, you said, 'Father, into your hands I commend my spirit'. You said, Lord, 'It is finished', signifying that the labours and sorrows which you bore for us wretches were completed. By all these things, I ask you, most gentle Lord Jesus Christ to keep me, thy servant King Richard, and defend me from all evil, from the devil and from all peril present, past and to come, and deliver me from all the tribulations, sorrows and troubles in which I am placed, and deign to console me, by your descent into hell, your resurrection, by your visits of consolation to your disciples, your wonderful ascension, by the grace of the Holy Spirit the Paraclete, and by your coming on the Day of Judgement. Lord, hear me, in the name of your goodness for which I give and return you thanks, and for all those gifts and goods granted to me, because you made me from

[192]

Richard III's Book of Hours: the Annunciation and the Hours of the Virgin.

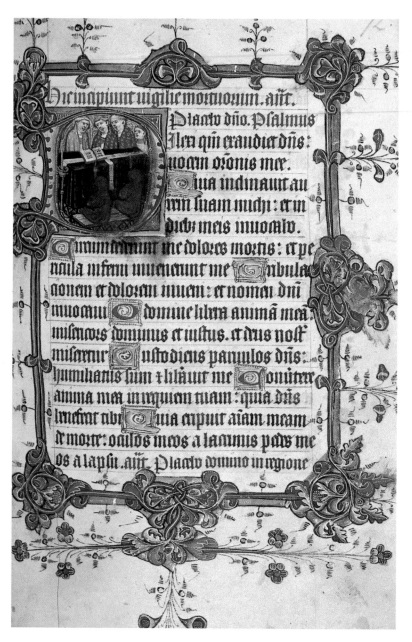

Richard III's Book of Hours: funeral scene with the Vigil of the Dead.

nothing and redeemed me through your most bounteous love and mercy from eternal damnation by promising eternal life. Because of these things and for others which the eye has not seen nor the ear heard, and which the heart of man cannot understand, I ask you, most gentle Lord Jesus Christ, to save me from all perils of body and soul by your love, and to deign always to deliver and help me, and after the journey of this life, to deign to bring me before you, the living and true God, who lives and reigns, O God. Through Christ the true Lord, Amen.[158]

Richard rewarded his confessor, John Roby, a Franciscan friar and doctor of theology, and the probable composer of the King's prayer, with a preferment:

Doctoure Roby, the Fre Chapelle of oure lady of Gissemond besides Newcastelle upon Tyne being voide by the decesse of Maister Lumley.[159]

Two letters of Richard's surviving from 1484 give some impression of his personality. The one to his mother, Cecily Neville, living a life of pious retirement, is the only example of his letters to her that remains.

The other relates to Elizabeth (Jane) Shore, the daughter of a City alderman and the mistress of Edward IV, imprisoned in Ludgate from mid June 1483. She appears to have been involved in the Marquis of Dorset's escape to Brittany and had possibly become his mistress after Edward's death. In Ludgate she engaged the affections of Thomas Lynom, Richard's Solicitor, and he wished to marry her, greatly to the King's surprise. Richard gave his consent to the marriage, however, and it duly took place. Lynom lost his legal office under Henry VII but appears to have continued to work for the crown in an administrative capacity.

Madam I recommaunde me to you as hertely as is to me possible, Beseching you in my most humble and effectuouse wise of youre daly blissing to my Synguler comfort & defence in my nede. And madam I hertely beseche you that I may often here from you to my Comfort. And suche Newes as bene here my servaunt, Thomas Bryane, this berere, shalle shew you, to whome please it you to yeve credence unto. And madam I beseche you to be good &

graciouse lady to my lord, my Chambreleyn, to be youre officer in Wilshire in suche as Colingbourne had. I trust he shalle therein do you good service And that it please you that by this berere I may understande youre pleasure in this behalve. And I pray god sende you thaccomplishement of youre noble desires. Written at Pountfreit the iij^{de} day of Juyne with the hande of Youre most humble Son, Ricardus Rex[160]

By the king

Righte Reverend fadre in god, etc. Signifyng unto you that it is shewed unto us that our servant and Sollicitor Thomas Lynom merveillously blynded and abused with the late wife of William Shore nowe being in Ludgate by our commandement hathe made contract of matrymony with hir, as it is said, and entendethe to our fulle grete mervaile to procede to theffect of the same. We for many causes wold be sory that hee soo shuld be disposed. Pray you therfore to sende for him. And in that ye goodly may exhorte and sture hyme to the contrary. And if ye finde him utterly set forto marye hur and noon othrewise wolbe advertised, than if it may stande with the lawe of the churche we be content, the tyme of mariage deferred to our commyng next to London, that upon sufficient suertie founde for hure good abering ye doo sende for hure keper and discharge hym of our said commaundement by warrant of thise, committing hure to the Rule and guyding of hur fader or any othre by your discrecion in the meane season yeven etc.

To the Righte Reverend fadre in god etc The Bisshop of Lincolne, our Chauncellor[161]

Richard's cultural interests appear to have included music:

Richard etc. To alle & every oure subgiettes aswele spirituelle as temporelle thise oure lettres hering or seing greting. We lat you wite that for the confidence & trust that we have in oure trusty and welbeloved servaunt John Melyonek, oon of the gentilmen of oure Chapelle, and knowing also his expert habilite and connyng in the science of Musique, have licenced him and by thise presentes licence and yeve him auctorite that within alle places in this oure reame aswele Cathedral churges, Coliges, Chappelles, houses of relegione and al other franchised & exempt places as elliswhere, oure colege roial at Wyndesore reserved & except, may take and sease for us and in oure name al suche singing mene & childre

[194]

being expart in the said science of Musique as he can finde and think sufficient and able to do us service. Wherfore etc yevene etc at Notingham the xvjth day of Septembre Anno secundo.[162]

William Catesby, originally councillor of Lord Hastings, later Chamberlain of the Exchequer and Esquire of the body to Richard III, and Speaker of Richard's only Parliament in 1484. He fought with Richard at Bosworth and was executed in Leicester three days after the battle on 25th August. Catesby is shown in armour covered by a tabard of his arms. His wife Margaret, daughter of William Lord Zouche, is in an heraldic mantle. Brass at Ashby St Ledgers, Northamptonshire.

[195]

December 1484 saw the trial in Guildhall, London, of William Colyngbourn and John Turburvyle for treason. Colyngbourn had been active all the year as an agent of Henry Tudor, encouraging invasion. He was found guilty and sentenced to death while Turburvyle was sent to prison. London chroniclers, such as the author of the Great Chronicle, forgot the treason and recorded only the famous rhyme pinned by Colyngbourn in July on the door of St Paul's:

> The Cat, the Rat, and Lovell our Dog,
> Rule all England under an Hog.

In these dayes were chieff Rulers abowth the kyng, The lord lovell, and ij Gentylmen beyng namyd Mr Ratcylff & Mr Catysby, Of the whych personys was made a sedicious Ryme & fastenyd upon the Crosse In Chepe & othir placys of the Cyte whereof the Sentence was as ffolowyth, The Catt the Ratt, and lovell owyr dogge Rulyn all Engeland, undyr an hogge, This was to meane that the fforenamyd thre personys as the lord lovell and the othir ij that is to meane Catysby and Rattclyff Rulid this land undyr the kyng whych bare a whyte boor ffor his conysaunce, Ffor the devysers of this Ryme much serch was made and sundry accusyd to Theyr Chargys, But ffynally two Gentylmen namyd Turburvyle & Colyngbourn were ffor that & othyr thyngys layd to theyr charge, arestid & cast In prison, ffor whom shortly afftyr as upon the [blank] was holdyn at the Guyldhalle an Oyer determyner where the said ij Gentylmen were aregnyd, and that oon off theym callid Colyngbourn convyct of that Cryme & othyr, ffor the which upon the [blank] ffoluyng he was drawyn unto the Towyr hyll and there ffull Cruelly put to deth, as ffyrst hangid and streygth Cutt doun & Ryppyd, & his bowellys cast Into a ffyre, . . .[163]

Christmas 1484 was celebrated in a festive fashion, much to the disapproval of the Croyland Chronicler. Soon after Christmas Richard's wife Anne fell ill. She died on 16 March 1485. From the remark of the Chronicler that Richard was advised to avoid her bed, and from the speed with which she sickened and died, it would appear possible that she suffered from tuberculosis.

So too, with many other things which are not written in this book, and of which I grieve to speak; although the fact ought not to be concealed that, during this feast of the Nativity, far too much attention was given to dancing and gaiety, and vain changes of apparel presented to queen Anne and the lady Elizabeth, the eldest daughter of the late king, being of similar colour and shape; a thing that caused the people to murmur and the nobles and prelates greatly to wonder thereat; while it was said by many that the king was bent, either on the anticipated death of the queen taking place, or else, by means of a divorce, for which he supposed he had quite sufficient grounds, on contracting a marriage with the said Elizabeth. For it appeared that in no other way could his kingly power be established, or the hopes of his rival be put an end to.

In the course of a few days after this, the queen fell extremely sick, and her illness was supposed to have increased still more and more, because the king entirely shunned her bed, declaring that it was by the advice of his physicians that he did so. Why enlarge? About the middle of the following month, upon the day of the great eclipse of the sun, which then took place, Anne, before-named, departed this life, and was buried at Westminster, with no less honors than befitted the interment of a queen.[164]

The moost nobyll lady and prynces . . ., wyfe furst to prynce Edward son and eyre to kynge Harre the Syxt. and after hys decese marvelowsly conveyed by all the corners and partyes of the whele fo fortune and eftsone exaltyd a geyne . . . to the moost hye trone and honour over all other ladys of thys nobyll realme anoyntyd and crownyd Quene of Ynglond wyfe unto the moost victoryus prince kynge Rychard the Thryd. In presene sche was semely ameabyll & bewteus and yn condycyons full commendabyll and ryght vertues and accordynge to the interpretacion of hur name anne full gracyows. Sho was second douhter and on of the eyrys of ye moost myghtty and nobyll lord Syr Rychard Nevyll Erle of Warrewyk and . . . was borne yn the castell of Warrewyk the xj day of the monythe of June the yere of owre Lord mcccclvj[165]

[197]

Soon after Anne's death rumours began to spread that Richard intended to marry his niece Elizabeth, eldest daughter of his brother Edward. This Richard denied publicly just before Easter 1485. There is some evidence that Elizabeth herself was desirous of this marriage, but the evidence, a letter said to have been written to her, is not now extant.

The king's purpose and intention of contracting a marriage with his niece Elizabeth being mentioned to some who were opposed thereto, the king was obliged, having called a council together, to excuse himself with many words and to assert that such a thing had never once entered his mind. There were some persons, however, present at that same council, who very well knew the contrary. Those in especial who were unwilling that this marriage should take place, and to whose opinions the king hardly ever dared offer any opposition, were Sir Richard Ratelyffe and William Catesby, Esquire of his body. For by these persons the king was told to his face that if he did not abandon his intended purpose, and that, too, before the mayor and commons of the city of London, opposition would not be offered to him by merely the warnings of the voice; for all the people of the north, in whom he placed the greatest reliance, would rise in rebellion against him, and impute to him the death of the queen, the daughter and one of the heirs of the earl of Warwick, through whom he had first gained his present high position; in order that he might, to the extreme abhorrence of the Almighty, gratify an incestuous passion for his said niece. Besides this, they brought to him more than twelve Doctors of Divinity, who asserted that the pope could grant no dispensation in the ease of such a degree of consanguinity. It was supposed by many, that these men, together with others like them, threw so many impediments in the way, for fear lest, if the said Elizabeth should attain the rank of queen, it might at some time be in her power to avenge upon them the death of her uncle, earl Antony, and her brother Richard, they having been the king's especial advisers in those matters. The king, accordingly, followed their advice a little before Easter, in presence of the mayor and citizens of London, in the great hall of the Hospital of Saint John, by making the said denial in a loud and distinct voice; more, however, as many supposed, to suit the wishes of those who advised him to that effect, than in conformity with his own.[166]

GENERALL COURTE OF OURE COMPENY HOLDEN THE
LAST DAYE OF MARCHE THE YERE ABOUEWRITTEN

Where as longe saying and muche symple Comunycacion amonge the peple by euyll disposed parsones contryved & sowne to verrey grete displesure of the Kyng shewyng how that the quene as by concent & will of the Kyng was poysoned for & to thentent that he myght than marry and haue to wyfe lady Elizabeth, eldest doughter of his broder, late Kyng of Englond decessed, whom god pardon &c. for the whiche & other the Kyng sende fore & had tofor hym at sent Johnes as yesterdaye the Mayre & Aldermen where as he in the grete Hall there in the presens of many of his lordes & of muche other peple shewde his grefe and displeasure aforsaid & said it neuer came in his thought or mynde to marry in suche maner wise nor willyng or glad of the dethe of his quene but as sorye & in hert as hevye as man myght be, with muche more in the premysses spoken, for the whiche he than monysshed & charged euery parson to ceas of suche untrue talkyng on parell of his indignacion. And what parson that from hensford tellith or reporteth any of theis forsaid untrewe surmysed talkyng, that the said parson therfore be had to preson unto the auctor be brought furth of whom the said parson harde the said untrue surmysed tale &c. And in this maner the Kyng hath geven comaundment & Charge unto the Mayre so for to punysshe and that he for the same to call tofore hym the Wardens of all craftes, Constables & other & to shewe unto them the mater of his displesure &c.[167]

But when the midst and more days of February were gone, the Lady Elizabeth, being very desirous to be married, and growing not only impatient of delays, but also suspicious of the success, wrote a letter to Sir John Howard, Duke of Norfolk, intimating first therein that he was the one in whom she most affied, because she knew the King her father much loved him, and that he was a very faithful servant unto him and to the King his brother then reigning, and very loving and serviceable to King Edward's children.

First she thanked him for his many courtesies and friendly offices, and then she prayed him as before to be a mediator for her in the cause of the marriage to the King, who, as she wrote, was her only joy and maker in this world, and that she was his in heart and in thoughts, in body, and in all. And then she intimated that the better half of February was past, and that she feared the queen would never die. And all these be her own words, written with her own hand, and this is the sum of her words, whereof I have seen

[199]

The Gate House of the Priory of the Knights Hospitaller of St John at Clerkenwell. Here Richard publicly denied that he had plans to marry his niece Elizabeth.

the autograph or original draft under her own hand, and by the special and honourable favour of the most noble and first count of the realm, and chief of his family, Sir Thomas Howard, and Baron Howard etc., Earl of Arundel and of Surrey.[168]

In late February Richard sent out urgent appeals for loans to the nobility and gentry of the realm to help pay the heavy costs in military operations he had incurred, and was about to incur. These were not 'Benevolences' (i.e. direct demands for money) such as his brother Edward IV had demanded; Richard had outlawed those in his 1484 Parliament. These were loans with a specific dated promise of repayment. Royal commissioners were appointed; they were given the form of words they were to use in approaching potential lenders, and letters already addressed to some named individuals. The sums named in the latter ranged downwards from £200, most of them being for £40. Other letters had blanks left for the sum to be written in.

By the king

Lettres directed to them that went with theym. Trusty etc. And for the singulere affiaunce & trust that we have in you we at this tyme have ordeigned & appoynted you to deliver certain oure lettres unto diverse oure subgiettes within oure Countie of Oxonford Berkshire and Bukingham and of theym to Receive suche sommes of money as we have written unto theym for. Whiche lettres we sende unto you by this berere and within the Corner & ende of every of the same ye shalle understande suche severelle sommes as bene conteigned therein part of the same bene superscribed and part ar blank. Whiche we wolle ye dericte unto suche persones within oure said Counties as by youre discrecions shalbe thoughte convenyent the copy wherof with the Remembraunce of suche wordes as ye shal use unto the persones to whom oure said lettres shalbe delyvered we sende unto you herein closed. Wherefore we wol and desire you that with al diligence to you possible ye put you in youre effectuelle devoirs to thaccomplisshing of oure message and entent in that behalve soo that the same by youre pollitique and wise meanes may take good effect and expedicion. As oure special trust is in you. Yeven etc at Westminstre the xxjth day of Fevrier[169]

Instruccions & credences. Sir the kinges grace gretethe you welle and desirethe and hertely prayethe you that be wey of loon ye wille let him have suche summe as his grace hathe writtene to you fore. And ye shalle truely have ayene at suche dayes as he hathe shewed and promysed to you in his lettres and this he desirethe to be emploied for the defence and suertie of his Roialle persone and the weele of this his Royaulme. And for that entent his

[201]

grace and alle his lordes thinking that every true Englissheman wolle help him in this behalve of whiche nombre his grace reputethe & takethe you for oon. And that is the cause he this writethe to you before other for the gret love confidence & substaunce that his grace hathe & knowethe in you whiche trustethe undoubtedly that ye like a lovyng subgiet wolle at this tyme accomplisshe this his desire.[170]

By the king

A lettre for money. Trusty and welbeloved we grete you wele. And for suche great and excessive costes and charges as we haistly must bere and susteign aswele for the keping of the see as othrewise for the defense of this oure Reame we desire and in oure hertiest wise pray you to send unto us by way of loone by oure trusti servaunt this berer   And we promitte you by these oure lettres signed with oure awne truely to recontent you therof at Martilmas next commyng and   residue at the feest of seint John Baptist than next folowing with out further delay. Assuring you that accomplisshing this oure instant desire and herty prayer ye shal finde us youre good and gracious souverain lord in any youre reasonable desires herafter yevyng ferthere credence to oure said servant in suche thinges as he shal openne unto you on oure behalve touching this matier. Yeven etc[171]

On 11 March of this year, Richard appointed his only remaining son, his bastard John of Gloucester, Captain of Calais. The wording of the patent seems once again (as with his son Edward's earlier, see No. 111) to reflect parental pride. John visited Calais later in the year, as an entry in the Chamberlains' Account of the City of Canterbury show.

The King, to all to whom etc, Greeting. Among the most notable our dear bastard son, John of Gloucester, whose disposition and natural vigour, agility of body and inclination to all good customs, promises us by the grace of God great and certain hope of future service. Know that we, by our special grace, and out of certain knowledge and our free volition ordain and appoint the same John Captain of our town and castle of Calais and of our Tower of Rysbank, and our Lieutenant in the Marches of the same. Reserving wholly to ourselves the gift and grant of offices and the power and authority of making and appointing all officers during the minority of the same John, before he reaches the age of 21 years. Having, occupying and exercising the offices of Captain and Lieutenant aforesaid the said John himself or through his sufficient deputy or deputies from the fourth day of March last past, for the term of his life with all rights, honours and profits, fees, wages, rewards and prerogatives, in all full power and form according as any other Captain of said town had before this time. . . .[172]

And paid for leavened bread allowed for the Lord Bastard riding to Calais 12d., and paid for a pike given to Master Brackenbury Constable of the Tower who at that time returned from Calais from the Lord Bastard 3s. 4d.[173]

Soon after these events Richard showed his anxiety to pay debts due to faithful servants in a privy seal warrant ordering payment to Sir Robert Brackenbury for services carried out.

Richard etc. For asmoche as by the reconyng and accompt taken of our right trusty and welbeloved counsellour Sir Robert Brakenbury knight for our body and Constable of our Towre of London from the laste daie of Maie the first yere of our reigne unto the last day of Novembre then next after that is to saie by half a yere and a daye. It is founden by the same that we be endetted unto him in the some of CCXV li vijs. vd. as money by him paied over alle manner somes of money by him received of Us or in our name of any manner personne or personnes by alle the said tyme aswele in his journeys riding to Sandwiche, Dover and Maidstone in the countie of Kent at two severell seasons and otherwise by our commaundment to our greate honnor, prouffite and pleasure with keping the fynding of our prisoners within our said Tower of London as for the provision and reparacion of our ordinances and artilleries with other divers particular charges by him had and doon within our said Tower by our commaundement. As in the said accompt right plainly dooth appere. We therefore having tendre respecte to the premisses. Willing him by noo meane to be uncontent of his said dutie Woll and straitly charge you that ye imediatly after the sight of these our lettres withoute delay content and pay unto our said counsaillor the said some of CCXV li vijs. vd. in redy money or elles that ye make unto him sufficient and sure assignement for the same some in such place or places as he most spedely maie atteigne his sure paiement of the same withouten prest or other charge to be sette upon him

[204]

for the same. And these our lettres shalbe unto you in this behalve warrant sufficient and discharge. Yeven undre our privie seell at our Paloys of Westminster the xv daie of Marche the seconde yere of our reigne [1485].[174]

The King seems to have been considerably troubled by malicious rumours, despite his efforts to quell them (as seen before) and on 19 April a letter from him was read to the York Council.

Trusty and welbeloved we grete you wele. And where it is soo that diverse sedicious and evil disposed personnes both in our citie of London and elleswher within this our realme, enforce themself daily to sowe sede of noise and disclaundre agaynest our persone and ayenst many of the lordes and astates of our land to abuse the multitude of our subgiettes and avertre ther myndes from us if they coude by any meane atteyne to that ther mischivous entent and purpose, some by setting up of billes some by messages and sending furth of false and abhominable langage and lyes some by bold and presumptuos open speech and communicacion oon with othre, wherthurgh the innocent people whiche wold live in rest and peas and truly undre our obbeissance, as they oght to doo, bene gretely abused and oft tymes put in daungier of ther lives, landes and goodes as ofte as they folowe the steppes and devises of the said seditious and mischevous persones to our grete hevynesse and pitie; for remedie wherof and to thentent the troth opinlye declared shuld represse all suche false and contrived invencions, we now of late called before us the maire and aldermen of our citie of London to togidder with the moost sadde and discrete persones of the same citie in grete nombre, being present many of the lordes spirituel and temporel of our land, and the substance of all our housland, to whome we largely shewed our true entent and mynd in all suche thinges as the said noise and disclaundre renne upon in suche wise as we doubt not all wel disposed personnes were and be therwith right wele content; where we also at the same tyme gafe straitly in charge aswell to the said maire as to all othre our officers, servauntes and feithful subgiettes whersoever they be, that fromhensfurth as oft as they find any persone speking of us or any othre lord or estate of this our land othrewise thane is according to honour, trouth and the peas and ristfulnesse of this our realme or telling of tales and tidinges whereby the people might be stird to

The page of a copy of the romance *Tristan* recording the ownership of Richard of Gloucester and of Elizabeth of York, his niece, with her motto *Sans removyr*.

commocions and unlawful assembles, or any strif and debate arrise betwene lord and lord or us and any of the lordes and estates of this our land they take and arrest the same persons unto the tyme he have he broght furth hyme or them of whom he understode that that is spoken and so proceding from oon to othre unto the tyme the furnisher, auctor and maker of the said sedicious speche and langage be taken and punyshed according to his desertes, and that whosoever furst finde any sedicious bille set up in any place he take it downe and without reding or shewing the same to any othre person bring it furthwith unto us or some of the lordes or othre of our counsaill; all which direccions, charges and commaundements soo by us taken and yeven by our mouthe en our citie of London, we notifie unto you by thies our lettres to thentent that ye shewe the same within all the places of your jurisdiction and see there the due execucion of the same from tyme to tyme as ye woll eschewe our grevous indignacion and answere unto us at your extreme perill. Yeven undre our signet at our citie of London the vth day of Aprill.

By the king   To our trusty and welbeloved the maire and his brethre of our citie of York[175]

Rumours persisted though, this time of imminent invasion, and the King, having finished his military preparations, went north from London on 12 May to make his headquarters at Nottingham, arriving there on 9 June. In late June he sent out Commissions of Array ordering the previously appointed Commissioners to array men for military service. These Commissions renewed those sent out the previous December. Richard also reissued a proclamation against Henry Tudor and his supporters.

Rumours at length increasing daily that those who were in arms against the king were hastening to make a descent upon England, and the king being in doubt at what port they intended to effect a landing, (as certain information thereon could be gained by none of his spies), he betook himself to the north, shortly before the feast of Pentecost; leaving lord Lovel, his chamberlain, near Southampton, there to refit his fleet with all possible speed, that he might keep a strict watch upon all the harbours in those parts; that so, if the enemy should attempt to effect a landing there, he might unite all the forces in the neighbourhood, and not lose the opportunity of attacking them.[176]

[206]

By the king

Trusty etc And for asmoche as certaine informacion is made unto us that oure Rebelles and traytors associat with oure auncyent ennemyes of Fraunce and othre straungiers entende hastely to invade this oure Royaulme purposing the distruccion of us, the subversione of this oure Royaulme and disheriting of al oure true subgiettes. We therefore wol and straitly commaunde you that in alle hast possible after the Receipt hereof ye doo put oure Commission heretofore directed unto you for the mustering and ordering of oure subgiettes in new execucion according to oure instruccions whiche we sende unto you at this tyme with thise oure lettres. And that this be doon with alle diligence. As ye tendre oure suertie the wele of youre self and of alle this oure Royaulme Yeven etc at Notingham the xxij day of Juyne.

To oure trusty and welbeloved oure Commissioners of array appointed within oure Counte of York

like lettres to al othre Commissioners in every Shire in England

Instruccions upon the same to the said Commissioners in alle the Royaulme

Furst. forasmoche as the kinges gode grace understandeth by the Reapoort of his Commissioners and othre the faithfulle disposicions and Redynesse that his subgiettes be of to doo him service and pleasire to thuttermost of theire powairs for the Resisting of his Rebelles traytors and ennemyes. The kinges highenesse therefore wil that his said Commissioners shal yeve on his behalf especialle thankinges unto his said subgiettes exhorting theim soo to contynue.

Item that the said Commissioners in alle hast possible Revieu the Souldiors late mustred before theim by force of the kinges Commission to theim late directed, and see that they be hable persones wele horsed and harneysed to doo the king service of werre. And if they be not to put othre hable men into theire places and that the money graunted and gadred for the waging of them in Townes Towneshippes villages or hundreds be redy in the handes of the Constables baillieffes or othre suffisaunt persones to be delyvred for the cause abovesaid when the caas shal Requier.

Item that the said Commissioners on the kinges behalf yeve straitly in commaundement to alle knightes Squiers and gentilmen to prepaire and arredy theimself in theire propre persones to doo the king service upon an houre warnyng when they shalbe thereunto commaunded by proclamacion

[207]

or othrewise. And that they faille not soo to doo upon the perille of lesing of theire lyfes landes & goodes. And that they be attending and awayting upon suche Capitaigne or Capitaignes as the kinges good grace shal appoint to have the Rule and leding of theim and upon othre.

Item that the Commissioners make proclamacion that al men be redy to doo the king service within an houre warnyng whensoever they be commaunded by proclamacion or othrewise.

Item to shewe to alle lordes noble men Capitaynes & othre that the kinges noble pleasire and commaundement is that they truely and honnorably almanere quarelles grugges Rancors & unkyndenesse layde aparte attende texecute the kinges commaundement, and every of theim to be lovyng & assisting to othre in the kinges quarelle & cause Shewing theim plainly that whosoever attempt the contrary, the kinges grace wille soo punysshe him that all othre shalle take example by him etc.

The tenor of the lettres directed to alle Shirieffes

Trusty and welbeloved we grete you wele. And forasmoche as we have commaunded oure Commissioners of array within oure Counties of Notingham & Derby to put oure Commission to them herebifore directed for mustering and ordering of oure subgiettes in newe execucion according to certaine Instruccions from us to theim directed. We therefore wol and straitly commaunde you that incontynently upon the Receipt hereof, ye fully dispose you to make youre contynuelle abode within the Shire Towne of youre Office or youre deputie for you to thentent that it may be openly knowen where ye or he shalbe surely founde for the performyng and fulfilling of suche thinges as on oure behalf or by oure said Commissioners ye shalbe commaunded to doo. Not failling hereof in any wise As ye wol answere unto us at youre uttermost perille. Yeven etc at Notingham the xxij day of Juyne.[177]

Richard etc., greetings. We order you etc.

Forasmoche as the Kyng our sovereign Lord hath certeyn knowledge that Piers, Bisshop of Exeter, Jasper Tydder, son of Owen Tydder, callyng hymself Erle of Pembroke, John, late Erle of Oxon, and Sir Edward Wodevyle, with other dyvers his rebelles and traytours, disabled and atteynted by the auctorite of the High Court of Parlement, of whom many be knownen for open murdrers, advoutrers [adulterers], and extorcioners, contrary to the pleasure of God, and a yenst all trouth, honour, and nature, have forsakyn there naturall contrey, takyng them first to be under

[208]

Elizabeth of York, later wife of Henry VII, and eldest child of Edward IV and Elizabeth Woodville. She was born in 1465 and died in 1503.

Portrait of Henry VII, showing him in late middle age (painted after 1504). Once owned by the Paston family.

th'obeisaunce of the Duke of Bretayn, and to hym promysed certeyn thyngs whiche by him and his counsell were thought thynggs to gretly unnaturall and abominable for them to graunt, observe, kepe, and perfourme, and therfor the same utterly refused.

The seid traytours, seyng the seid Duke and his counsell wolde not aide nor socour theym ner folowe there wayes, privily departed oute of his contrey in to Fraunce, and there takyng theym to be under the obeisaunce of the Kynggs auncient enemy, Charlys, callyng hymself Kyng of Fraunce, and to abuse and blynde the comons of this seid Realme, the seid rebelles and traitours have chosyn to be there capteyn one Henry Tydder, son of Edmond Tydder, son of Owen Tydder, whiche of his ambicioness and insociable covetise encrocheth and usurpid upon hym the name and title of royall astate of this Realme of Englond, where unto he hath no maner interest, right, title, or colour, as every man wele knoweth; for he is discended of bastard blood bothe of ffather side and of mother side, for the seid Owen the graunfader was bastard borne, and his moder was doughter unto John, Duke of Somerset, son unto John, Erle of Somerset, sone unto Dame Kateryne Swynford, and of ther indouble avoutry [adultery] gotyn, whereby it evidently apperith that no title can nor may in hym, which fully entendeth to entre this Reame, purposyng a conquest. And if he shulde atcheve his fals entent and purpose, every man is lif, livelod, and goddes shulde be in his hands, liberte, and disposicion, whereby sholde ensue the disheretyng and distruccion of all the noble and worshipfull blode of this Reame for ever, and to the resistence and withstondyng whereof every true and naturall Englishman born must ley to his hands for his owen suerte and wele.

And to th'entent that the seid Henry Tydder myght the rather atcheve his fals intent and purpose by the aide, supporte, and assistence of the Kynggs seid auncient enemy of Fraunce, hath covenaunted and bargayned with hym and all the counsell of Fraunce to geve up and relese inperpetuite all the right, title, and cleyme that the Kyng of Englond have, had, and ought to have, to the Crowne and Reame of Fraunce, to gether with the Duchies of Normandy, Anjoy, and Maygne, Gascoyn and Guyne, castell and townys of Caleys, Guysnes, Hammes, with the marches apperteynyng to the same, and discevir and exclude the armes of Fraunce oute of the armes of Englond for ever.

And in more prove and shewing of his seid purpose of conquest, the seid Henry Tidder hath goven as well to dyvers of the seid Kynggs enemys as to his seid rebelles and traitours, archebisshoprikes, bisshoprikes, and other dignitees spirituels, and also the ducheez, erledomez, baronyes, and other possessions and inheritaunces of kynghts, squyres, gentilmen, and other the Kynggs true subjetts withynne the Reame, and entendith also to chaunge and subverte the lawes of the same, and to enduce and establisse newe lawes and ordenaunces amongez the Kynggs seid subjetts. And overthis, and beside the alienacions of all the premyssez into the possession of the Kynggs seid auncient enemys to the grettest anyntisshment, shame, and rebuke that every myght falle to this seid land, the seid Henry Tydder and others, the Kynggs rebelles and traitours aforeseid, have extended at there comyng, if they may be of power, to do the most cruell murders, slaughterys, and roberys, and disherisons that ever were seen in eny Cristen reame.

For the wich, and other inestymable daungers to be escheuved, and to th'entent that the Kynggs seid rebelles, traitours, and enemys may be utterly put from there seid malicious and fals purpose and sone discomforted, if they enforce to land, the Kyng our soveraign Lord willith, chargeth, and comaundith all and everyche of the naturall and true subgetts of this his Reame to call the premyssez to there mynds, and like gode and true Englishmen to endever themselfs with all there powers for the defence of them, there wifs, chylderyn, and godes, and heriditaments ayenst the seid malicious purposes and conspiracions, which the seid auncient enemes have made with the Kynggs seid rebelles and traitours for the fynall distruccion of this lande as is aforeseid. And our said soveraign Lord, as a wele willed, diligent, and coragious Prynce, wel put his moost roiall persone to all labour and payne necessary in this behalve for the resistence and subduyng of his seid enemys, rebells, and traitours to the moost comforte, wele, and suerte of all his true and feithfull liege men and subgetts.

And over this, our seid soveraign Lord willith and comaundith all his seid subgetts to be redy in there most defensible arraye to do his Highnes servyce of werre, when thy be opyn proclamacion, or otherwise shall be comaunded so to do, for the resistence of the Kynggs seid rebelles, traitours and enemyes. And this under peril, etc. Witness myself at Westminster, 23 day of June, in the second year of our reign.[178]

At the end of July Richard sent to Bishop Russell, the Chancellor, for the Great Seal, in order to have it ready to hand, as he had done in 1483 during the Buckingham rebellion.

Memorandum, that on 24 July, 3 Richard III, emanated letters missive of the king sealed with his signet directed to John bishop of Lincoln, the chancellor, in which it is contained that the said chancellor for certain reasons moving him despatched the great seal then in his custody to the king by Thomas Barowe, keeper of the rolls, whom the king had assigned to receive the seal from the chancellor and to carry it to him: and the chancellor, by command of the king, on Friday, 29 July, at the eighth hour, in presence of Richard Skypton, Christopher Hanyngton, William Nanson, Walter Wheler and Thomas Snowe, at the Old Temple in the lower oratory, delivered the seal enclosed in a white leather bag sealed with the chancellor's eagle signet, to Thomas Barowe to carry to the king.[179]

Memorandum, that on 1 August, 3 Richard III, Thomas Barowe, keeper of the chancery rolls, came to the king at Nottingham, and there in his oratory within the chapel and castle of the said town, on the first day about seven of the evening, in presence of Thomas archbishop of York, John earl of Lincoln, Thomas Scrope, lord Scrope of Upsale, George lord Straunge

Great Seal of Richard III. This seal was held by the King's Chancellor and used to authenticate the most important official documents.

[211]

and John Kendall, secretary to the king, delivered the great seal to the king. Whereupon the king, for causes and considerations him moving, in presence of the above persons, delivered the seal to the aforesaid Thomas Barowe to seal all manner of writs and letters patent, and appointed him keeper of the great seal then and there.[180]

A few weeks later, on Sunday the 7th of August, the waiting ended, and Henry Tudor, with a small army of exiles and French and Scottish mercenaries, landed at Milford Haven in Pembroke. The King immediately sent out letters summoning his adherents, and his major supporters, for example the Duke of Norfolk, did the same. The City of York (and probably other places) was also anxious to send troops.

On hearing of their arrival, the king rejoiced, or at least seemed to rejoice, writing to his adherents in every quarter that now the long wished-for day had arrived, for him to triumph with ease over so contemptible a faction, and thenceforth benefit his subjects with the blessings of uninterrupted tranquillity. In the meantime, in manifold letters he despatched orders of the greatest severity, commanding that no men, of the number of those at least who had been born to the inheritance of any property in the kingdom, should shun taking part in the approaching warfare; threatening that whoever should be found in any part of the kingdom after the victory should have been gained, to have omitted appearing in his presence on the field, was to expect no other fate than the loss of all his goods and possessions, as well as his life.[181]

Richard III to Henry Vernon, squire for his body, Richard Vernon, and . . . . . Vernon, squires, and to every of them

Trusty and welbeloved we grete you wele. And forasmuche as our rebelles and traitours accompanyed with our auncient enemyes of Fraunce and othre straunge nacions departed out of the water of Sayn the furst day of this present moneth making their cours westwardes ben landed at Nangle besides Mylford Haven in Wales on Soneday last passed, as we be credibly enfourmed, entending our uttre destruccion, thextreme subversion of this oure realme and disheriting of oure true subgiettes of the same, towardes whoes recountring, God being our guyde, we be utterly determined in our owne persone to remeove in all hast goodly that we can or may. Wherfor we

[212]

wol and straitely charge you that ye in your persone with suche nombre as ye have promysed unto us sufficiently horssed and herneised be with us in all hast to you possible, to yeve unto us your attendaunce without failling, al manere excuses sette apart, upon peyne of forfaicture unto us of all that ye may forfait and loose. Yeven undre our signet at oure logge of Beskewode the xj day of August.

[sign manual][182]

To my welbelovyd frend, John Paston, by thys byll delyveryd in hast.

Welbelovyd frend, I cummaunde me to yow, letyng yow to undyrstond that the Kyngs enmysse be a land, and that the Kyng wold hafe set for the asuppon Monday but only for Howre Lady Day; but for serten he gothe forward as uppon Tewsday, for a servant of myne browt to me the sertente.

Wherfor, I pray yow that ye met with me at Bery, for, be the grace of God, I purposse to lye at Bery as uppon Tewsday nyght, and that ye brynge with yow seche company of tall men as ye may goodly make at my cost and charge, be seyd that ye have promysyd the Kyng; and I pray yow ordeyne them jakets of my levery, and I shall contente yow at your metyng with me.   Yower lover,

J. NORFFOLK.[183]

Friday after the feast of the Assumption etc, that is 19th August, in the third year

Wer assembled in the counsaill chambre, where and when it was determyned upon the report of John Nicholson, which was commen home from the kinges grace fro Beskwod, that iiij^{xx} [80] men of the citie defensible araiyed, John Hastings gentilman to the mase being capitayn, shuld in all hast possible depart towards the kinges grace for the subduying of his ennemyes forsaid, wherapon evere parish in the citie was sessid as it appereth herafter. And that eevere sogiour shuld have x^s for x days being furth xij^d by day. And also that the consaill shuld mete at ij of the clok at after none the same day at the yeld hall ther to poynt such personnes as shuld take waiges and ther to receve the same.[184]

[213]

The Blue Boar Inn at Leicester. Tradition says that Richard stayed here (it then being known as the White Boar) while collecting his army in August 1485.

Finally, King Richard left Nottingham and marched to Leicester, arriving there on the 19th of August. Here he gathered his army. Two days later he marched out to meet Henry Tudor at Bosworth Field on the 22nd of August. Here he fought his last battle, supported by the Duke of Norfolk, who was killed, but betrayed by Thomas Lord Stanley and his brother Sir William Stanley, whose sudden switch to Tudor's side at a crucial moment lost Richard the battle and his life. Richard died fighting bravely.

On the Lord's day before the feast of Bartholomew the Apostle, the king proceeded on his way, amid the greatest pomp, and wearing the crown on his head; being attended by John Howard, duke of Norfolk, and Henry Percy, earl of Northumberland and other mighty lords, knights, and esquires, together with a countless multitude of the common people. On

[214]

departing from the town of Leicester, he was informed by scouts where the enemy most probably intended to remain the following night; upon which, he encamped near the abbey of Mirival, at a distance of about eight miles from that town.

The chief men of the opposing army were the following: – in the first place, Henry earl of Richmond, whom they called their king, Henry the Seventh; John Vere, earl of Oxford, John lord Wells, of Wells, uncle to king Henry the Seventh, Thomas lord Stanley and William his brother, Edward Wydville, brother of queen Elizabeth, a most valiant knight, John Cheyne, John Savage, Robert Willougby, William Berkeley, James Blunt, Thomas Arundel, Richard Edgcumbe, Edward Poynings, Richard Guilford, and many others of knightly rank, who had been distinguished before these troubles, as well as at the commencement of the present war. Of the ecclesiastical orders, there were present, for the purpose of giving their advice, the following persons, who had similarly suffered banishment – the venerable father, Peter, bishop of Exeter, the flower of the knighthood of his country, Master Robert Morton, clerk of the Rolls of Chancery, Christopher Urswyk, and Richard Fox, of whom the one was afterwards appointed to the office of Almoner, and the other to that of Secretary, together with many others.

At day-break, on the Monday following there were no chaplains present to perform Divine service on behalf of king Richard, nor any breakfast prepared to refresh the flagging spirits of the king; besides which, as it is generally stated, in the morning he declared that during the night he had seen dreadful visions, and had imagined himself surrounded by a multitude of daemons. He consequently presented a countenance which, always attenuated, was on this occasion more livid and ghastly than usual, and asserted that the issue of this day's battle, to whichever side the victory might be granted, would prove the utter destruction of the kingdom of England. He also declared that it was his intention, if he should prove the conqueror, to crush all the supporters of the opposite faction; while, at the same time, he predicted that his adversary would do the same towards the well-wishers to his own party, in case the victory should fall to his lot. At length, the prince and knights on the opposite side now advancing at a moderate pace against the royal army, the king gave orders that the lord Strange before-mentioned should be instantly beheaded. The persons, however, to whom this duty was entrusted, seeing that the issue was doubtful in the extreme, and that matters of more importance than the destruction of one individual were about to be decided, delayed the performance of this cruel order of the king, leaving the man to his own disposal, returned to the thickest of the fight.

A battle of the greatest severity now ensuing between the two sides, the earl of Richmond, together with his knights, made straight for king Richard; while the earl of Oxford, who was next in rank to him in the whole army and a most valiant soldier, drew up his forces, consisting of a large body of French and English troops, opposite the wing in which the duke of Norfolk had taken up his position. In the part where the earl of Northumberland was posted, with a large and well-provided body of troops, there was no opposition made, as not a blow was given or received during the battle. At length a glorious victory was granted by heaven to the said earl of Richmond, now sole king, together with the crown, of exceeding value, which king Richard had previously worn on his head. For while fighting, and not in the act of flight, the said king Richard was pierced with numerous deadly wounds, and fell in the field like a brave and most valiant prince[185]

Standard of Richard III, showing his badges of the white boar and the *rose-en-soleil*. The standard was parted and fringed murrey and blue.

In the meane time king Richard, hearing that thennemy drew neare, came first to the place of fight, a little beyond Leycester (the name of that village ys Boswoorth), and ther, pightching his tentes, refresshyd his soldiers that night from ther travale, and with many woords, exhortyd them to the fyght to coome. Yt ys reportyd that king Rycherd had that night a terryble dreame; for he thowght in his slepe that he saw horryble ymages as yt wer of evell spyrytes haunting evydently abowt him, as yt wer before his eyes, and that they wold not let him rest; which visyon trewly dyd not so muche stryke into his brest a suddane feare, as replenyshe the same with heavy cares: for furthwith after, being troublyd in mynde, his hart gave him theruppon that thevent of the battale folowing wold be grevous, and he dyd not buckle himself to the conflict with such lyvelyness of corage and countenance as before, which hevynes that yt showld not be sayd he shewyd as appallyd with feare of his enemyes, he reportyd his dreame to many in the morning. But (I beleve) yt was no dreame, but a conscyence guiltie of haynous offences, a conscyence (I say) so muche the more grevous as thoffences wer more great, which, thowght at none other time, yeat in the last day of owr lyfe ys woont to represent to us the memory of our sinnes commyttyd, and withall to shew unto us the paynes immynent for the same, that, being uppon good cause penytent at that instant for our evell led lyfe, we may be compellyd to go hence in heavynes of hart. Now I return to my purpose. The next day after king Richerd, furnysshyd throwghly with all maner of thinges, drew his whole hoste owt of ther tentes, and arraieth his vanward, stretching yt furth of a woonderfull lenght, so full replenyshyd both with foote men and horsemen that to the beholders afar of yt gave a terror for the multitùde, and in the front wer placyd his archers, lyke a most strong trenche and bulwark; of these archers he made leder John duke of Norfolk. After this long vanward folowyd the king himself, with a choyce force of soldiers. In this meane time Henry, being departyd bak from the conference with his frinds, began to take better hart, and without any tary encampyd himself nighe his enemyes, wher he restyd all night and well early in the morning commandyd the soldiers to arm themselves, sending withall to Thomas Stanley, who was now approchyd the place of fight, as in the mydde way betwixt the two battaylles, that he wold coom to with his forces, to sett the soldiers in aray. He awnsweryd that the earle showld set his owne folkes in order, whyle that he should coome to him with his army well apoyntyd. With which answer, geaven contrary to that was looked for, and to that which thoportunytie of time and weight of cause requyryd, thowghe Henry wer no lyttle vexyd, and began to be soomwhat appallyd, yeat withowt lingering he of necessytie orderyd his men in this sort. He made a sclender vanward for the smaule number of his people; before the same he placyd archers, of whom he made captane John erle of Oxfoord; in the right wing of the vanward he placyd Gilbert Talbot to defend the same; in the left veryly he sat John Savage; and himself, trusting to thayd of Thomas Stanley, with one troup of horsemen, and a fewe footemen dyd folow; for the number of all his soldiers, all manner of ways, was scarce v.[M.] besydes the Stanleyans, whereof about 3.[M.] wer at the battaill, under the

[217]

conduct of William. The kings forces were twyse so many and more. Thus both the vanwardes being arrayed, as soone as the soldiers might one se an other afur of, they put on ther head peces and preparyd to the fyght, expectyng thalarme with intenyve eare. Ther was a marishe betwixt both hostes, which Henry of purpose left on the right hand, that yt might serve his men instede of a fortresse, by the doing therof also he left the soon upon his bak; but whan the king saw thenemyes passyd the marishe, he commandyd his soldiers to geave charge uppon them. They making suddanely great showtes assaultyd thennemy first with arrowes, who wer nothing faynt unto the fyght but began also to shoote fearcely; but whan they cam to hand strokes the matter than was delt with blades. In the meane tyme therle of Oxfoord, fearing lest hys men in fyghting might be envyronyd of the multitude, commandyd in every rang that no soldiers should go above tenfoote from the standerds; which charge being knowen, whan all men had throng thik togethers, and stayd a whyle from fighting, thadversaryes wer therwith aferd, supposing soom fraude, and so they all forbore the fight a certane space, and that veryly dyd many with right goodwill, who rather covetyd the king dead than alyve, and therfor fowght fayntly. Than therle of Oxforth in one part, and others in an other part, with the bandes of men closse one to an other, gave freshe charge uppon thenemy, and in array tryangle vehemently renewyd the conflict. Whyle the battayll contynewyd thus hote on both sydes betwixt the vanwardes, king Richard understood, first by espyalls wher erle Henry was a farre of with smaule force of soldiers abowt him; than after drawing nerer he knew yt perfytely by evydent signes and tokens that yt was Henry; wherfor, all inflamyd with ire, he strick his horse with the spurres, and runneth owt of thone syde withowt the vanwardes agaynst him. Henry perceavyd king Richerd comme uppon him, and because all his hope was than in valyancy of armes, he receavyd him with great corage. King Richerd at the first brunt killyd certaine, overthrew Henryes standerd, toygther with William Brandon the standerd bearer, and matchyd also with John Cheney a man of muche fortytude, far exceeding the common sort, who encountered with him as he cam, but the king with great force drove him to the ground, making way with weapon on every syde. But yeat Henry abode the brunt longer than ever his owne soldiers wold have wenyd, who wer now almost owt of hope of victory, whan as loe William Stanley with thre thowsand men came to the reskew: than trewly in a very moment the resydew all fled, and king Richerd alone was killyd fyghting manfully in the thickkest presse of his enemyes.[186]

[218]

. . . with his crown and all his treasure this wretched creature was killed as by lightning in the midst of his army by a comparative few. Yet if I should speak the truth to his credit, he defended himself as a noble knight with great courage to his last breath, although small in body and weak in strength, often shouting out and crying 'Treson, treson, treson'. Thus, tasting what others had often drunk, he finished his life most miserably, and finally was buried in the choir of the church of the Friars Minor in Leicester.[187]

Processional Cross, found at Bosworth in 1778, and possibly used in a battlefield service in 1485. The roundels contain symbols of the evangelists.

[219]

King Richard did in his army stand,
   he was n[u]mbred to 40000 and 3
of hardy men of hart and hand,
   that vnder his banner there did bee.

Sir William Stanley wise & worthie
   remembred the brea[k]ffast he hett to him;
downe att a backe then cometh hee,
   & shortlye sett vpon the Kinge.

then they countred together sad & sore;
   archers they lett sharpe arrowes fflee,
they shott guns both ffell & ffarr,
   bowes of yewe bended did bee,

springalls spedd them speedylye,
   harquebusiers pelletts throughly did thringe;
soe many a banner began to swee
   that was on Richards partye, their King.

then our archers lett their shooting bee,
   with ioyned weapons were growden ffull right,
brands rang on basenetts hye,
   battell-axes ffast on helmes did light.

there dyed many a doughtye Knight,
   there vnder ffoot can thé thringe;
thus they ffought with maine & might
   that was on Heneryes part, our King.

then to King Richard there came a Knight,
   & said, "I hold itt time ffor to fflee;
ffor yonder Stanleys dints they be soe wight,
   against them no man may dree.

"heere is thy horsse att thy hand readye'
   another day thou may thy worshipp win,
& ffor to raigne with royaltye,
   to weare the crowne, and be our King."

[220]

A battle scene of the 1480s, from the Beauchamp Pageant, probably written and illustrated as a gift for Richard's son.

he said, "giue me my battell axe in my hand,
 sett the crowne of England on my head soe hye!
ffor by him that shope both sea and Land,
 King of England this day I will dye!

"one ffoote will I neuer fflee
 whilest the breath is my brest within!"
as he said, soe did itt bee;
 if hee lost his liffe, if he were King.

about his standard can thé light,
 the crowne of gold thé hewd him ffroe,
with dilffull dints his death thé dight,
 the Duke of Norffolke that day thé slowe.

the Lord Ferrers & many other moe,
 boldlye on bere they can them bringe;
many a noble Knight in his hart was throwe,
 that lost his liffe with Richard the King.[188]

The York City Council had (slightly inaccurate) reports of the battle on the day after it was fought. In their own Minutes they provided Richard III with a lasting epitaph.

On the 22nd day of August *Anno Domini* 1485 at Redemore near Leicester there was fought a battle between our Lord King Richard III and others of his nobles on the one part, and Harry Earl of Richmond and others of his followers on the other part. In this battle the foresaid King Richard in the third year of his reign, John Duke of Northfolc, Thomas Earl Lincoln, Thomas Earl Surr', son of the aforesaid duke, Francis Viscount Lowell, Lord Walter Deveres Lord de Ferez, Sir Richard Ratcliff and Sir Robert Brakanbury, the Lord King at Sandeforth near Leicester and others in the same field, with many other nobles, knights, squires and gentlemen were killed.[189]

Tuesday the vigil of St Bartholomew,
that is 23rd August in the year etc, the throne being vacant

Wer assembled in the counsaill chamber, where and when it was shewed by diverse persones and especially by John Sponer send unto the feld of Redemore to bring tidinges frome the same to the citie that king Richard late mercifully reigning upon us was thrugh grete treason of the duc of Northfolk and many other that turned ayenst hyme, with many other lordes and nobilles of this north parties was piteously slane and murdred to the grete hevynesse of this citie, the names of whome foloweth herafter. Wherfor it was determyned for somoch as it was said that therle of Northumberland was commen to Wressill that a letre shuld be consaved unto the said erle, beseking hyme to yeve unto them his best advise how to dispose them at this wofull season both to his honour and worship and well and proufitt of this citie.[190]

Overleaf: Memorial stone to Richard III at the foot of Ambion Hill, Bosworth. Here at Sandford Richard's last charge ended in a hand to hand fight with Tudor and Stanley supporters. The stone was erected in 1974.

[223]

Richard, the last
Plantagenet King of
England was slain here
22nd. August 1485

REFERENCES

1 James Gairdner, *Life of Richard III*, Cambridge 1898, p. 5.
2 Charlotte D'Evelyn (ed.), *Peter Idley's Instructions to his Son*, Boston 1935, p. 81, lines 8–28.
3 James Gairdner (ed.), *The Historical Collections of a Citizen of London in the Fifteenth Century*, Camden Society 1876, pp. 205, 206, 207, from William Gregory's 'Chronicle of London'.
4 James Gairdner (ed.), *The Paston Letters*, London 1872–5 (3 vols), vol. 1, p. 525.
5 A.B. Hinds (ed.), *Calendar of State Papers and Manuscripts existing in the Archives Collection of Milan 1359–1618*, London 1913, p. 73.
6 Corporation of London Records Office, Journal 6, f. 54 (photograph 488).
7 *Calendar of Patent Rolls 1461–67*, London 1897, p. 214.
8 John Rous, *The Rous Roll*, (ed. W. Courthope), new edition Gloucester 1980, item 56.
9 F. Devon (ed.), *Issues of the Exchequer*, London 1837, p. 490.
10 Richard Warner, *Antiquitates Culinariae*, London 1791, pp. 94, 96.
11 Richard Bentley (ed.), *Excerpta Historica*, London 1831, pp. 227–8.
12 Historical Manuscripts Commission, *The Manuscripts of R.R. Hastings*, London 1928, vol. 1, pp. 290–1. Names of manors left out by present editors.
13 Henry Ellis (ed.), *Original Letters*, Series 2, London 1827, vol. 1, pp. 143–4, letter 46. (BL. Ms. Cotton Vespasian F III, item 19 (modern reference)).
14 *Calendar of Patent Rolls 1467–77*, London 1900, p. 178.
15 Ibid., p. 180.
16 John Warkworth, *A Chronicle of the First Thirteen Years of the Reign of Edward the Fourth*, (ed. J.O. Halliwell), Camden Society 1839, p. 11.
17 Philip de Commines, *The Memoirs*, (ed. Andrew R. Scoble), London, 1911, vol. 1, pp. 193–4.

18 From the accounts of the City of Ter Veere, for the second week of November 1470, quoted in *The Ricardian*, 1974, vol. 3, no. 44, p. 10.

19 *Historie of the Arrivall of Edward IV, etc.*, (ed. John Bruce), Camden Society 1838, pp. 2–3.

20 *Arrivall*, p. 11.

21 Polydore Vergil, *Anglica Historia*, (ed. Henry Ellis), Camden Society 1844, p. 141.

22 *The Great Chronicle of London*, (ed. A.H. Thomas and I.D. Thornley), London 1938, p. 216.

23 Warkworth, p. 16.

24 Thomas Wright (ed.), *Political Poems and Songs*, Rolls Series 1861, vol. 1, pp. 271–81.

25 Warkworth, pp. 17–8.

26 *Arrivall*, pp. 28–30.

27 Warkworth, p. 18.

28 *Arrivall*, p. 30.

29 A passage written after the Battle in *Rental of all the Houses in Gloucester 1455*, (ed. W.H. Stevenson), Gloucester 1890, p. 125.

30 Historical Manuscripts Commission, *The Manuscripts of the Duke of Rutland*, London 1888, vol. 1, p. 4.

31 *Arrivall*, p. 38.

32 Warkworth, p. 21.

33 *Ingulph's Chronicle of the Abbey of Croyland*, (ed. Henry T. Riley), London 1893, pp. 467–8.

34 *Rolls of Parliament*, London 1783, vol. 6, p. 234.

35 *Calendar of Patent Rolls 1467–77*, p. 266.

36 *Paston Letters*, vol. 3, p. 38.

37 *Croyland*, pp. 469–70.

38 *Paston Letters*, vol. 3, p. 98.

39 *Paston Letters*, vol. 3, p. 102.

40 Thomas Hearne (ed.), *A Remarkable Fragment of an Old English Chronicle*, Oxford 1715, p. 304.

41 *Rolls of Parliament*, vol. 6, pp. 100–1.

42 *Paston Letters*, vol. 3, p. 39.

43 *Paston Letters*, vol. 3, p. 92.

44 Historical Manuscripts Commission, *Sixth Report*, London 1877–8, pp. 223–4.

45 F.P. Barnard (ed.), *Edward IV's French Expedition of 1475*, Oxford 1925, p. (iv).

46 *Croyland*, p. 473.
47 Commines, vol. 1, p. 277.
48 Francis Sandford, *A Genealogical History of the Kings and Queens of England*, 2nd Edition, London 1707, pp. 391–2.
49 W.G. Searle, *The History of the Queens' College of St Margaret and St Bernard*, Cambridge Antiquarian Society 1867, pp. 89–92.
50 *The Narrative of the Marriage of Richard Duke of York with Anne of Norfolk 1477*, from *Illustrations of Ancient State and Chivalry*, (ed. W.H. Black), Roxburgh Club 1840, pp. 28–31.
51 *Croyland*, pp. 479–80.
52 Dominic Mancini, *The Usurpation of Richard the Third*, (ed. C.A.J. Armstrong), 2nd edition, Oxford 1969, pp. 63–5.
53 J.B. Sheppard (ed.), *Christ Church Letters*, Camden Society 1877, p. 37 (Thomas Langton to Prior Sellyng).
54 Eric E. Barker (ed.), *Register of Archbishop Rotherham*, Canterbury and York Society 1974–5, pp. 194–5.
55 James Raine (ed.), *Testamenta Eboracensia*, Surtees Society 1864, vol. 3, pp. 238–41.
56 James Raine, The Statutes . . . for the College of Middleham, dated July 4, 1478, *Archaeological Journal*, 1857, vol. 14, pp. 160–70.
57 York House Books, Book 1, f. 42b, transcription by Dr Lorraine Attreed.
58 York House Books, Book 1, f. 76, transcription by Dr Attreed.
59 York House Books, Books 2/4, f. 56b, transcription by Dr Attreed.
60 PRO E404/77/1/28, transcription by P.B. and R.C. Hairsine in preparation for their forthcoming edition of the E404 file for 1478–1485.
61 Thomas Rymer (ed.), *Foedera, etc*, London 1707, vol. 12, p. 157.
62 *Issues of the Exchequer*, pp. 501–4.
63 R. Brown (ed.), *Calendar of State Papers and Manuscripts relating to English Affairs existing in the Archives and Collections of Venice, etc 1202–1509*, London 1864, no. 483.
64 *Rolls of Parliament*, vol. 6, pp. 204–6.
65 *Croyland*, p. 483.
66 L. Lyell and F. Watney (eds.), *The Acts of Court of the Mercers' Company 1453–1527*, Cambridge 1936, pp. 146–7.
67 *Croyland*, pp. 484–6.
68 Mancini, pp. 75–9.
69 *Croyland*, pp. 486–7.

70 Ibid., p. 487.
71 *Acts of Court*, p. 147.
72 *Croyland*, pp. 487–8.
73 *Acts of Court*, pp. 152–153.
74 *Facsimiles of National Manuscripts*, part 1, Southampton 1865, item 53.
75 Angelo Raine (ed.), *York Civic Records*, Yorkshire Archaeological Society 1939, vol. 1, pp. 73–4.
76 *Paston Letters*, vol. 3, p. 306.
77 Richard Firth Green, Historical Notes of a London Citizen 1483–8, *English Historical Review*, vol. 96, (1981), p. 588.
78 Mancini, pp. 89–91.
79 *Croyland*, p. 488.
80 Mancini, p. 89.
81 *Croyland*, pp. 479–80.
82 Mancini, p. 95.
83 *York Civic Records*, Vol. 1, p. 75.
84 *Acts of Court*, p. 155.
85 *Facsimiles of National Manuscripts*, part 1, item 56.
86 Mancini, p. 95.
87 John Rous, *Historia Regum Angliae*, Oxford 1745, pp. 213–4. Translation by the present editors.
88 *Croyland*, p. 489.
89 Ibid., p. 489.
90 *Great Chronicle*, p. 232.
91 Richard Grafton, *History of the Reigns of Edward IV, etc*, (ed. H. Ellis), London 1812, p. 113.
92 R. Horrox and P.W. Hammond (eds.), *British Library Harleian Manuscript 433*, Upminster and London 1979–83 (4 vols), vol. 3, p. 29.
93 Mancini, p. 99.
94 *Acts of Court*, pp. 155–6.
95 *Great Chronicle*, p. 233.
96 Anne F. Sutton and P.W. Hammond (eds.), *The Coronation of Richard III*, Gloucester 1983, pp. 275–82.
97 *Harleian MS 433*, vol. 1, p. 3.
98 Westminster Abbey Muniments 9482, editors' own transcript.
99 Public Record Office C81/1392/1, transcript by R.C. and P.B. Hairsine.

100 N.M. Herbert, Charter of Richard III to Gloucester, in *The 1483 Gloucester Charter in History* (ed. N.M. Herbert *et al.*), Gloucester 1983, pp. 9–15.

101 James Gairdner (ed.), *Letters and Papers Illustrative of the Reigns of Richard III and Henry VII*, Rolls Series, London 1861–3, vol. 1, pp. 25, 35–6.

102 *Harleian MS 433*, vol. 3, p. 35.

103 *Calendar of Patent Rolls 1476–1485*, London 1901, p. 403.

104 *Harleian MS 433*, vol. 3, p. 38.

105 Ibid., vol. 3, p. 36.

106 Ibid., vol. 2, pp. 108–9.

107 J.B. Sheppard (ed.), *Christ Church Letters*, Camden Society 1877, p. 46, Thomas Langton to Prior Sellyng.

108 *Harleian MS 433*, vol. 2, p. 19.

109 Ibid., vol. 2, p. 20.

110 Ibid., vol. 2, p. 28.

111 Ibid., vol. 2, pp. 82–3.

112 *Croyland*, p. 490.

113 *Harleian MS 433*, vol. 2, p. 42.

114 York Minster Library, Bedern College Statute Book, p. 48, transcript by the present editors.

115 *Croyland*, pp. 491–2.

116 Mancini, p. 93.

117 *Great Chronicle*, p. 234.

118 Public Record Office C81/1392/6, transcript by R.C. and P.B. Hairsine.

119 *Foedera*, vol. 12, p. 204.

120 *Croyland*, pp. 492–3.

121 *Harleian MS 433*, vol. 2, pp. 48–9.

122 *Calendar of Close Rolls 1476–1485*, London 1954, no. 1152.

123 *Calendar of Patent Rolls 1476–1485*, p. 413.

124 Corporation of London Records Office, Journal of Common Council, 9, f. 43.

125 Canterbury City Archives, Chamberlains' Accounts, Michaelmas 1483 – Michaelmas 1484, f. 13b, quoted in *The Ricardian*, 1980, vol. 5, p. 283.

126 *Rolls of Parliament*, vol. 6, pp. 240–2.

127 *Statutes of the Realm, 1101–1713*, Record Commission 1810–1828, Richard III, chapter 2.

128 Ibid., chapter 3.

129 Ibid., chapter 9.

130 *Rolls of Parliament*, vol. 6, pp. 244–9, quoted in the modernised summary from C.A. Halsted, *Richard III as Duke of Gloucester and King of England*, 2 vols, London 1844, vol. 2, pp. 546–8, with a few corrections by the present editors.

131 *Croyland*, pp. 495–6.

132 Ibid., p. 496.

133 Ibid., p. 496.

134 *Harleian MS 433*, vol. 3, p. 190.

135 Public Record Office, Exchequer Warrants for Issue, E404/78/2/28 and 33, transcript by R.C. and P.B. Hairsine.

136 British Library, Harleian MS. 258, f. 11b, as given by C. Halsted, vol. 2, pp. 569–70.

137 *Harleian MS 433*, vol. 1, p. 269.

138 Ibid., vol. 2, p. 137.

139 C.H. Cooper, *Annals of Cambridge*, Cambridge 1842, vol. 1, p. 230, corrected by present editors.

140 *Harleian MS 433*, vol. 2, p. 207.

141 Ibid., p. 192.

142 British Library Cottonian Manuscript Faustina, C.iii, f. 405, as quoted in *Annals of Cambridge*, vol. 1, pp. 228–9.

143 Guildhall Library MS 16988, vol. 1, Ironmongers' Company Wardens' Accounts and Memoranda 1454–1533, f. 45b, as given in *The Ricardian*, vol. 4, no. 57 (June 1977), p. 2.

144 *Rous Roll*, item 63.

145 *Croyland*, pp. 496–7.

146 William Langland, *The Vision of Piers Plowman*. Done into English by W.W. Skeat, London 1922, pp. 17–18, lines 61–70.

147 *Harleian MS 433*, vol. 2, pp. 24–5.

148 Ibid., vol. 2, pp. 106–7.

149 Ibid., vol. 2, p. 146.

150 *Croyland*, pp. 497–8.

151 *Harleian MS 433*, pp. 105–6.

152 Ibid., vol. 3, pp. 107–8.

153 M. Hemmant (ed.), *Select Cases in the Exchequer Chamber before all the Justices of England*, vol. 2, *1461–1509*, Selden Society 1948, pp. 86–90.

154 *Harleian MS 433*, vol. 3, pp. 118–20.

155 Ibid., vol. 3, pp. 116–18.
156 A.T.B. Byles (ed.), *The Book of the Ordre of Chyvalry printed by William Caxton*, Early English Text Society OS 168 (1926), pp. 121–5.
157 *Harleian MS 433*, vol. 3, p. 139.
158 The original prayer is in Richard III's Book of Hours, Lambeth Palace Library MS 474, ff. 181–3. Translation by present editors.
159 *Harleian MS 433*, vol. 1, p. 104.
160 Ibid., vol. 1, p. 3.
161 Ibid., vol. 3, p. 259.
162 Ibid., vol. 2, p. 163.
163 *The Great Chronicle*, p. 236.
164 *Croyland*, p. 499.
165 *Rous Roll*, item 62.
166 *Croyland*, p. 499.
167 *Acts of Court*, pp. 173–4.
168 George Buck, *The History of King Richard the Third*, (ed. A.N. Kincaid), Gloucester 1979, p. 191. Buck says he saw the letter in the cabinet of the Earl of Arundel.
169 *Harleian MS 433*, vol. 3, p. 129.
170 Ibid., vol. 3, p. 130.
171 Ibid., vol. 3, p. 128.
172 *Foedera*, vol. 12, p. 265, translation by the present editors.
173 Chamberlains' Accounts of the City of Canterbury, Michaelmas 1484 – Michaelmas 1485, f. 26, transcription and translation by the present editors.
174 Public Record Office E404/78/3/46, transcript by R.C. and P.B. Hairsine.
175 York House Books, Books 2/4, f. 163b, transcription by Dr Attreed.
176 *Croyland*, p. 500.
177 *Harleian MS 433*, vol. 2, pp. 228–9.
178 *Paston Letters*, vol. 3, pp. 316–20.
179 *Calendar of Close Rolls 1476–1485*, no. 1457.
180 Ibid., no. 1458.
181 *Croyland*, p. 501.
182 Historical Manuscripts Commission, *Manuscripts of the Duke of Rutland*, pp. 7–8.
183 *Paston Letters*, vol. 3, p. 320.
184 York House Books, Books 2/4, f. 169, transcription by Dr Attreed.

185 *Croyland*, pp. 502–4
186 Vergil, pp. 221–4.
187 Rous, *Historia Regum Angliae*, p. 218, translation by the present editors.
188 Ballad of Bosworth Field, from *Bishop Percy's Folio Manuscript*, (eds. J.W. Hales and F.J. Furnivall), London 1868, vol. 3, pp. 256–7.
189 York House Books, Books 2/4, f. 169, transcription by Dr Attreed, translation by the present editors.
190 York House Books, Books 2/4, f. 169b, transcription by Dr Attreed.

INDEX

[233]